IMAGES
of America

SPRECKELS

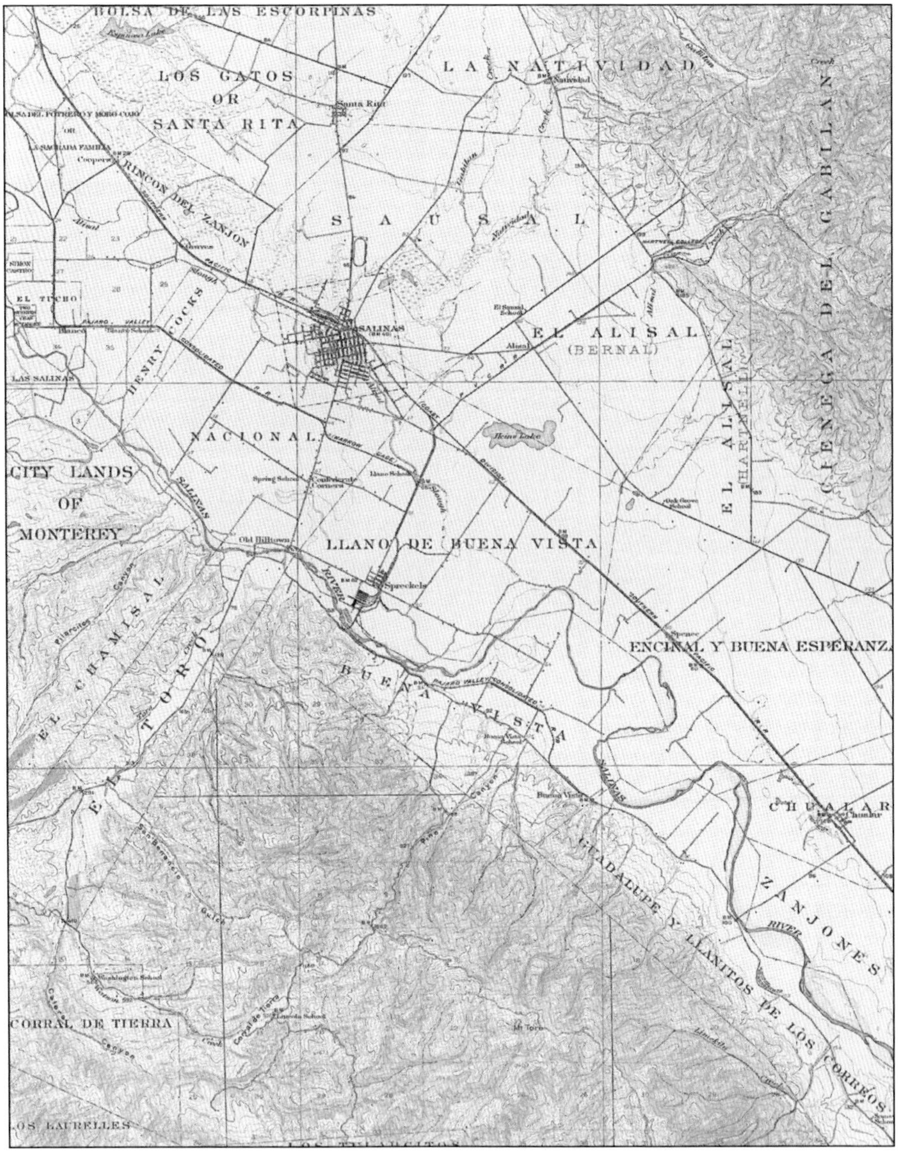

This United States Geological Survey quadrangle map shows the Salinas area in 1912. Note the boundaries of Salinas at that time, along with the location of Spreckels to the south. It also shows the route of the Pajaro Valley Consolidated Railroad, a narrow-gauge line that was built by Claus Spreckels. The tracks ran northeast from Spreckels and branched southeast of Salinas, with one branch turning northeast to the foothills and the other continuing on to Moss Landing. This railroad was important for hauling sugar beets and other resources to the factory and transporting refined sugar to the docks at Moss Landing.

ON THE COVER: This is the Spreckels Sugar Factory, with the town of Spreckels and a portion of the Salinas Valley in the background; the city of Salinas is out of the photograph to the left. It was taken in approximately 1898. Within the town, "The Store" building has been constructed, but the Louvre Saloon and the school have not. The Salinas River is in the foreground.

IMAGES
of America

SPRECKELS

Gary S. Breschini, Mona Gudgel,
and Trudy Haversat

ARCADIA
PUBLISHING

ISBN 978-0-7385-4684-1

Published by Arcadia Publishing
Charleston, South Carolina

Printed in the United States of America

Library of Congress Catalog Card Number: 2006929372

For all general information contact Arcadia Publishing at:
Telephone 843-853-2070
Fax 843-853-0044
E-mail sales@arcadiapublishing.com
For customer service and orders:
Toll-Free 1-888-313-2665

Visit us on the Internet at www.arcadiapublishing.com

Contents

ACKNOWLEDGMENTS

This work is being produced on behalf of the Monterey County Historical Society. The authors wish to thank all of the hardworking members of the society and the community, who have contributed so much to gather and maintain the early photographs, memorabilia, and stories from Salinas's beginnings. We wish we had room to name them all, but the list would be far too long. Special thanks to Barbara Brown, Ruth Dios, Robert Drake, Sandy and Earl Legate, James Perry, Sharon Richardson, James Ross Riley III, Corey Sanchez, Tom Tarp, and the Spreckels Sugar Company.

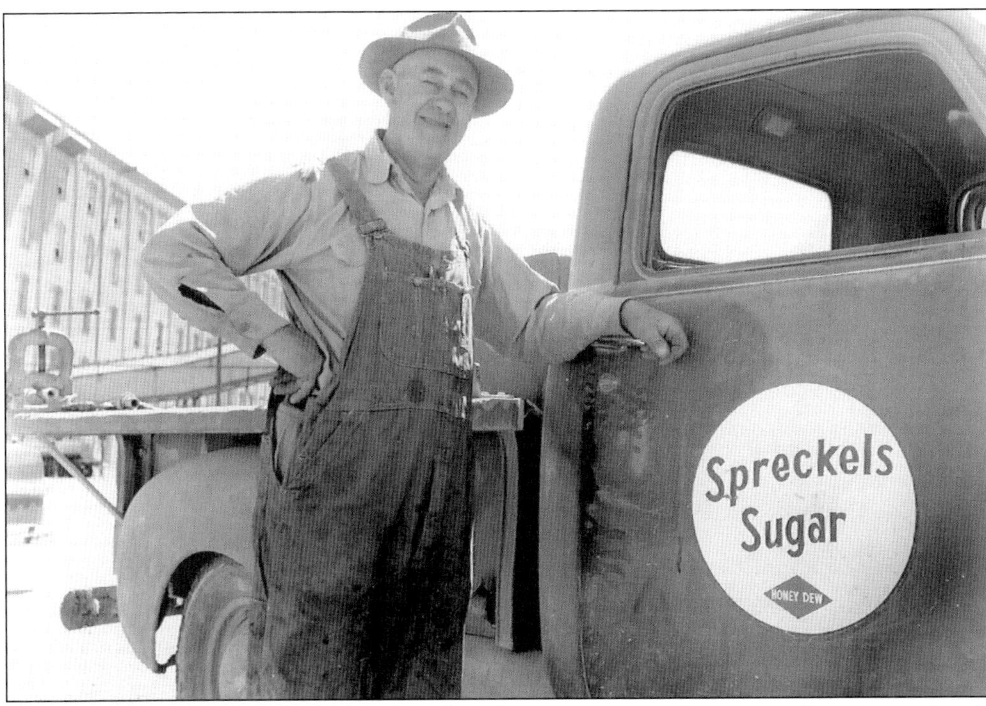

Claus Spreckels may have built the plant, but the maintenance department kept it running. If something broke in the plant or the town, Virgil Wallace was one of the folks who would be summoned to fix it. (Courtesy of Monterey County Agricultural and Rural Life Museum.)

INTRODUCTION

The story of Spreckels, California, began on August 1, 1896. Claus Spreckels, already well known as the "Sugar King" of Hawaii, addressed a massed assembly of about 2,000 Salinas Valley farmers and ranchers at a meeting at Agricultural Hall in Salinas. They could little guess how their lives and their valley were about to change.

Spreckels was well known in the sugar industry, having run successful ventures in San Francisco, Hawaii, and Philadelphia. By 1887, he was the leading sugar refiner on the Pacific Coast. Although his success was based on sugar cane, the contracts with Hawaiian growers came up for renewal every three years. He felt the conditions were finally right to use sugar beets.

He had called a similar meeting in Watsonville on November 5, 1887, and signed up local growers. His Western Beet Sugar Company plant in Watsonville could handle 350 tons of beets a day and produced about three million pounds of raw sugar during the 1888 campaign. The raw sugar had to be shipped to the San Francisco factory for refining.

Spreckels expanded the plant to handle 1,000 tons of beets per day, but even that was not enough. In 1896, he began making plans for an even larger and finer factory. He tentatively selected the Salinas area for its site and summoned the farmers to the August 1, 1896, meeting. Salinas city leaders, anxious to secure the plant, spread the word.

Spreckels knew that he could only build the new factory if he obtained guarantees from the farmers to grow the quantities of beets he needed to keep the factory running. He told the assembled crowd, "Raise the beets, and I will do the rest. . . . It will be a factory with a capacity of 3,000 tons daily, and do you know what that means to you? It means an expenditure of $12,000 per day for 100 days in the year. It means $5,000 a day for labor, fuel, etc., for the same period. . . . But I want two things, beets and protection. The former I will make the sugar out of and the latter I will need until the industry becomes fully established. We must have some law whereby the manufacturer in the United States who pays $2 or more to his labor in men will have some protection from the countries where labor is paid 50 cents a day." (*San Francisco Chronicle*, August 2, 1896, p. 20.)

At a banquet held at the Abbott House in Salinas after the meeting, someone addressed Spreckels as "Sir Claus," but he refused the title, saying, "If you want to give me a title, I have two. I was a colonel on the Governor's staff and I am the 'sugar king.' When I shall have built this big refinery, however, I will no longer be the 'sugar king,' but the 'emperor of the sugar industry.'" (*San Francisco Call*, August 2, 1896, p. 27.)

Once valley farmers had signed their pledges to grow beets and arrangements were made to begin construction of the new factory, Spreckels sold a half interest in his Pacific Coast operations to the American Sugar Company, also known as the Sugar Trust, an eastern firm that controlled nearly all Atlantic Coast sugar refineries. This allowed him to leverage his finances and spread the risk. By this time, Spreckels's interests were being increasingly handled by his sons John and Adolph.

A site for the new factory, and the new town to support it, was selected some five miles south of Salinas. But at that time there was no transportation between Salinas and the new site, just horse-and-buggy. To help solve the transportation problem, Spreckels extended his narrow-gauge railroad, already serving his Watsonville factory, to the new site in 1897. The combined operation was known as the Pajaro Valley Consolidated Railroad. When the factory was finished, Spreckels would also need the capacity for moving beets and raw materials to the plant and hauling processed sugar to the docks at Moss Landing.

In short order, a 61-room hotel and 40 cottages, using 12 different designs, were constructed. Noted architect William H. Weeks was employed to handle most of the design work. The main factory building was 582 feet long, 102 feet wide, and five stories high. This one building alone used 3,500 tons of steel and four million bricks; the latter brought in by ship from Germany. There were many other support buildings as well as the infrastructure to supply 13 million gallons of water a day—a figure equal to the total water consumption of San Francisco at the time.

The factory's first year of operation was 1899. By 1952, capacity had increased from 3,000 to nearly 7,000 tons of beets per day.

Claus Spreckels died on December 26, 1908. He had accomplished a significant goal: the Spreckels Sugar Factory was the largest refinery in the world when finished in 1899. He truly was the "Sugar King!"

His massive factory survived the 1906 earthquake. By the time the 1989 Loma Prieta earthquake hit central California, the building was no longer in use, but the damage from that quake was the beginning of the end, and it was demolished just a few years later.

The town of Spreckels was formed as a company town. Even as late as 1972, nearly half of the houses and 40 percent of the land were still owned by the company. While the factory has ceased operations, the town created by Spreckels continues to thrive. This book presents a part of its history.

One

Claus Spreckels, Immigrant

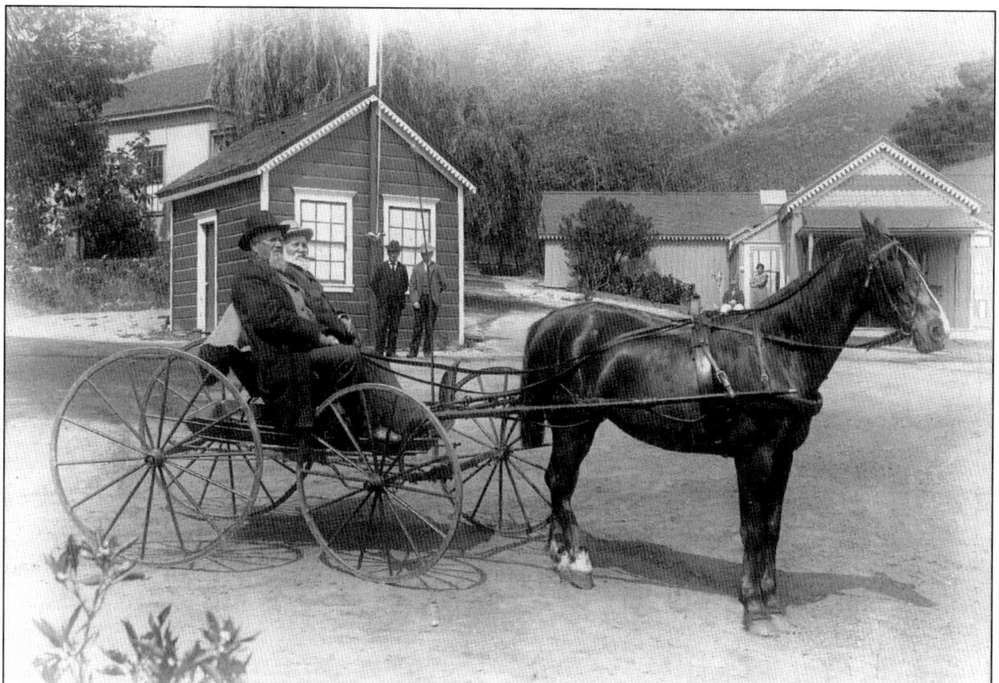

Claus Spreckels and former Monterey County supervisor Charles T. Romie, a prominent landowner, are most likely at Paraiso Hot Springs, a resort south of Soledad that Romie owned. Fort Romie, the first Salvation Army colony, was founded in the fall of 1897 on land purchased from Romie. Spreckels supported the colony, as he expected its farmers to produce sugar beets for his factory.

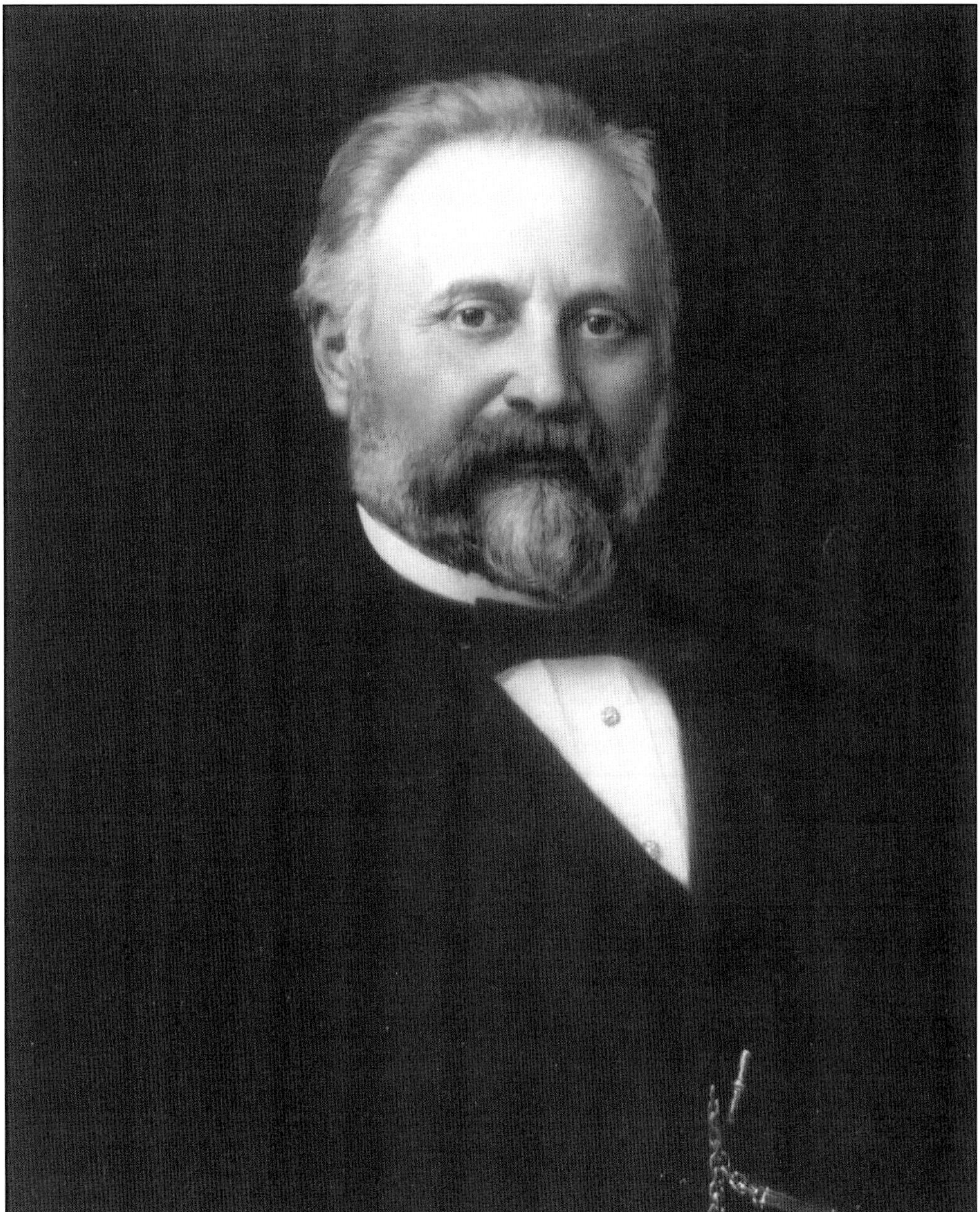

Claus Spreckels was born on July 9, 1828, in Lanstedt, Germany, the eldest of six children. Because of their poverty, the Spreckels family followed the local custom of loaning their children out to work in the fields during harvest season so there would be fewer mouths to feed at home. It is possible that this early poverty led to Spreckels's subsequent obsession with wealth, success, and power. At the age of 18, Claus borrowed money from a friend and sailed to Charleston, South Carolina. He arrived in 1846, virtually broke. He took a job in a grocery store, and within just six years, he had bought and paid for that store, moved to New York, where he purchased the Samson Moore grocery, and married his childhood sweetheart, Anna. He owned the New York store until he moved to San Francisco in 1856. There he continued in the grocery business and started a brewery as well. He sold both by 1863 and at age 35 was already a fairly wealthy man.

Anna Christina Mangels was Claus Spreckels's childhood sweetheart. As soon as Spreckels began to prosper in America, he probably followed the tradition of many immigrants by sending a ticket back home for others to follow. Anna came to New York and probably stayed with her brother until she and Claus were married on August 11, 1852.

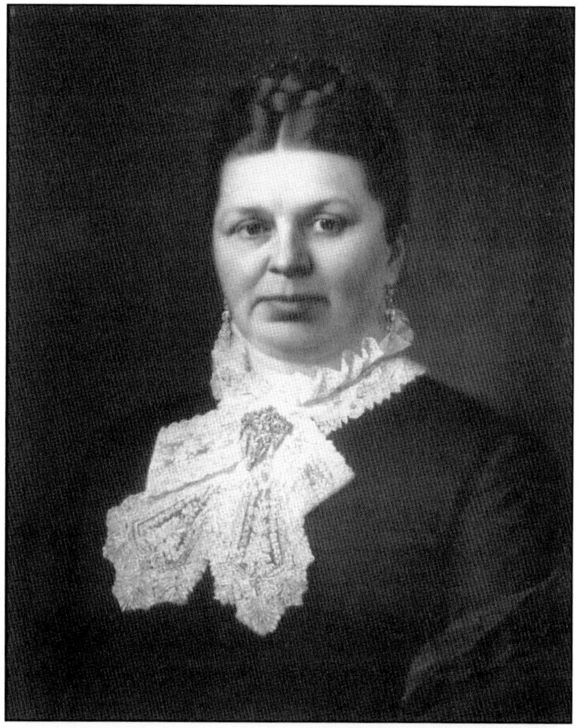

This was Claus Spreckels's new California Sugar Refinery in San Francisco as illustrated in 1881. This facility, completed in 1867, processed sugar cane from Hawaii, and after 1888 raw beet sugar from the Watsonville factory. Its initial capacity was 25,000–30,000 pounds of sugar per day. The text at the top reads, "Issued with the S.F. News Letter, Christmas Number 1881."

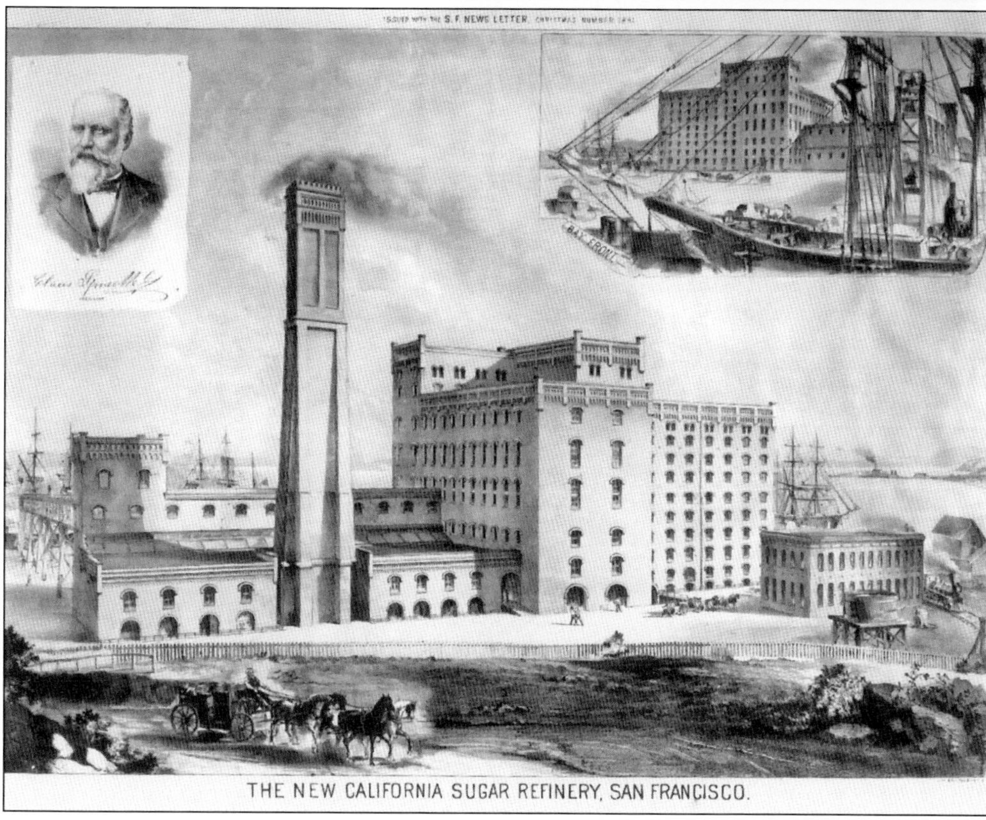

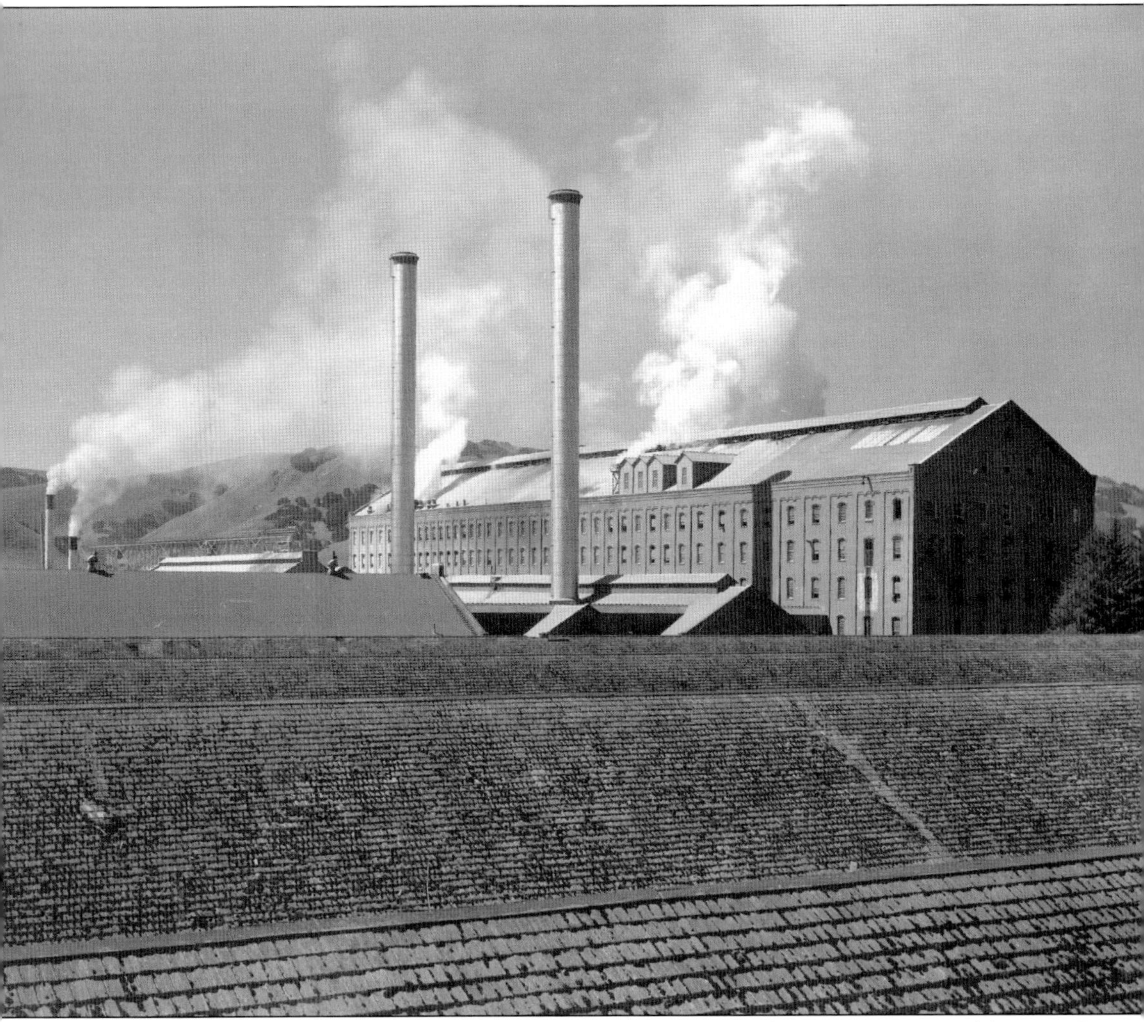

As Cordray noted in his 1955 dissertation, "Spreckels directed his activities toward bigness. It was a symbol of success to him. He liked being pointed out as the founder of the largest sugar refinery in San Francisco, and he pointed with pride to the fact that the beet sugar factory at Spreckels was the largest in the world. As he once stated, after its building he would no longer be the 'Sugar King,' but the 'emperor of the sugar industry.' The 'Claus Spreckels Building' was the tallest building in San Francisco. The Spreckels home was one of the largest and finest in the city. His gifts to unemployment, the German Fair, and to earthquake relief were the most generous. He subscribed the most to the stock of the San Francisco and San Joaquin Valley Railroad. Thus, doing things in a big way was Spreckels' method of demonstrating his success."

Two

BEGINNINGS

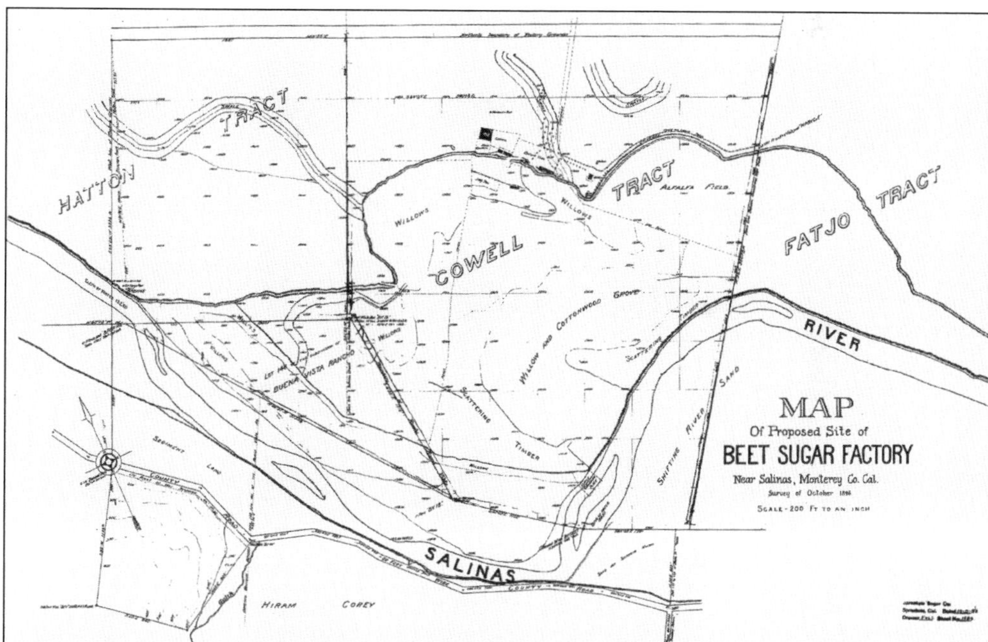

This October 1896 map shows the proposed site of the Spreckels Beet Sugar Factory. Beginning in 1865, Carlysle S. Abbott leased this land for a dairy. By 1875, Abbott was milking 1,500 cows and producing 200,000 pounds of butter annually, and he owned the land. Abbott noted, "I had lumber hauled from Watsonville, and built a residence and out-buildings at the present site of Spreckels Sugar Company's big factory." This and other such drawings in this book are among hundreds of blueprints and architectural drawings donated to the Monterey County Historical Society by the Spreckels Sugar Company.

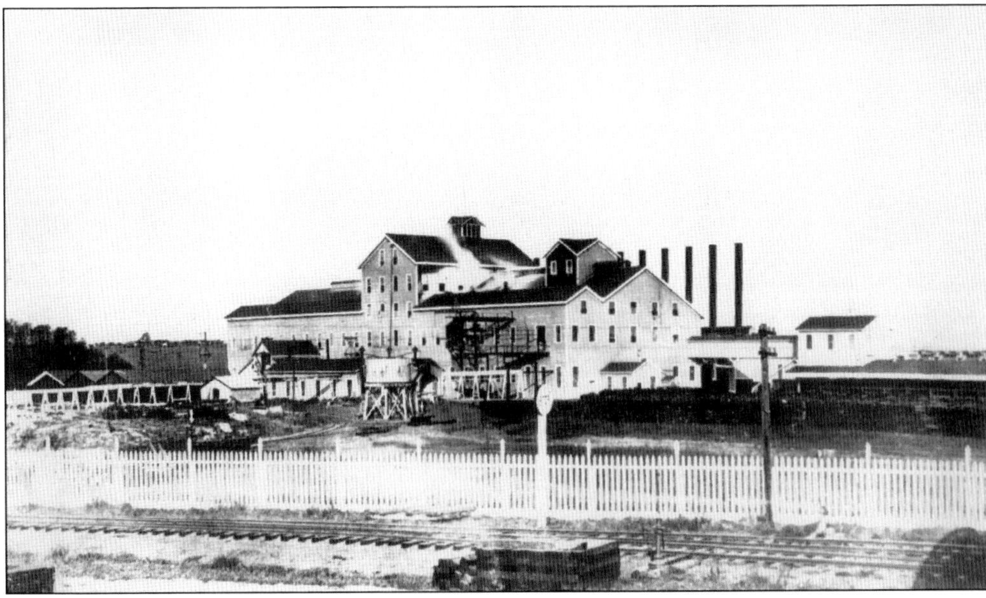

Spreckels's Watsonville refinery was incorporated on October 15, 1887, and began processing beets in 1888; it was closed shortly after the new factory at Spreckels began production. The raw beet sugar was shipped to the San Francisco factory for final processing.

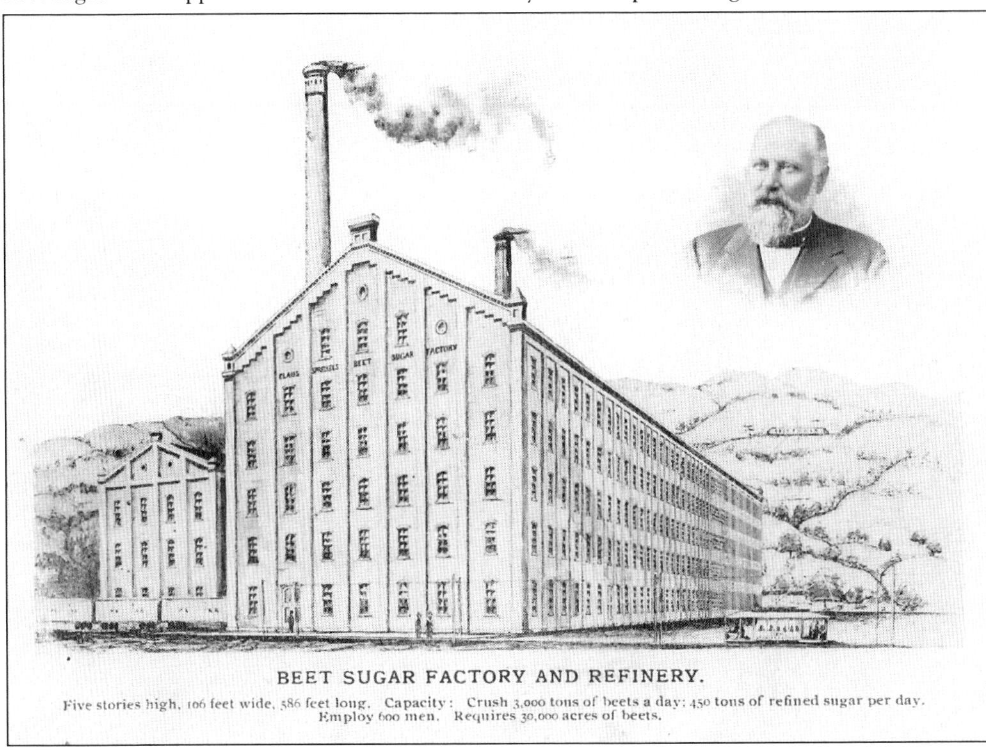

A promotional drawing, apparently prepared by Spreckels, appeared in the *Salinas Index* and in a promotional leaflet. The Salinas Valley did not need much encouragement as it seemed to see the sugar beet as their salvation. Times had been hard recently for many farmers and ranchers.

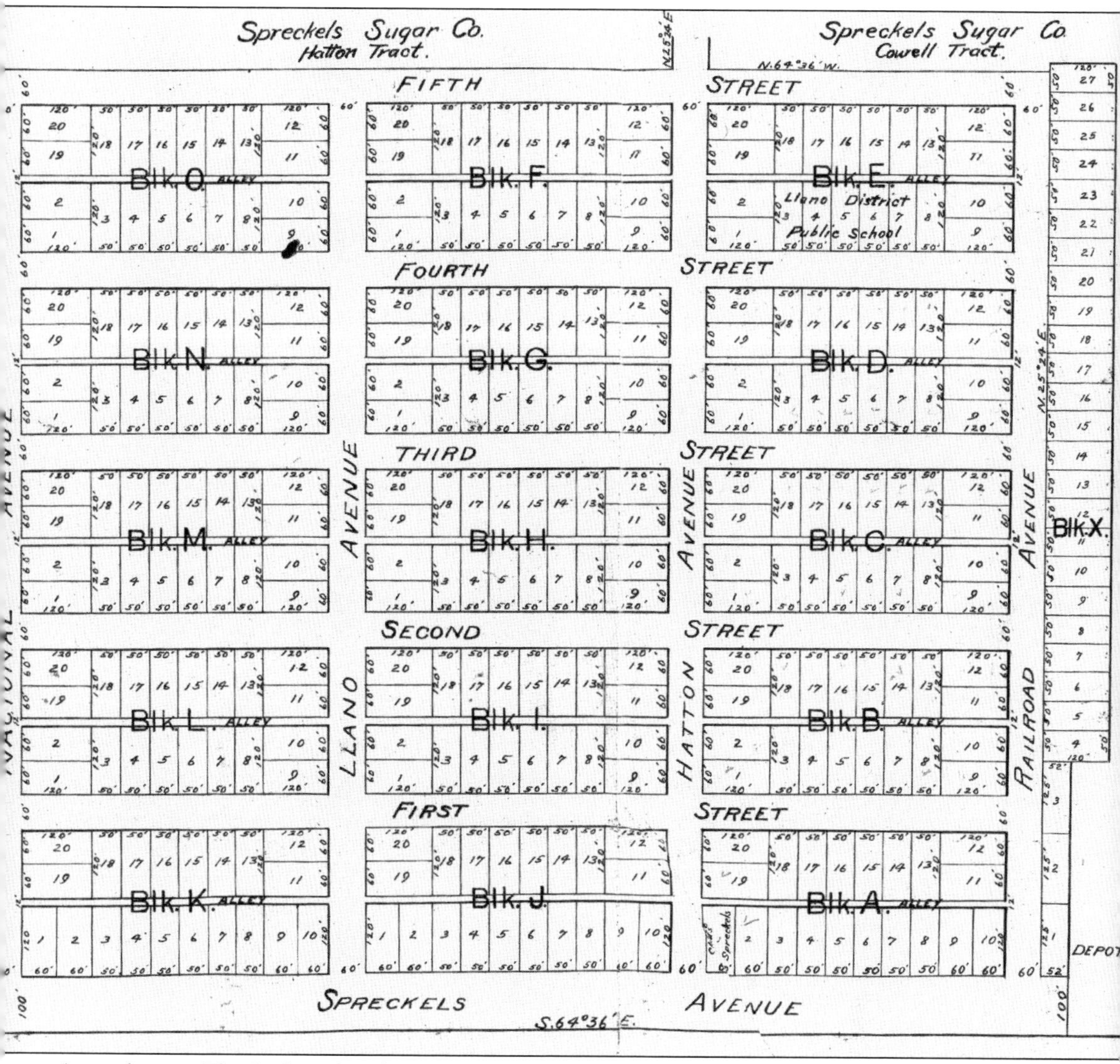

According to *The Owl* on October 14, 1897, "Architect Weeks prepared plans for 40 four-room farm houses to be erected on subdivisions of Spreckels's old Cowell ranch. With each building, there will be an outhouse to match, also a barn." Nacional Avenue and the five blocks to the west were never completed. According to an early assessment book, some initial buildings were: Block A, lots 9–17, hotel; Block A, lot 19, real estate office; Block E, lots 1–7, school; Block G, lots 9–10, church; and Block I, lot 20, church. A full list of property owners includes the following: Spreckels Sugar Company, J. M. Juhler, Catherine Schrouder, Palilha Cooper, Alexander Mills, Llano District Public School, United Presbyterian Church of America, Catholic Church, Claus A. Spreckels et al., C. E. Bradley, Lillie B. Madsen, Leo Schlytes, J. Braga, W. H. Moore, D. Stanghellini, V. Panilli, P. Brusaca, John C. Freitas, Jacob Sorenson, Jennie E. Moore, Ernest Steinfartz, C. W. Gandy, ? Anderson, W. Y. Wilson, and Antone J. Camera.

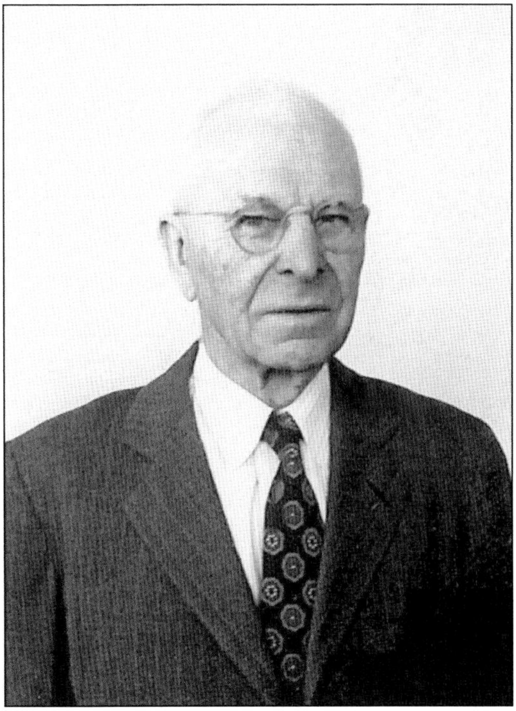

Charles L. Pioda was the civil engineer for the sugar factory. He surveyed the site of the future town of Spreckels in 1897. He later became the resident manager and was in the company's employ for 48 years. He was often referred to as Spreckels's engineer in newspaper articles. He had worked for Spreckels on the Pajaro Valley Consolidated Railroad before moving to Salinas. (Courtesy of Monterey County Agricultural and Rural Life Museum.)

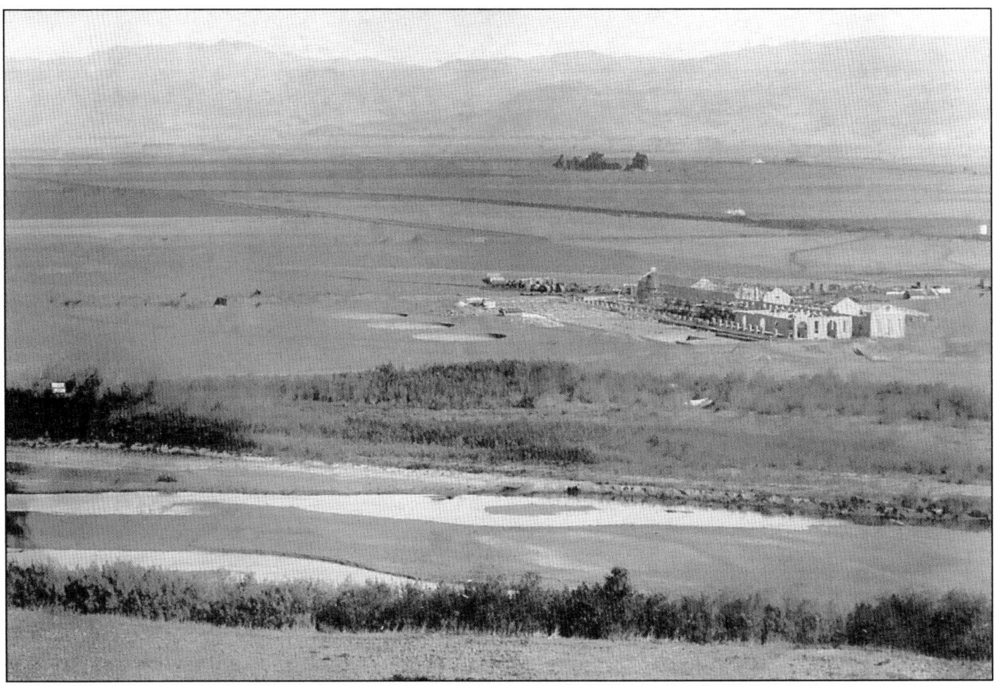

This is a very early view of the Spreckels Sugar Factory under construction, looking across the riparian corridor of the Salinas River toward the northeast. On the right is a farm building, most likely associated with the earlier Abbott dairy but part of the Logwood dairy when Spreckels bought the property. The ground has been cleared, but the steel framework of the factory has not yet been assembled. The future site of the town of Spreckels strongly resembles a hay field.

This advertisement appeared in *The Owl*, a Salinas newspaper, on Saturday, August 22, 1896, obviously commemorating Spreckels's decision to locate his new sugar factory in the Salinas area.

JEFFERY HOUSE.

BILL OF FARE.

Sunday, Aug. 23rd. Dinner 12 to 2 P. M.

SOUP.

New Enterprise.

SALAD.

Prosperity Crab Salad.

ENTREES.

Sugar Factory Stew.
Chicken a la Claus Spreckels.
Breast of Mutton Refinery Style.

ROASTS.

Prime Beef a la Neuf Salinas.
Mutton with Salinas Export Sauce.
Fricandau of Veal au Sugar Beets.

VEGETABLES.

Sugar Peas, String Beans,
Mashed Potatoes.

PASTRY.

Mass Meeting Ice Cream.
Farmers Pie. Citizens Pie.

Tea Fruits Coffee Cheese

Constructed in 87 working days, this large steel frame represented the most modern construction techniques of the time. Claus Spreckels was personally involved with the design; he returned from his European factory tour with a "hastily" sketched factory design that was reportedly done in France. Local architect W. H. Weeks was closely associated with the final design and construction.

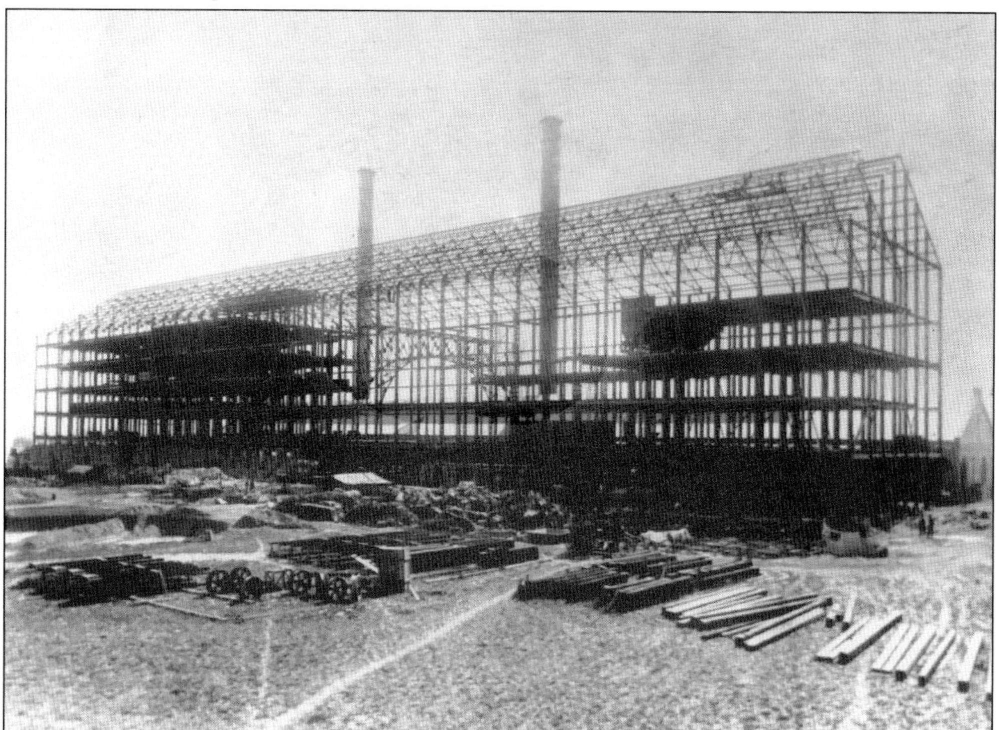

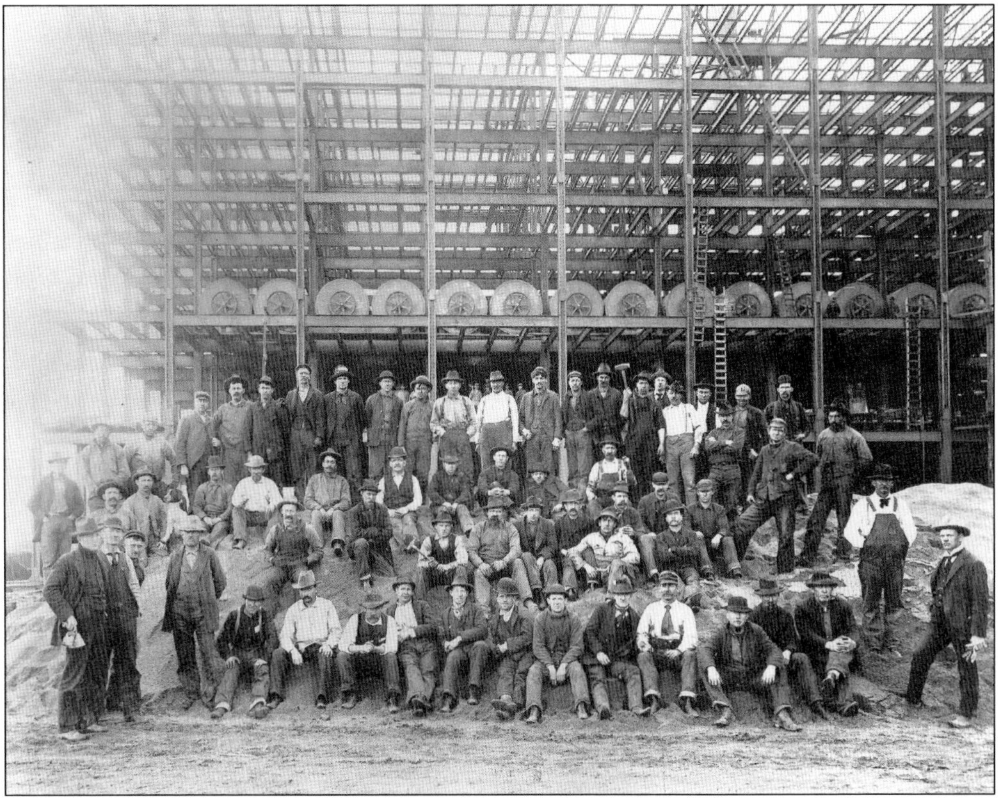

Steel workers used forges to construct the factory's interior steel frames. Rivets were heated in the forges until they were red hot before being pounded into holes that had been drilled into the steel beams. It took 200 train cars of steel and reportedly over a half million rivets to assemble this superstructure. The contractor for the main factory building and the boiler house was Risdon Iron Works of San Francisco, and they completed the job in 87 working days. To the right is crew supervisor G. R. Field.

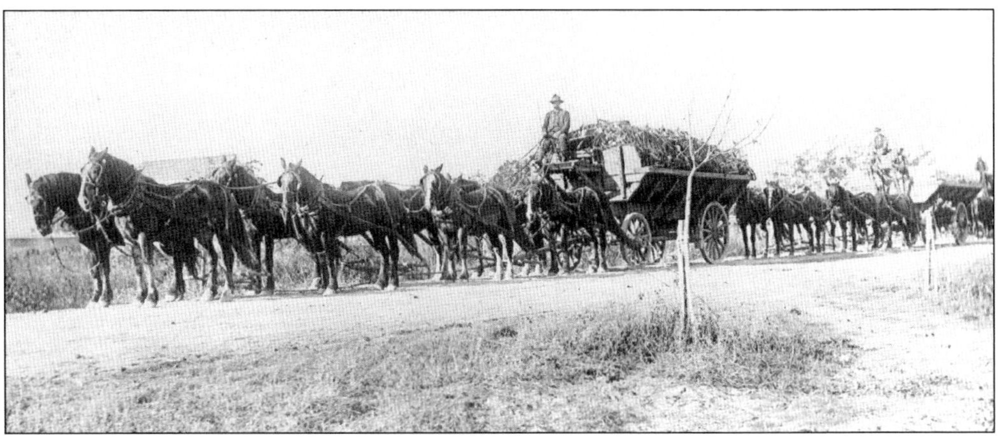

Horse teams pulled wagonloads of beets down Spreckels Boulevard. The famous row of black walnut trees are but saplings in the foreground. Before the automobile age, horse- and mule-drawn wagons hauled most of the produce in the Salinas Valley. Soil excavated from factory construction and the quarry was used to pave the early roadways and railroad beds.

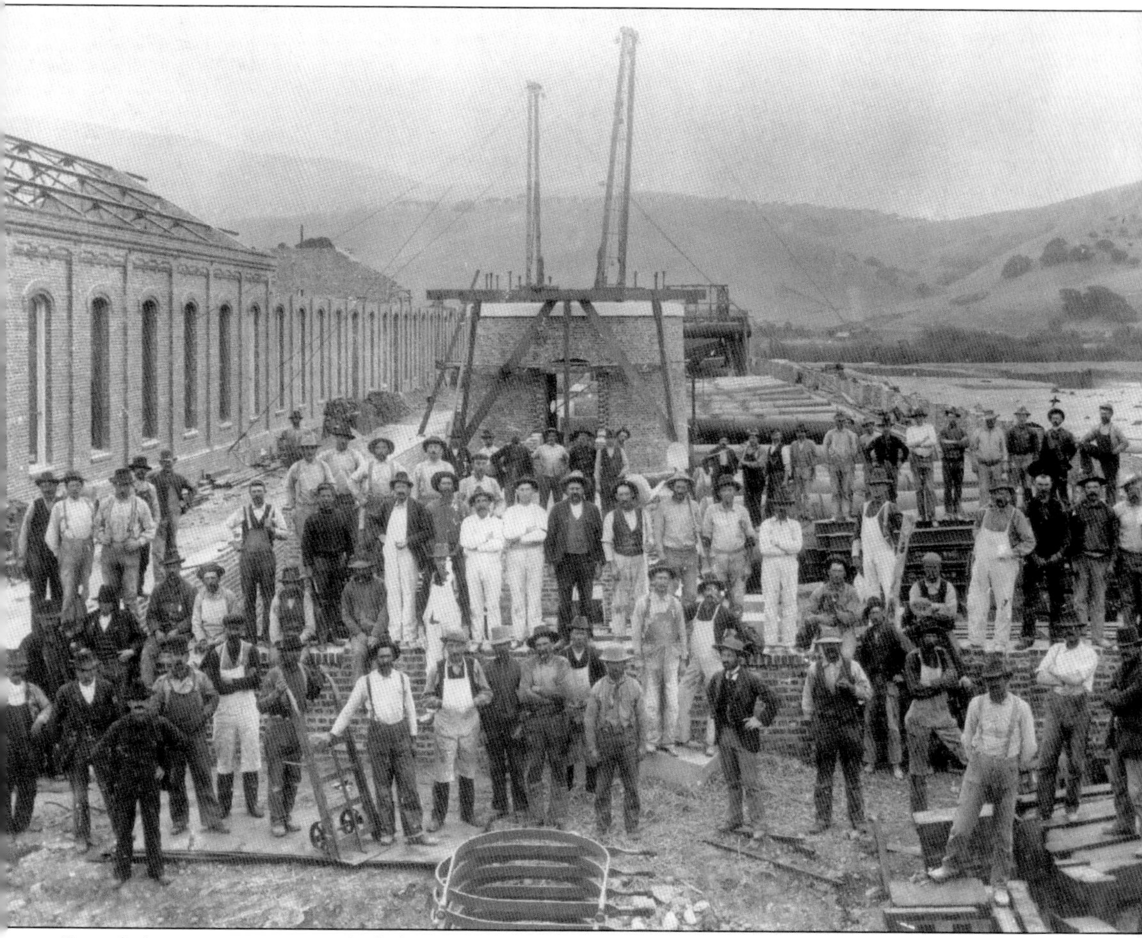

Spreckels erection crew included Joe Kavanaugh, who supervised the excavation and masonry crews for contractor James A. McMahon of San Francisco. McMahon's company was contracted to provide excavation and concrete work for the main building as well as the smaller buildings of the factory. Overseeing the construction were Spreckels engineers and architect William H. Weeks. Engineer W. C. Waters was brought in from the Watsonville plant, where he was general manager. A phone line was run down the newly created railway beds so that Waters could be in constant contact at both plants. The construction plans were drawn by chief draftsman Joseph Rhyner and a team of 27 other draftsmen. The cranes in the background were imported from New York by Spreckels and had a lifting capacity of 20,000 pounds each. McMahon's crews were also responsible for building six miles of railroad between the factory and the quarry site in Alisal Canyon (northeast of Salinas). This branch line passed within a few yards of the current terminal at the Salinas Municipal Airport.

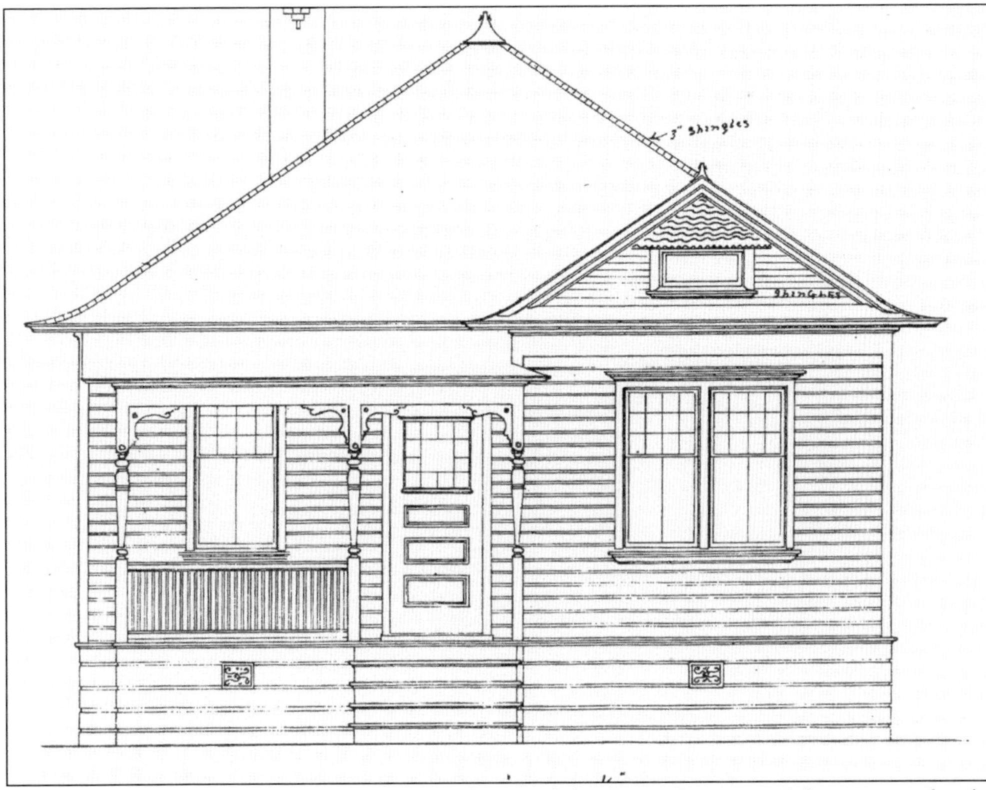

Architect William H. Weeks, around 1898, designed the front elevation of this cottage for the Spreckels Sugar Company. Initial plans called for 40 of these to be built. Each building included an outhouse and a barn. This is but one of 12 designs created by Weeks for the first homes in Spreckels. A. W. Wyman, a builder from Soquel, was the initial contractor for this construction.

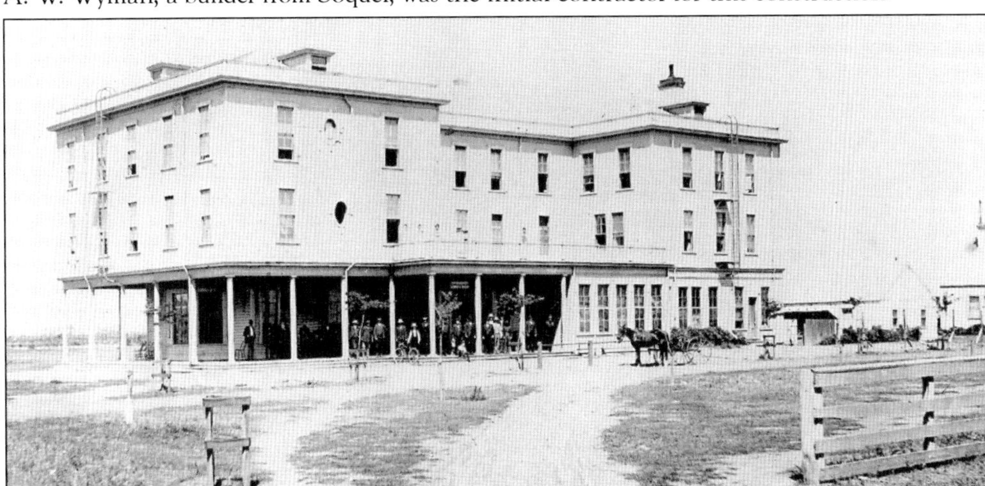

The Spreckels Hotel opened on August 7, 1898, under the operation of Mrs. James Huff. There were 61 rooms in the building, 50 of which were bedrooms. Some held as many as four beds. In short order, Huff had 61 guests at the hotel and could not accept any more. The hotel had a barbershop, four private baths, a bar, fire escapes, waitresses, and Chinese cooks. The building was only a few months old when fire destroyed the upper two stories. It was immediately restored.

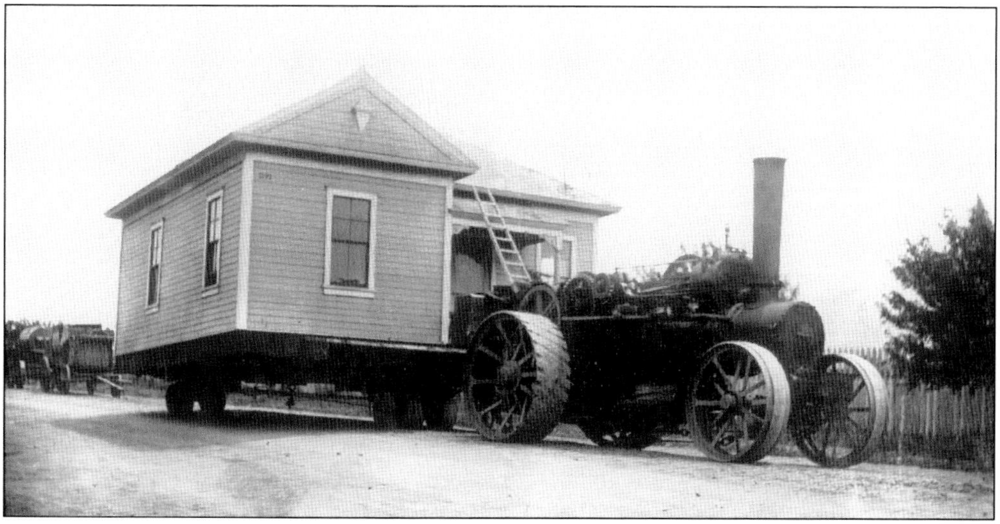

The town of Spreckels was growing rapidly. To ease the housing shortage, buildings were regularly moved in from other locations, particularly from Spreckels's other facilities. This house is being towed by a steam tractor. The company had some houses cut in two and loaded on railroad cars for transport from Gilroy to Spreckels.

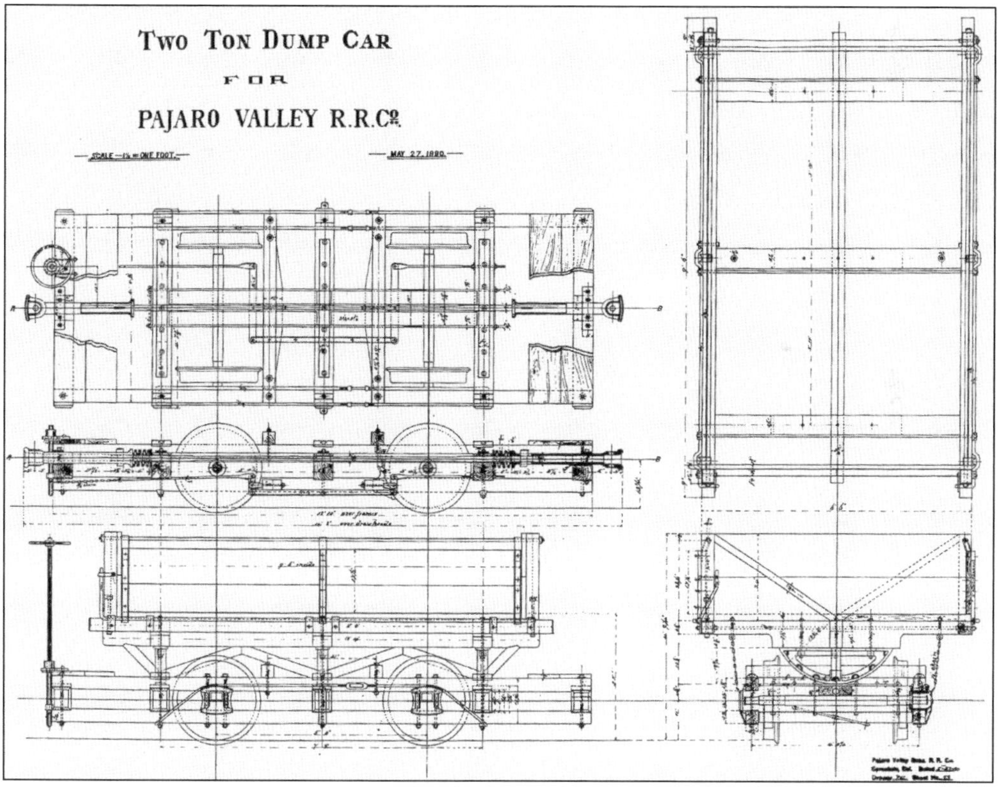

The architectural drawing for a two-ton dump car, designed for the Pajaro Valley Railroad Company, is dated May 27, 1890. This car is the type used for the Spreckels factory when it was built in the late 1890s. The cars included dump mechanisms that allowed them to be turned on their sides for unloading.

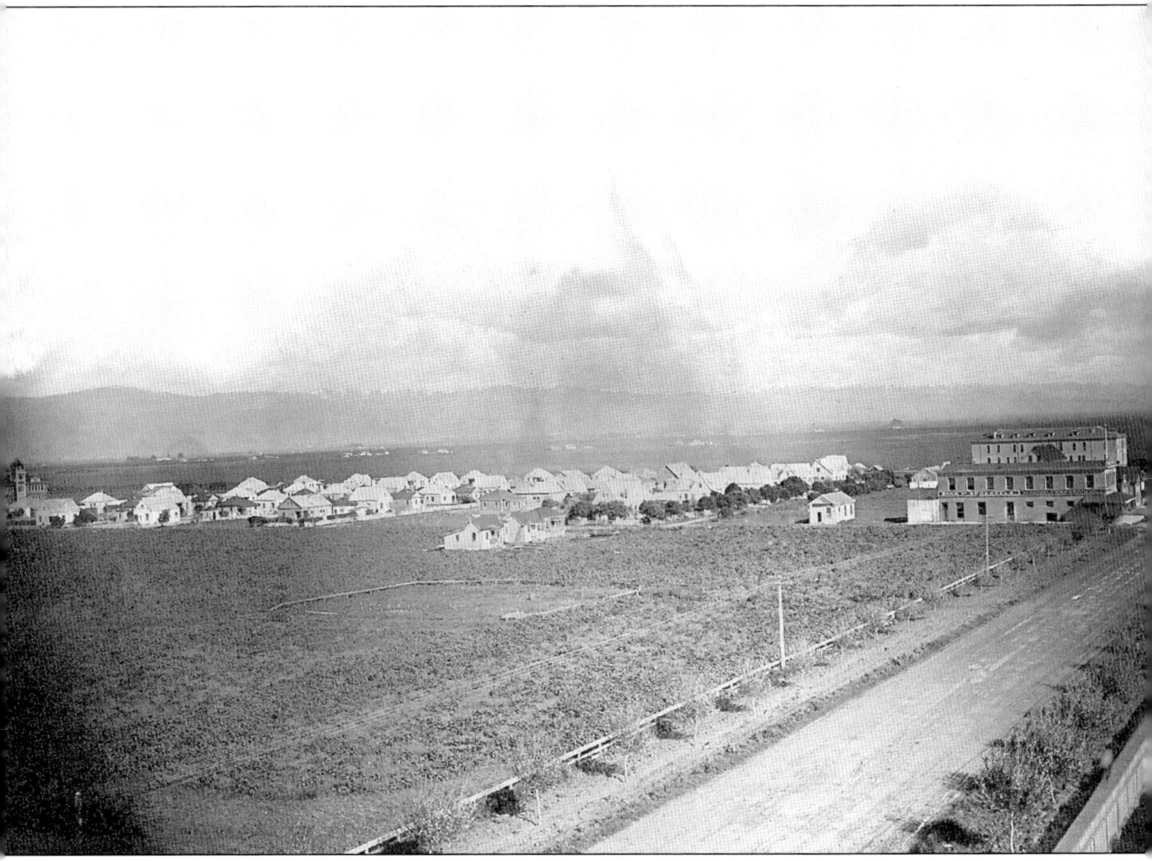

In the fledgling town of Spreckels, this former hay field has been growing houses at a rapid rate. This view shows that the three-story hotel (1897) has been joined by a two-story brick commercial building that came to be known as the Emporium/Bank of Spreckels (1898) and the three-story brick school with a bell tower (1899). It also shows the row of young black walnut trees along Spreckels Boulevard. The *Salinas Daily Index* on July 24, 1898, read, "Within full view of Mr. Water's residence the new town of Spreckels is rapidly assuming definite shape. Immense piles of lumber are on the ground, the foundations of numerous buildings are ready and about 40 carpenters are at work on others. Already four of the cottages are up and enclosed, four are partially enclosed and seven will be ready to enclose the middle of this week. As fast, as they are enclosed they are being lathed and plastered. The cottages are being built in various sizes, some having five rooms, while others will have six, seven and eight rooms. The designs are nearly similar."

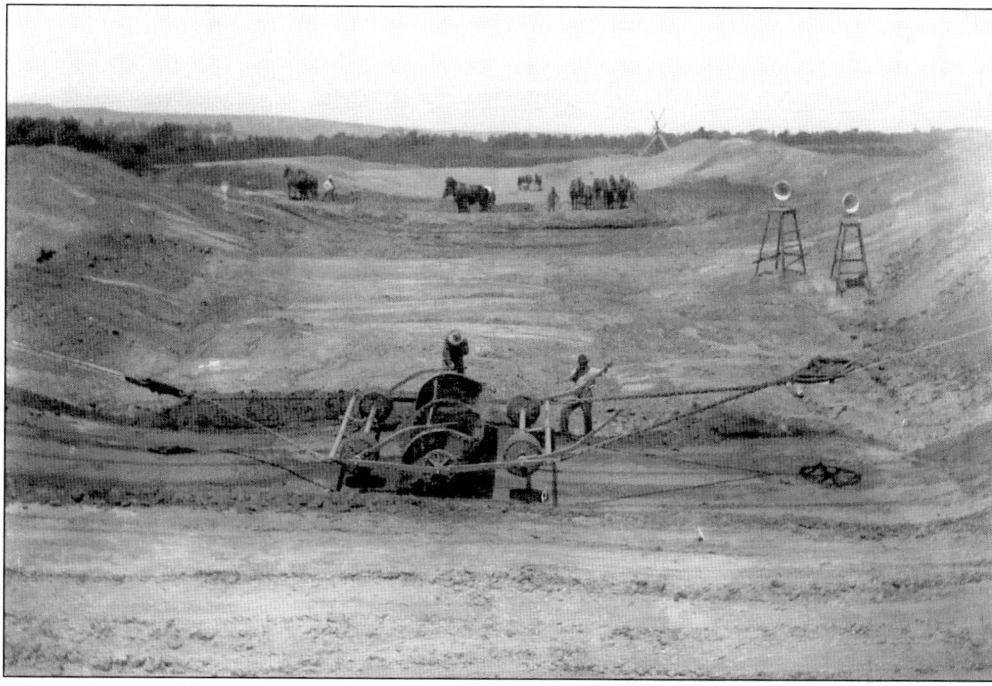

The method used for excavating the site for Silo No. 3 involved a grader, which was pulled laterally back and forth by means of cables hooked to steam tractors. In the background, teams of horses are also engaged in land leveling. Excavated soil was used to make roads and railroad beds.

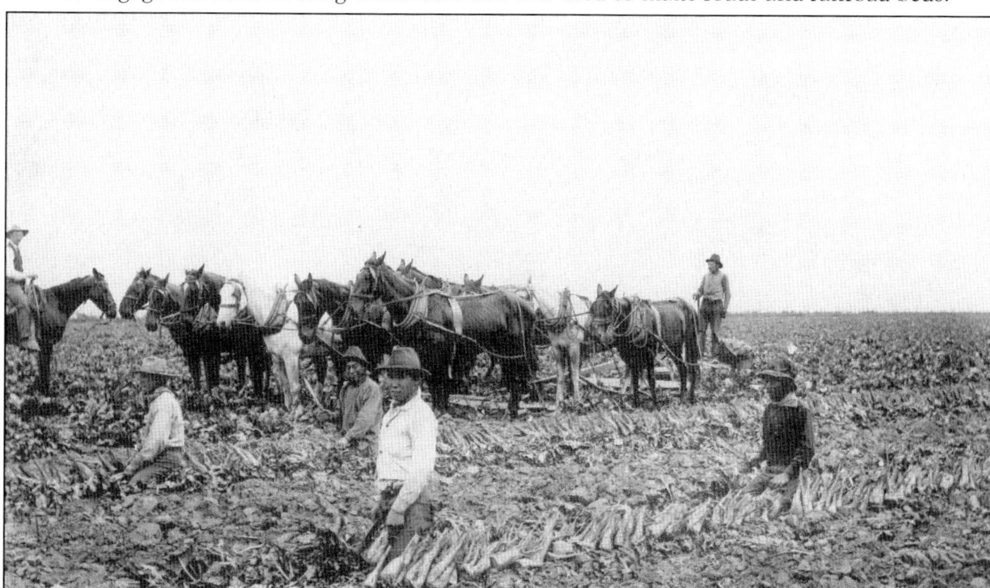

Until the late 1890s, Chinese men provided much of the labor required to grow and transport beets. A contractor usually hired out the beet workers to local growers. A fee was paid to the contractor for each man the grower hired. Contract labor began with the Chinese. After the Exclusion Act of 1882 barred Chinese laborers from entering the United States, other immigrant groups eventually replaced them. Japanese, Filipinos, Indians, and Europeans all worked as field labor. Mexican nationals became a source of labor beginning in 1942, during World War II.

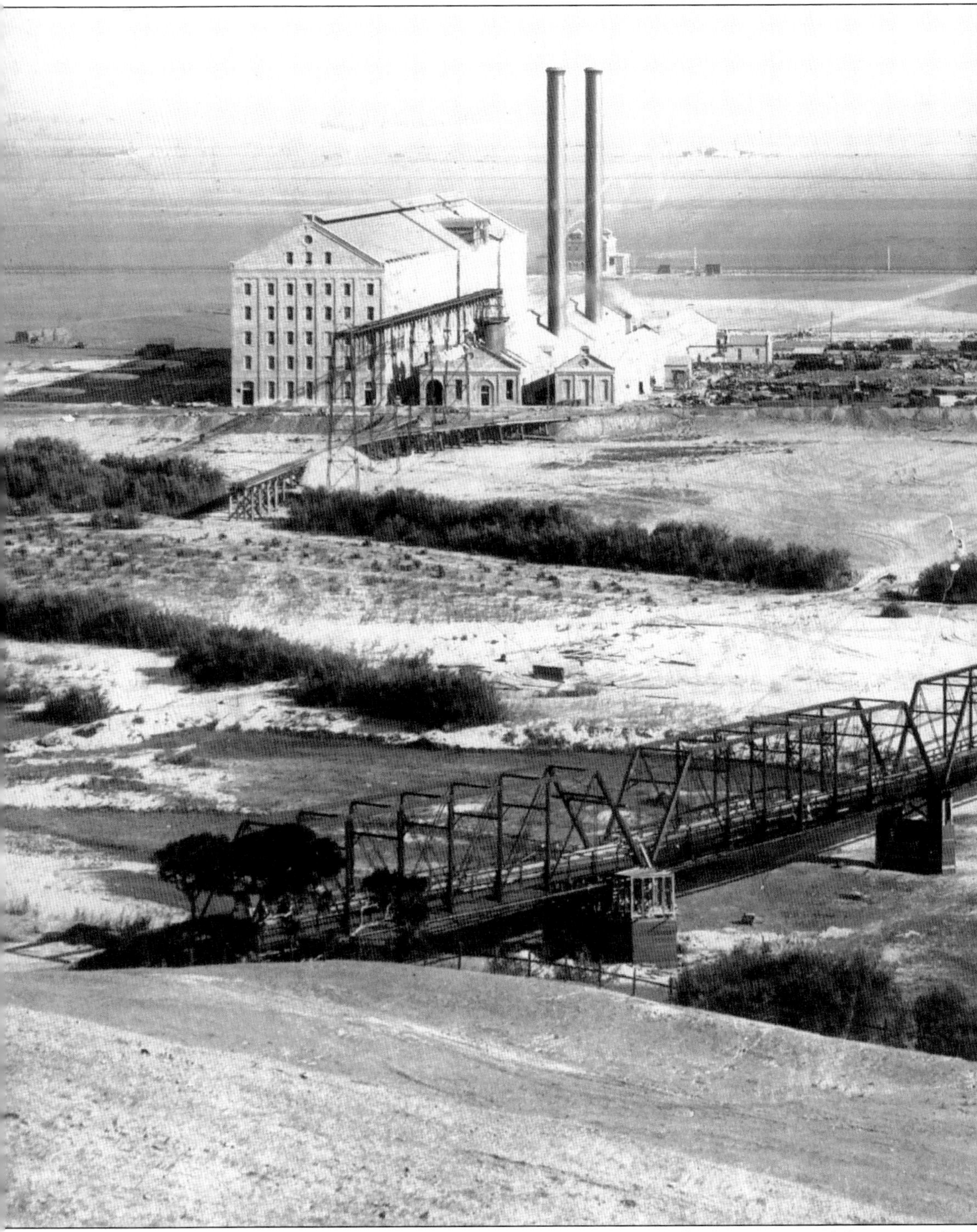

This early photograph shows Spreckels Sugar Factory No. 1 and the beginnings of the town of Spreckels. "The Store" and school have not yet been constructed. In the early years, discharge from the factory went into the river. When the factory had its first "campaign"—a term used to refer to the annual beet harvest and processing—the effluent from the factory went directly into the

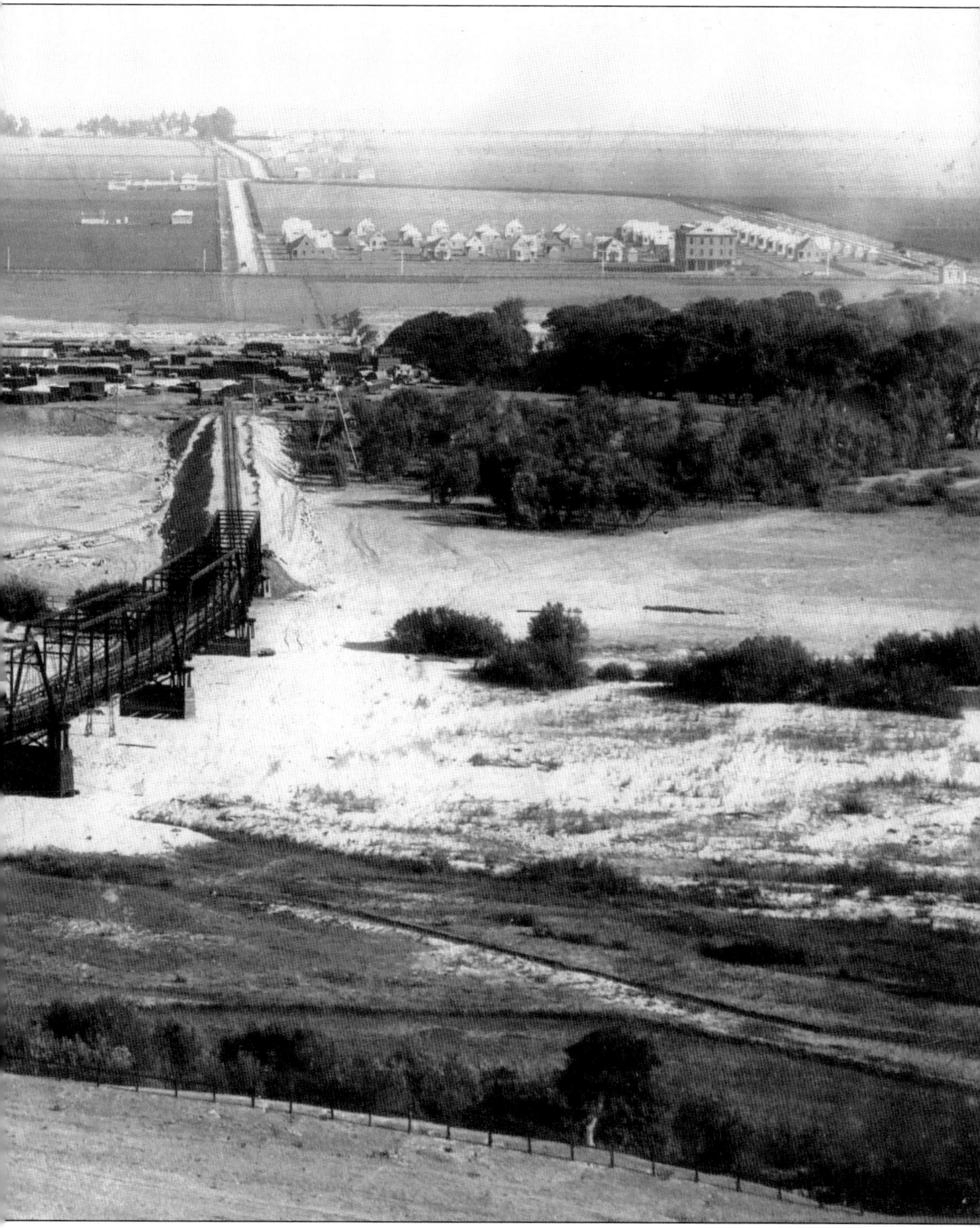

Salinas River. This resulted in a "big stink," both figuratively and literally, and a major fish kill. Thereafter, a reservoir pond system was developed whereby wastewater went into holding ponds and was then recycled as irrigation water for the fields rather than being dumped into the river.

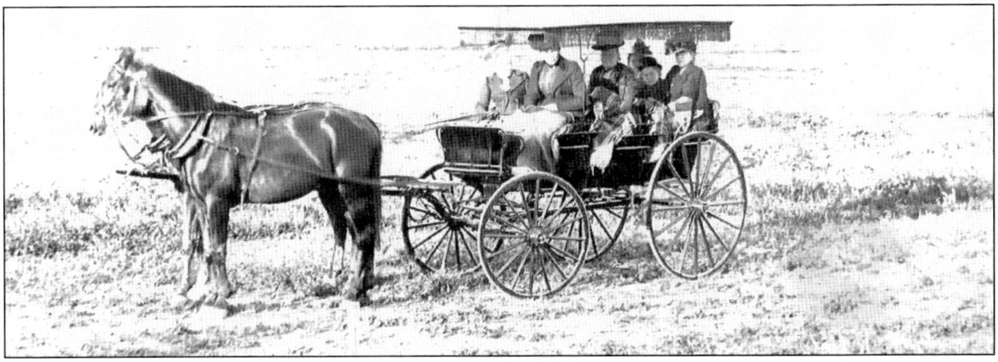

These women and children, in a three-seater hired from a Salinas livery stable, had their photograph taken just before they left for a ride to Monterey. Arriving at their destination, the horses were watered, fed, and allowed to rest before returning to Spreckels. The photograph shows the factory yard fence and the beet bins in the background. (Courtesy of Monterey County Agricultural and Rural Life Museum.)

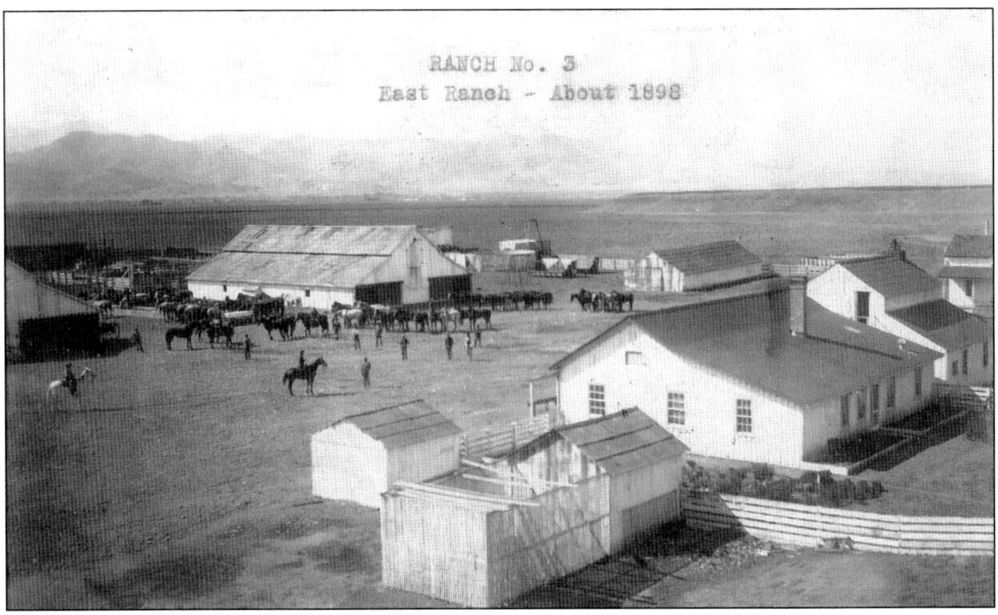

In addition to all the private landholders whose tenants were growing beets for the factory, Spreckels bought large tracts of land, which were then divided into "ranches." These were more like management districts, as not all the lands held were contiguous. Ranch No. 1 was in Spreckels, and Ranch No. 3 was near King City. Large numbers of field hands lived and worked on the outlying ranches.

Three

The Town

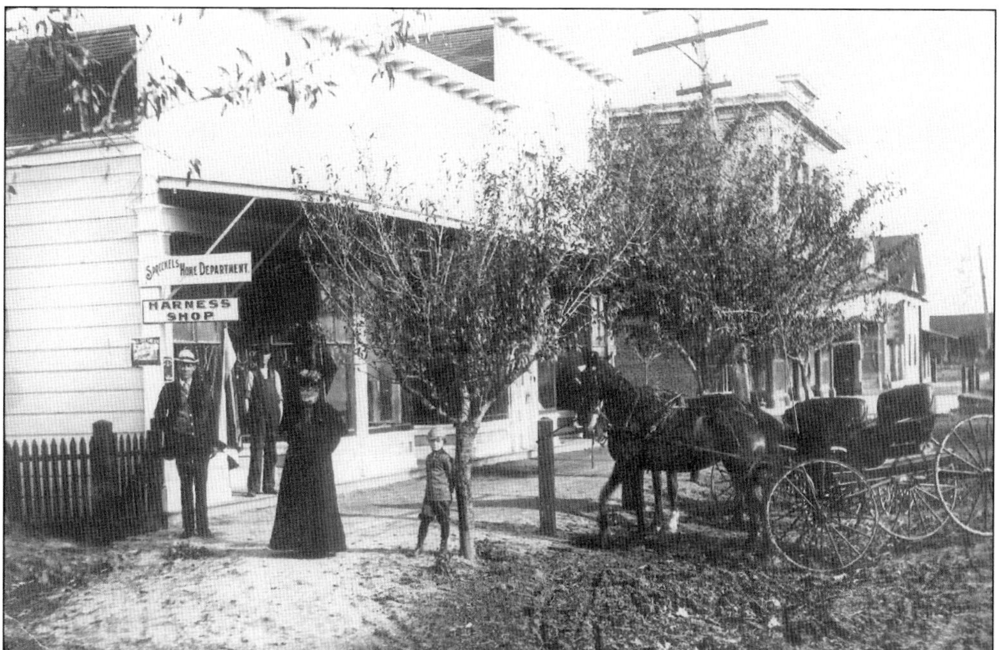

Waxy McDougal's harness shop was one of the businesses that moved into the newly created business district. Note the impatient horse fidgeting; he is tied to the hitching post in front of the shop. Most businesses closed during the curly top blight in the early decades of the 20th century.

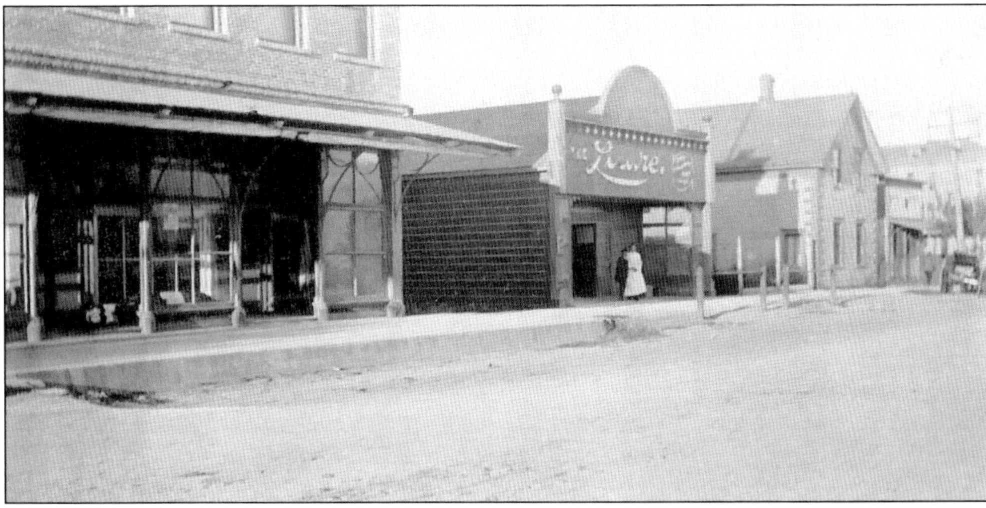

The early Spreckels Post Office was housed in the two-story building on the left; the Ford and Sanborn Company operated this structure as "The Store." Perhaps the most famous building in town was the Louvre Saloon. This was a popular place for many of the factory workers. The women in town became disenchanted with the time and money the men spent in the saloon and circulated a petition demanding that after the its liquor license expired in 1912 that Spreckels become a dry town. The two-story building to the right was occupied by a family, and next to that was the Spreckels Meat Market.

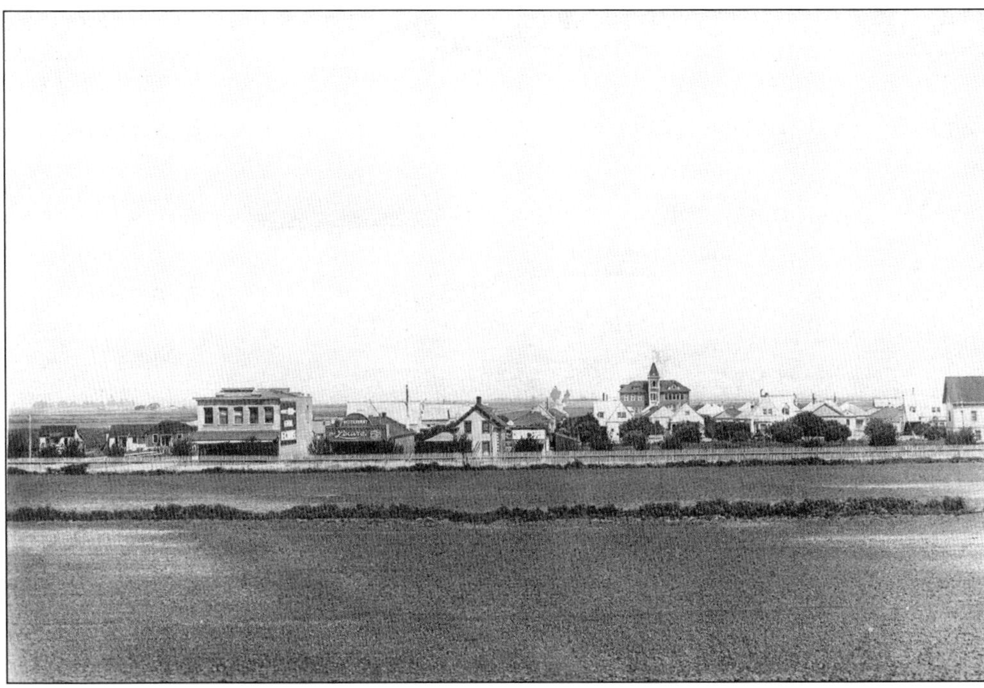

A view of the newly created business district shows, on the left, the two-story brick commercial building known as "The Store." The lower portion was part store, bank, and post office. Upstairs was a recreation hall. In the background is the three-story school, and to the right is the hotel.

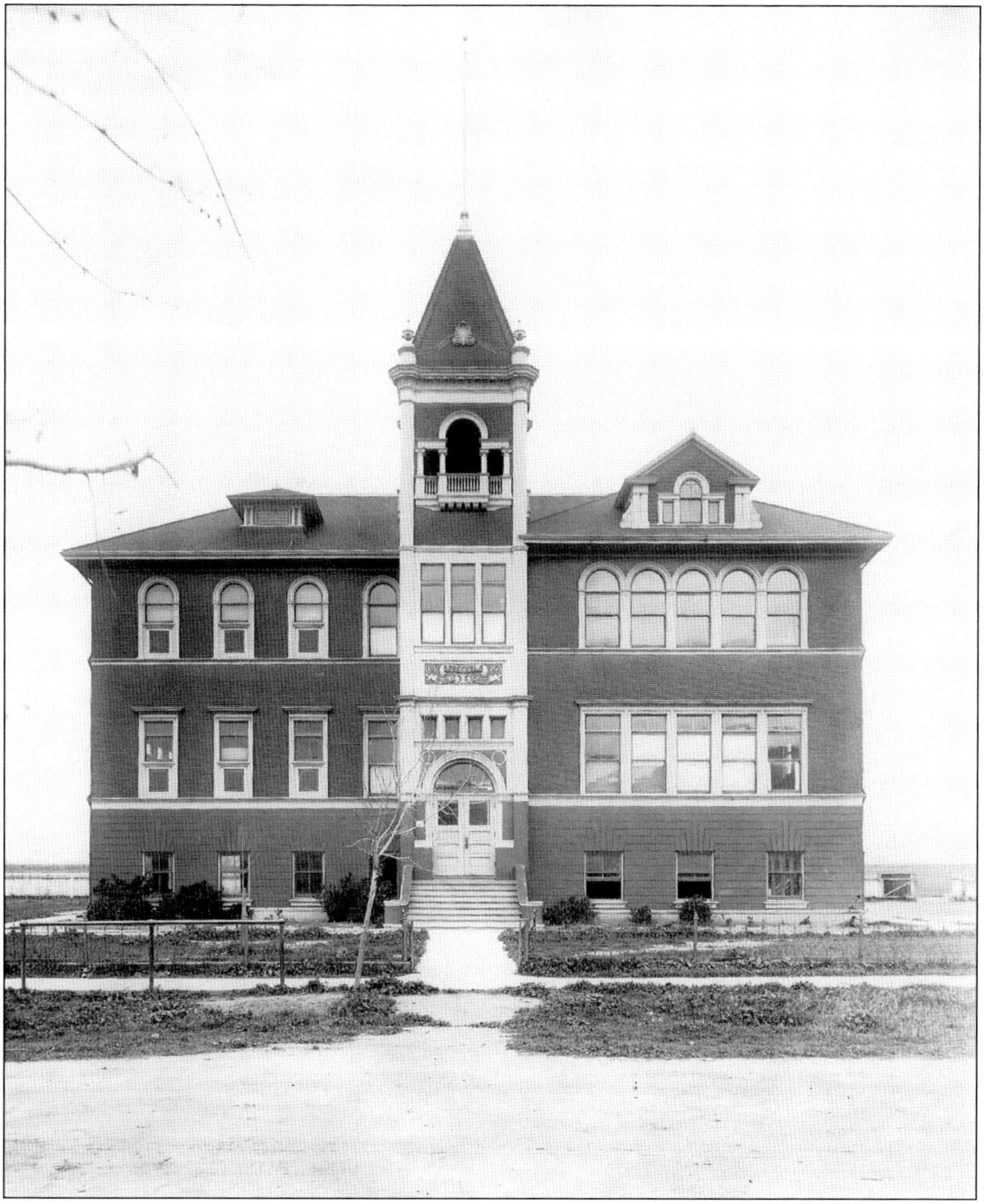

The little red schoolhouse was three stories high and designed by W. H. Weeks. The school started with two teachers, Lena Forden and Lilian Lang. The pigeons thought the bell tower was a fine place to roost. This structure served as the local schoolhouse from 1899 to 1936, when it was replaced. The bell was taken to University of California (UC) Davis where it is still used to signal scores at football games. The school was also used for Sunday school classes, organized by a group of young people, since the only religious services in Spreckels at that time were conducted by the Catholic church. Edwin T. Dahlberg said, "It was in the room just below the tower, the room with the three windows, above the sign 'Spreckels' that I had my first experience as a Sunday school teacher, at the age of 17. I had a class of seven or eight boys, about 12 years old. The bell rope from the bell in the tower hung right down in the middle of my class, so when anything got out of my control as a teacher the whole town knew it!"

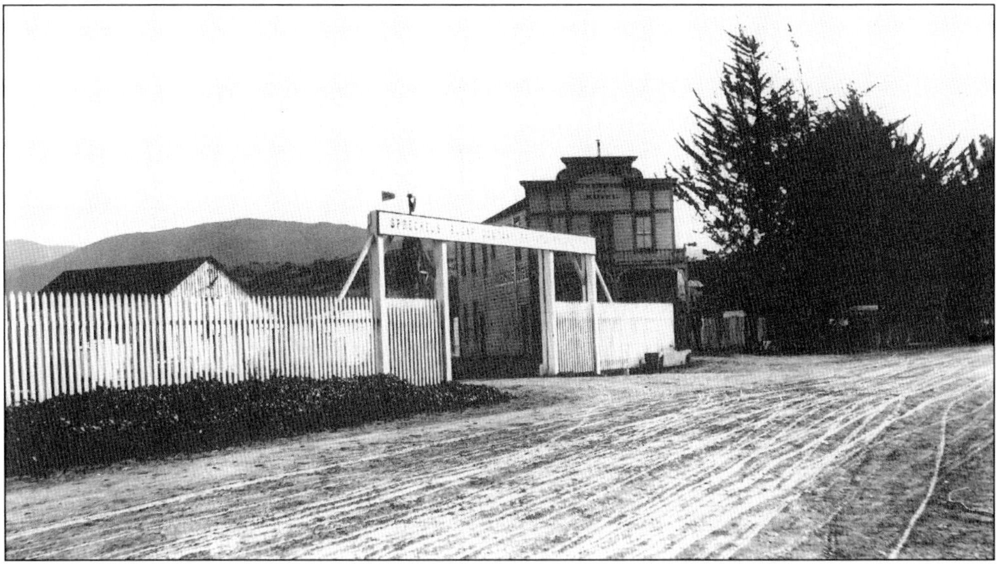

The Riverside Hotel, built around 1898, stood in Hilltown at the west end of Spreckels Boulevard. This was the site of the original ford over the Salinas River and later the site of a ferry. This land was purchased by James Bryant Hill in 1852, and he started a small community that came to be called Hilltown. This area marked the beginnings of Salinas, as Hill was named the first postmaster for the Salinas Post Office in 1854. The sign above the entry to the adjacent property reads "Spreckels Sugar Company Private Property."

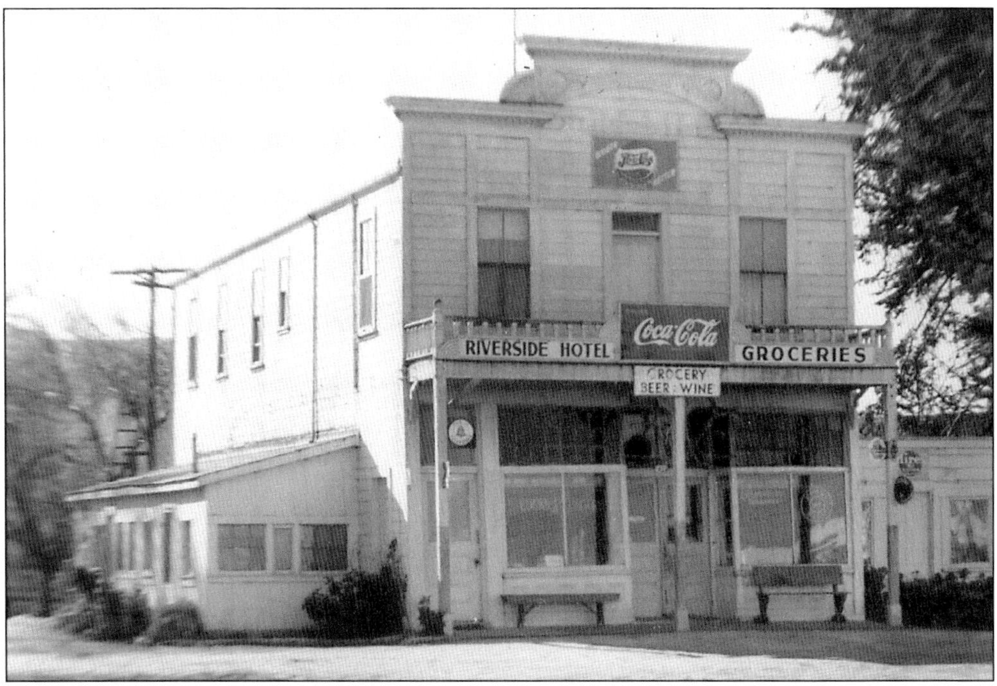

The Riverside Hotel at nearby Hilltown was used to ease the housing crunch while the town of Spreckels was under construction. Hilltown also had a saloon, which probably saw its share of business as early stories indicate that some of the workers liked to imbibe, particularly after they received their paychecks.

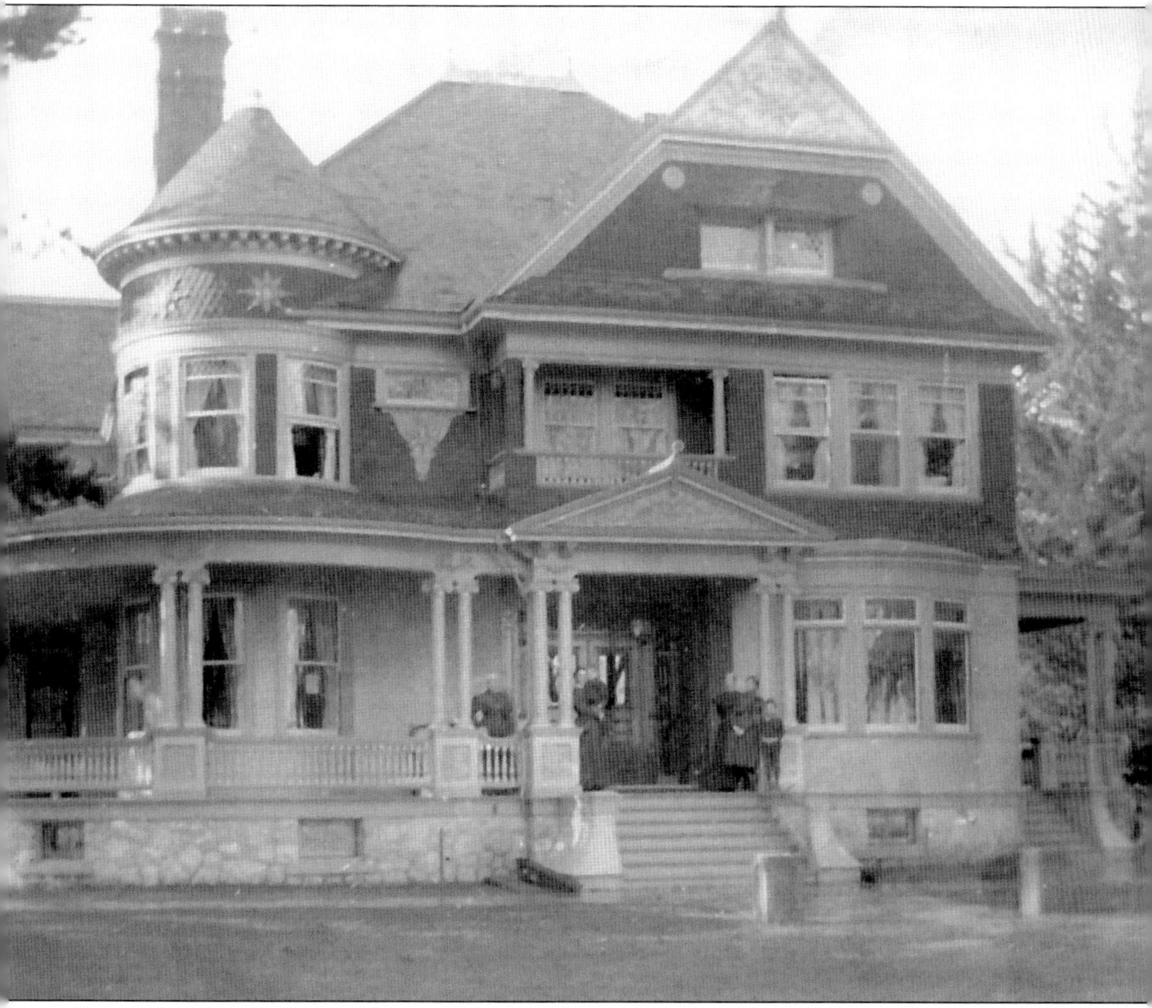

Architect William H. Weeks designed the Spreckels supervisor's home. Mr. and Mrs. Waters, the first residents, held a large housewarming party in 1898 to show off their new residence. "Again crossing the river and just as the old Logwood barn is reached, a turn to the left shows a path leading to a grove of cypress and pine trees. Within this grove and almost in its center Architect Weeks is engaged in the erection of one of the finest houses in the county for Superintendent Waters. . . . On the first floor are seven fine rooms, kitchen, pantries, bathroom and toilet-rooms. On the second floor are seven rooms, a library, large hall and bathroom with toilets. There will be two rooms furnished in the finest style for use by Claus Spreckels whenever he visits the factory," wrote the *Salinas Daily Index* on July 24, 1898. W. C. Waters selected the homesite overlooking the Salinas River, east of the factory. This reportedly was at the site of the Logwood house, associated with the Logwood dairy begun by Carlisle S. Abbott around 1865. The Waters family resided here until he retired in 1904. J. M. Taylor took over during his term as general manager, followed by R. H. Moore. In 1912, during the term of F. E. Sullivan, the residence caught fire and was destroyed.

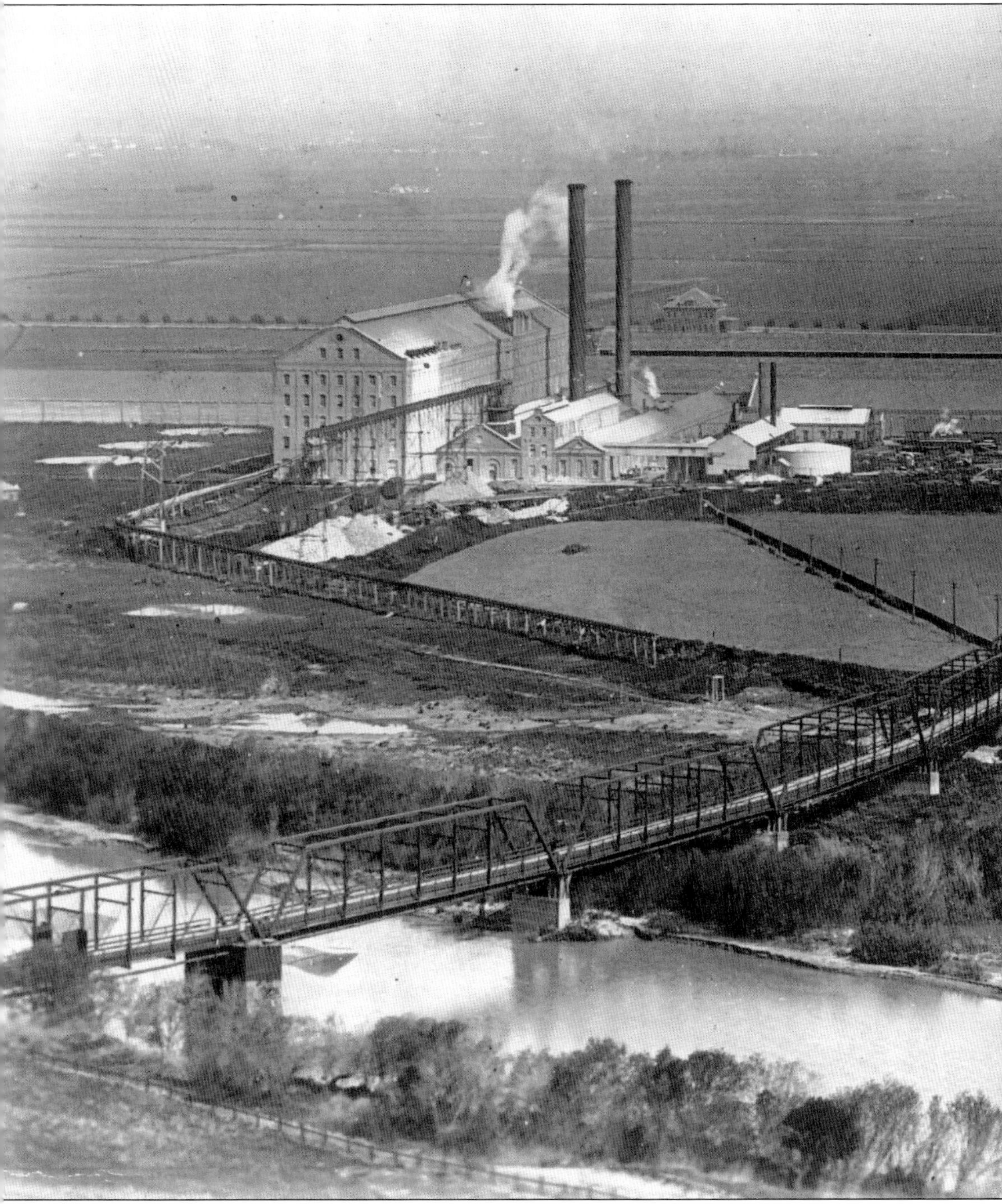

At the time of his death in 1908, this was the crown jewel of Spreckels's sugar empire. Claus had fulfilled his promises to the people of the Salinas Valley. In the 12 years since the mass meeting in which he laid out his plan, Spreckels had built not only the largest sugar plant in the world but the town to go with it. There was also the infrastructure of intertwining network of roads, railways, dump stations, irrigation canals, wells and pumps, and pipelines. The entire Salinas Valley was enjoying an unprecedented level of prosperity thanks to this Hanoverian immigrant

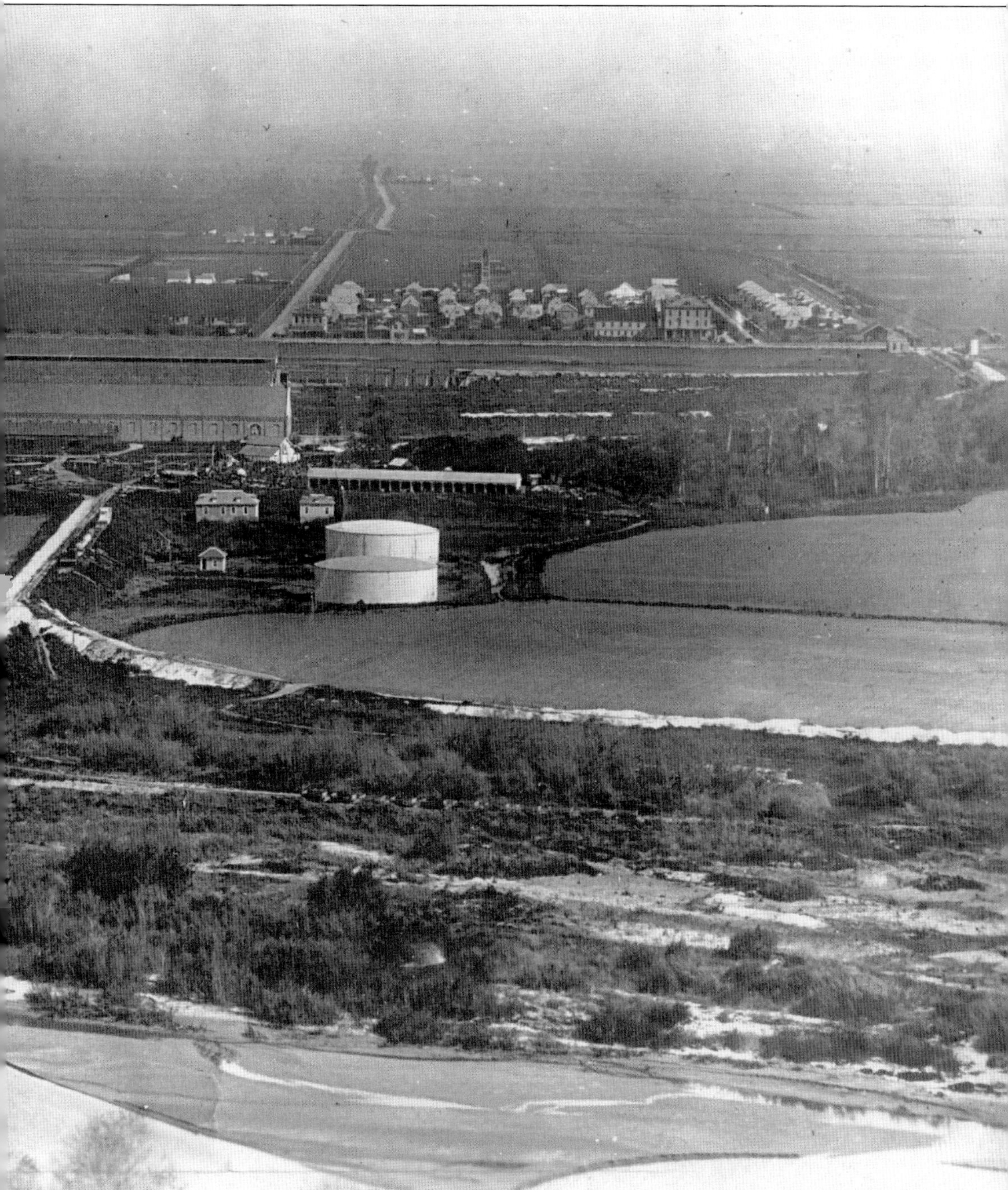

who came to this country on borrowed money. In his lifetime, he fulfilled the "American dream" of immigrating to this country and becoming successful, not only for himself but for many others as well. All of this created a lasting legacy that persists even to this day. Although the factory is now gone—it remained in operation for over 80 amazing years—the town and the community carry on the Spreckels legacy.

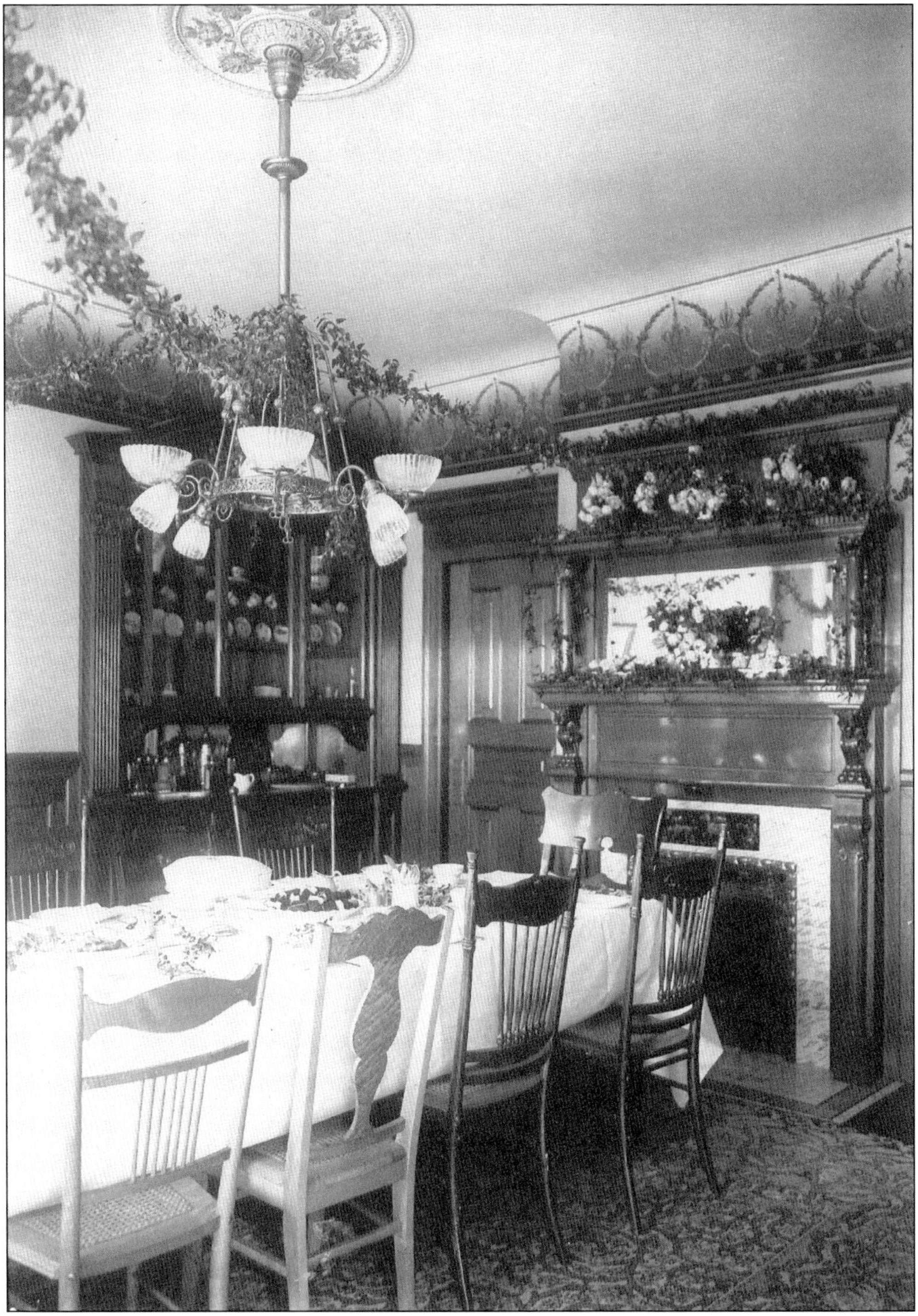

This was the breakfast setting for the Bullene wedding in the dining room at factory superintendent Waters's residence. Note the Victorian-style ceiling with the painted tin embellishment at the top of the hanging chandelier. Indoor plumbing and electricity were rare when this house was constructed, particularly for a home located five miles from the nearest city.

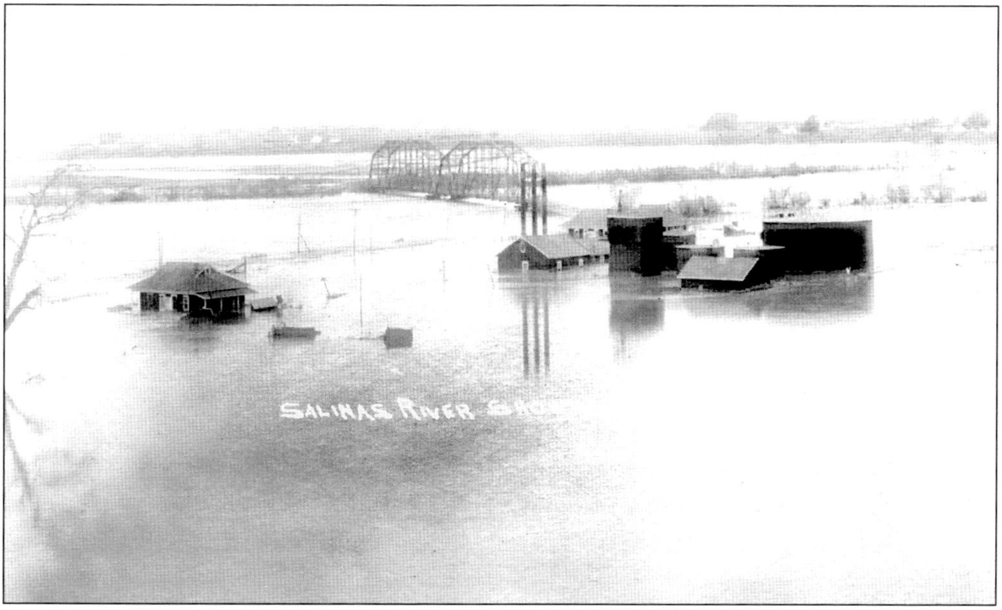

Flooding is always a problem near the Salinas River. Notable floods are recorded for 1911 and 1914, but the area pictured has been flooded as recently as 1995. This is the Hilltown area, showing the old iron bridge. A new four-lane, elevated highway has long since replaced the bridge, but it too was rendered temporarily unusable in 1969 shortly after it was built.

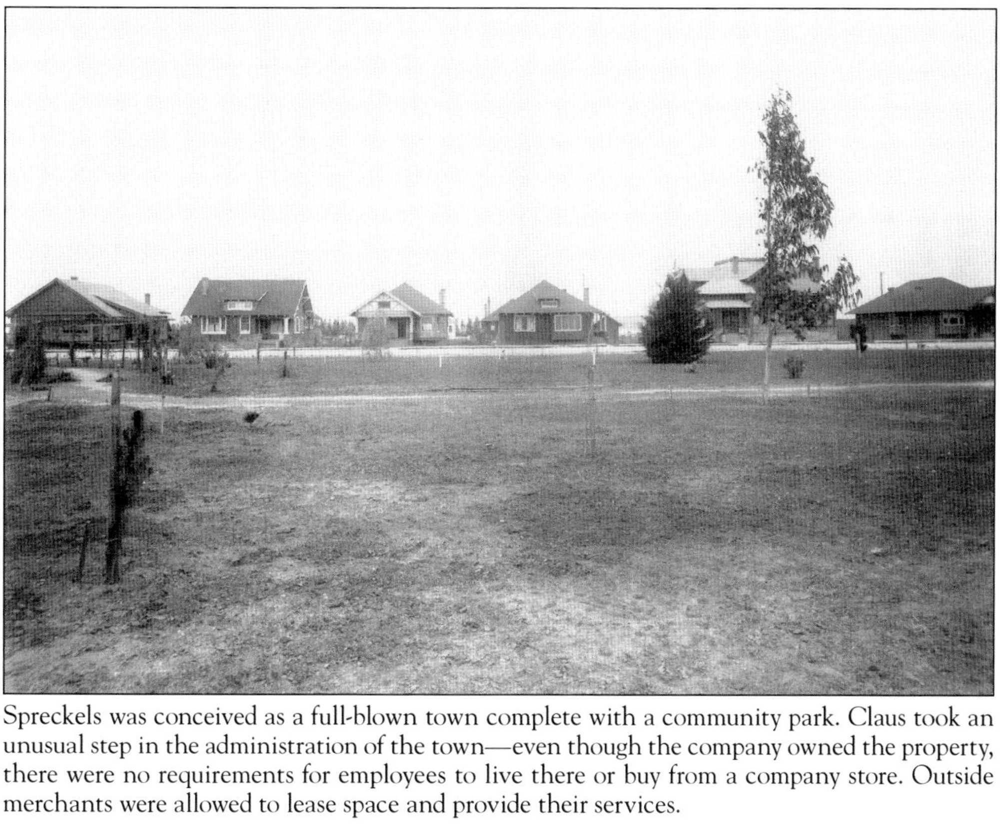

Spreckels was conceived as a full-blown town complete with a community park. Claus took an unusual step in the administration of the town—even though the company owned the property, there were no requirements for employees to live there or buy from a company store. Outside merchants were allowed to lease space and provide their services.

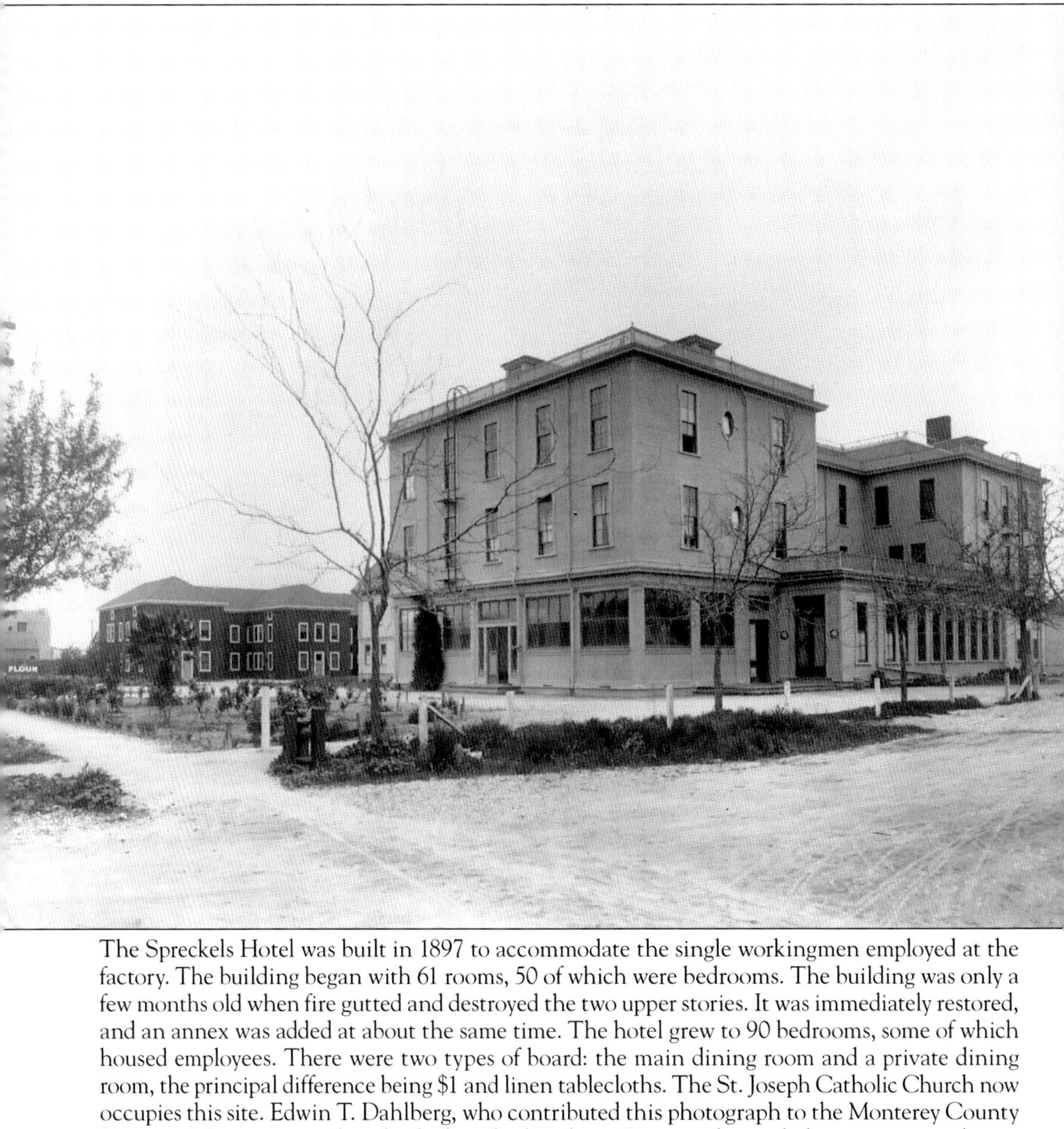

The Spreckels Hotel was built in 1897 to accommodate the single workingmen employed at the factory. The building began with 61 rooms, 50 of which were bedrooms. The building was only a few months old when fire gutted and destroyed the two upper stories. It was immediately restored, and an annex was added at about the same time. The hotel grew to 90 bedrooms, some of which housed employees. There were two types of board: the main dining room and a private dining room, the principal difference being $1 and linen tablecloths. The St. Joseph Catholic Church now occupies this site. Edwin T. Dahlberg, who contributed this photograph to the Monterey County Historical Society, noted on back that the hotel was "occupied mainly by migrant employees of the Sugar Company. They were known as 'sugar tramps,' since they were employed by the company for only three or four months of the year—a period called 'the campaign'—during the times the sugar beets were being harvested and being made into sugar. Eventually all of us who were employed by the company during the entire year were also called 'sugar tramps.'"

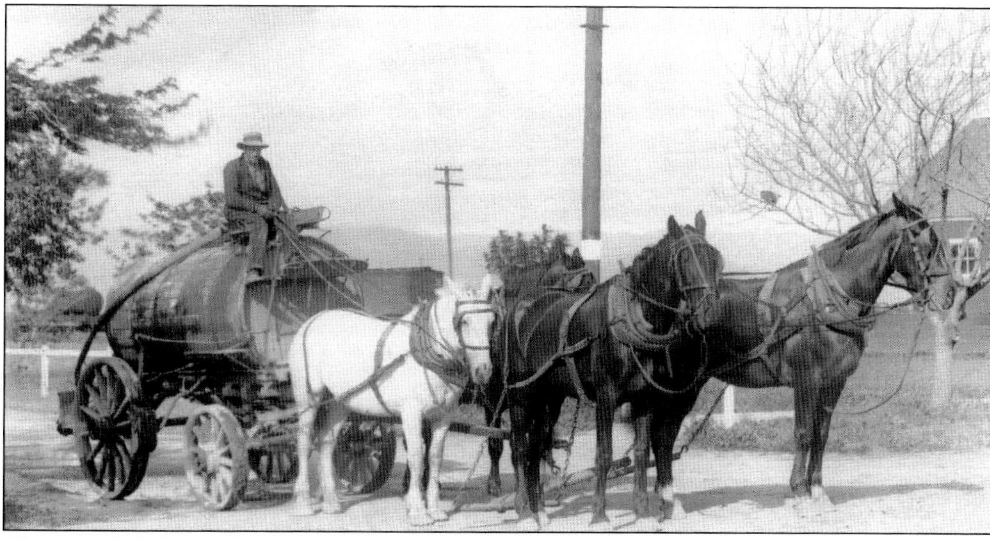

The Spreckels horse-drawn wagon was used to haul potable water to the residents of Spreckels and to the steam tractors in the fields. It is now in the collection of the Monterey County Historical Society.

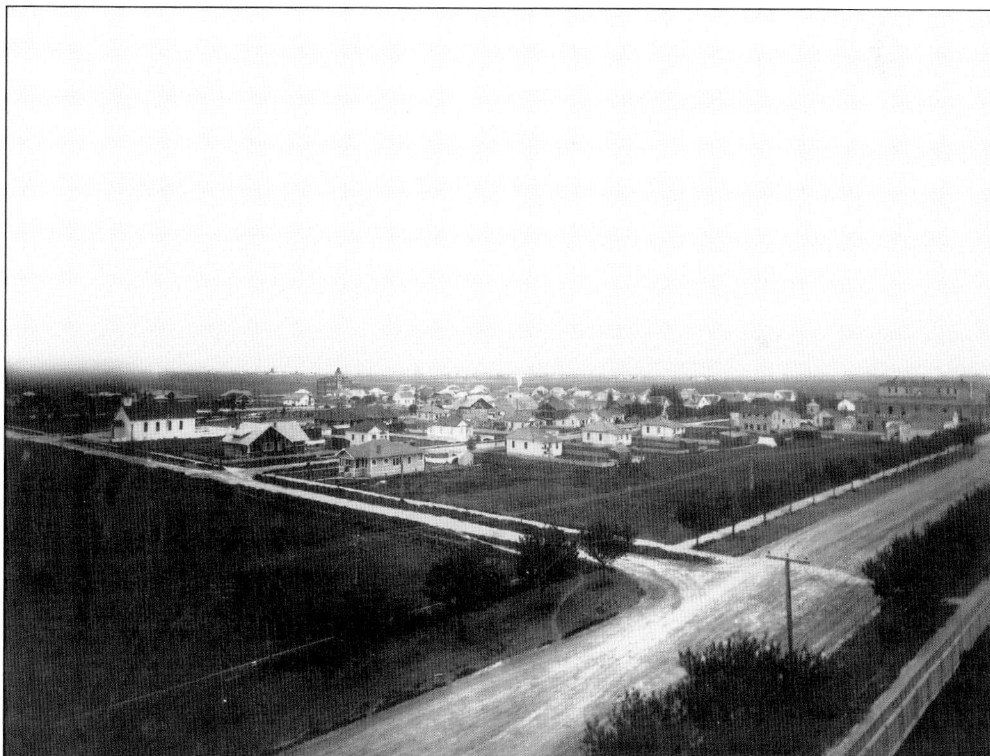

A view of the town of Spreckels was taken from the top of the office/weigh-station building. Claus Spreckels was a shrewd businessman and found efficient and cost-saving ways to build the company town by using materials from a hotel he owned in Aptos and moving 25 cottages in from different company ranches.

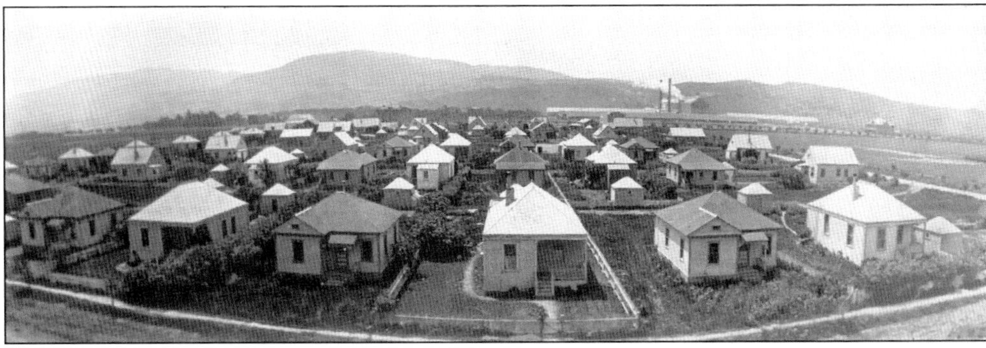

An unusual southerly view of Spreckels is seen here. This photograph was taken from an upper story or the bell tower of the school. Note the alternating designs of the cottages. The town flourished, and 20 years after it started, the businesses included Spreckels Meat Market, Toomey's Shoe and Men's Clothing Store, Nilson's Cabinet Shop, Rouse's Plumber's Shop, Decorating and Tinting Service, Wincey Yancey Wilson's Grocery, Nihaus' Spreckels Lumber Yard, Smith's Livery, Bergstrom and Company's Painting, a bicycle shop, a Chinese laundry, and a local barber.

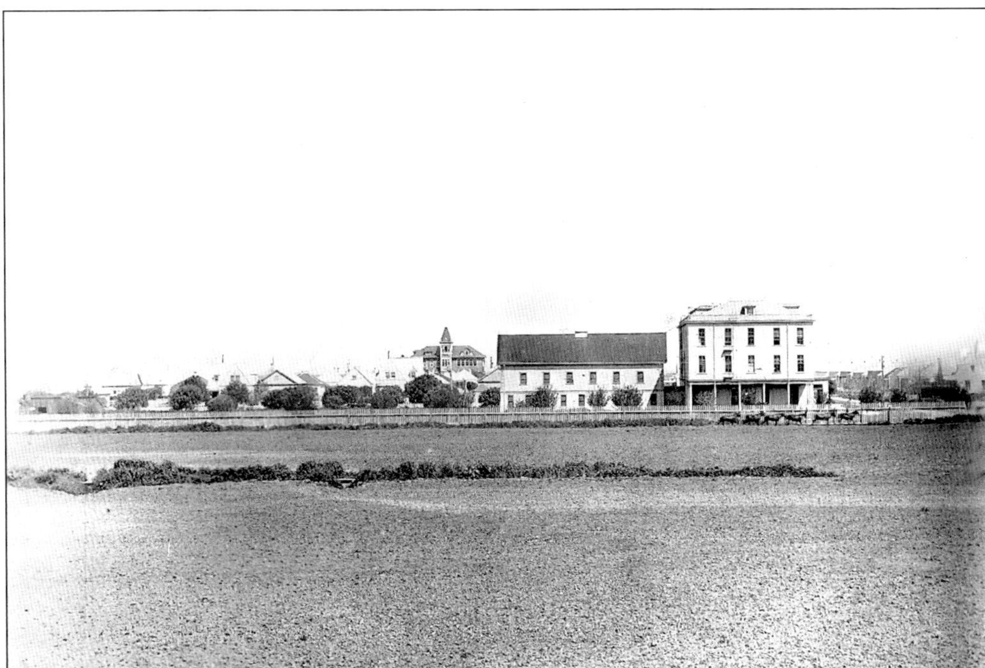

This view of the town shows the hotel and school. A small herd of horses runs next to the fence in front of the hotel. An annex has been constructed, but the lower portion of the hotel has not yet been enclosed in the constant effort to house the tremendous influx of workers.

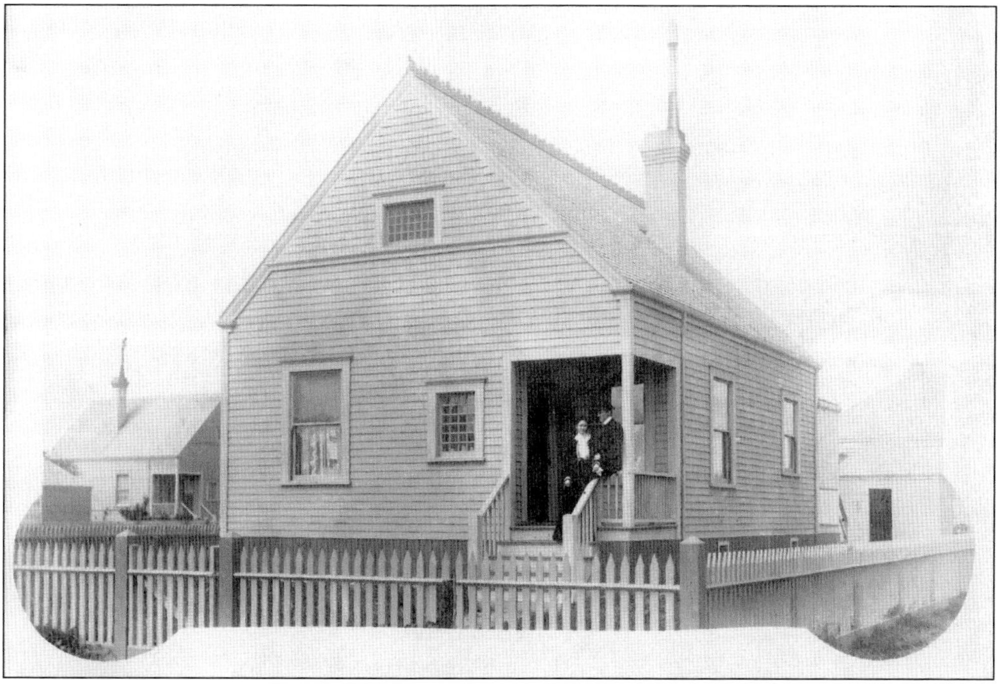

This *c.* 1898 residence on Third Street, a Victorian cottage with a cutout porch, was designed by W. H. Weeks. This appears to be one of the more basic models. Note the outbuilding in the back yard and the classic white-picket fence. On the left is another similar structure.

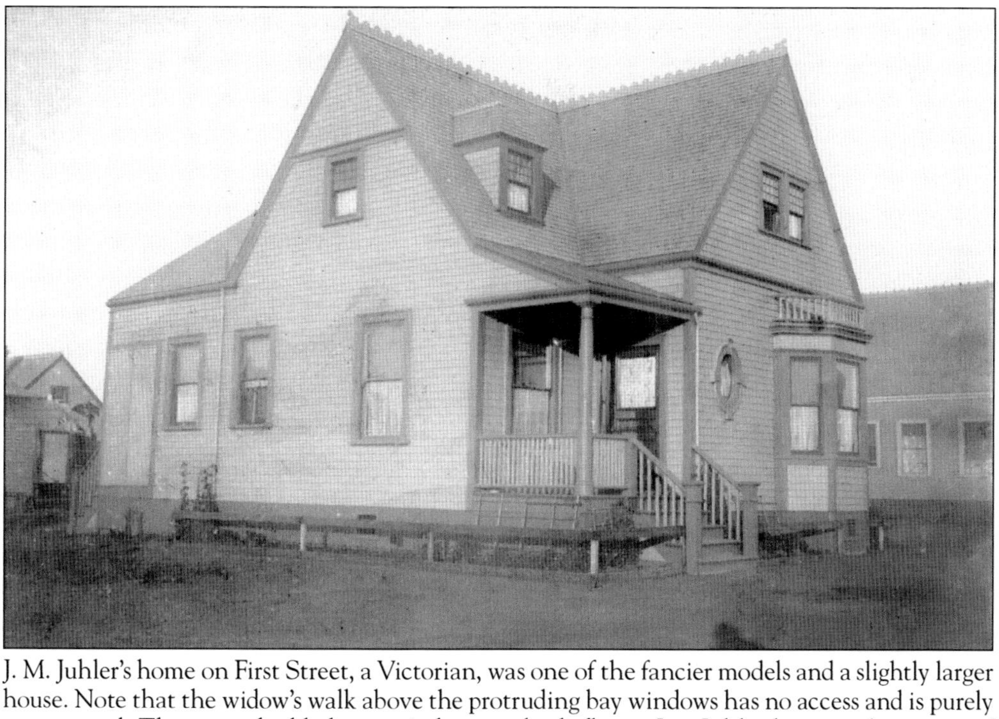

J. M. Juhler's home on First Street, a Victorian, was one of the fancier models and a slightly larger house. Note that the widow's walk above the protruding bay windows has no access and is purely ornamental. There are double-hung windows on both floors. Jess Juhler became the owner of "The Store," which he renamed the Emporium.

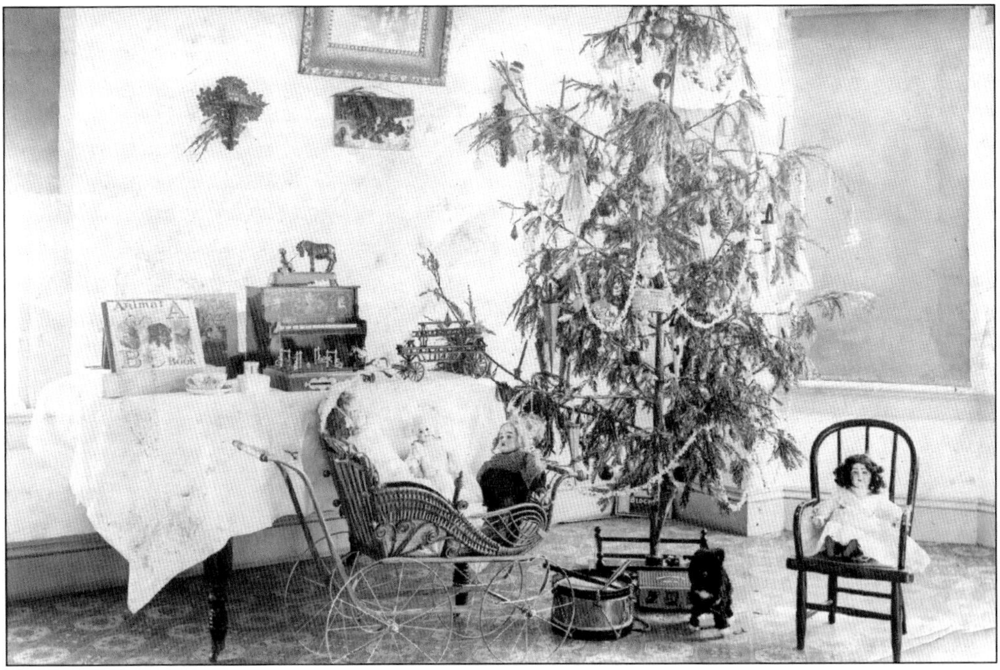

This Christmas scene is at the Rhyners' Spreckels home. The Rhyner family moved to the new town, becoming a "sugar" family and some of its earliest residents. Joseph Rhyner worked at the factory, and his daughter Rose spent a good many years in the old brick offices on Spreckels Boulevard.

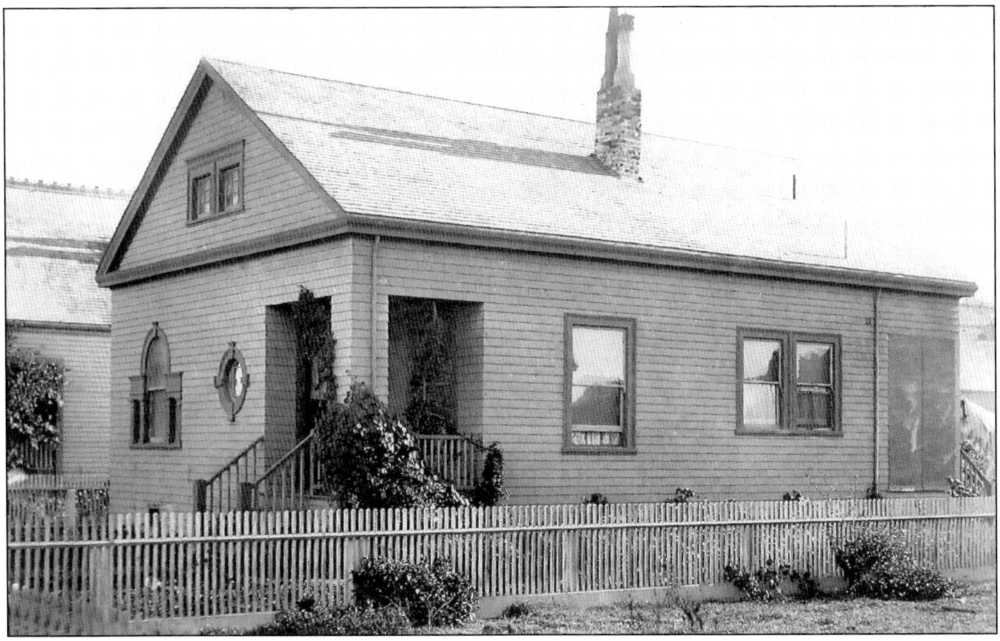

This is another example of an early Spreckels home, *c.* 1898. This Victorian cottage has a cutout porch and slightly more ornamental-rounded windows. This slight stylistic difference helps to separate the otherwise similar structures. On the side, however, the double-hung windows are the more traditional rectangular style. (Courtesy of James Ross Riley III.)

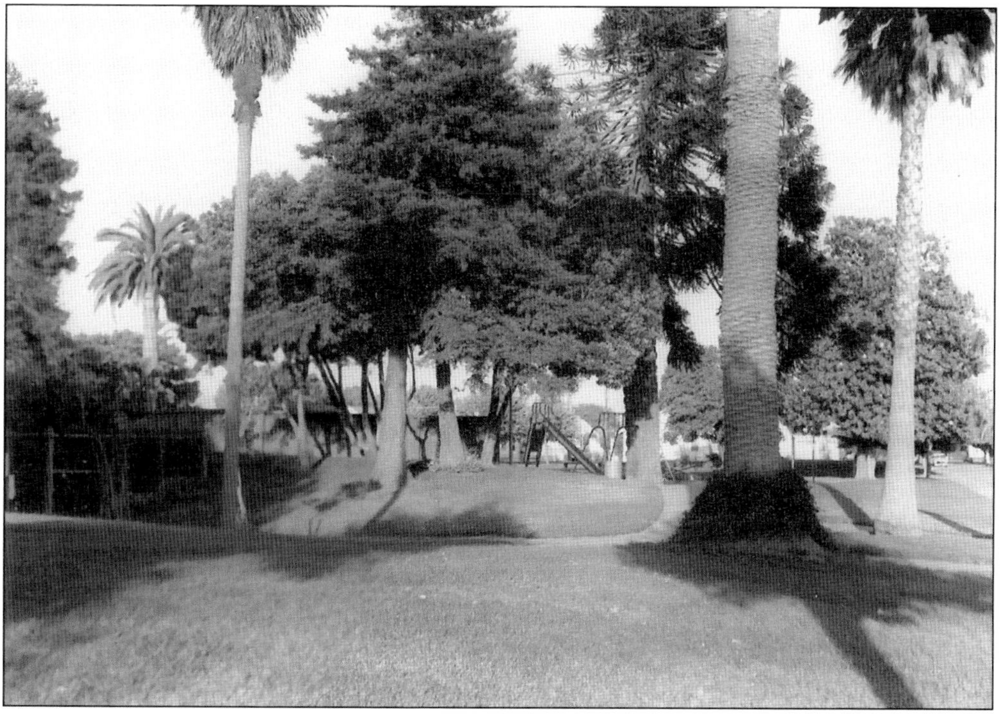

Here is a recent view of Spreckels Park, which was started between the years of 1906 and 1907 for the children to play in and the adults to enjoy a day under the shade of the trees. In 1911, the beginning of a new playground with a baseball diamond, sandpile, and swing sets was put in place for the children.

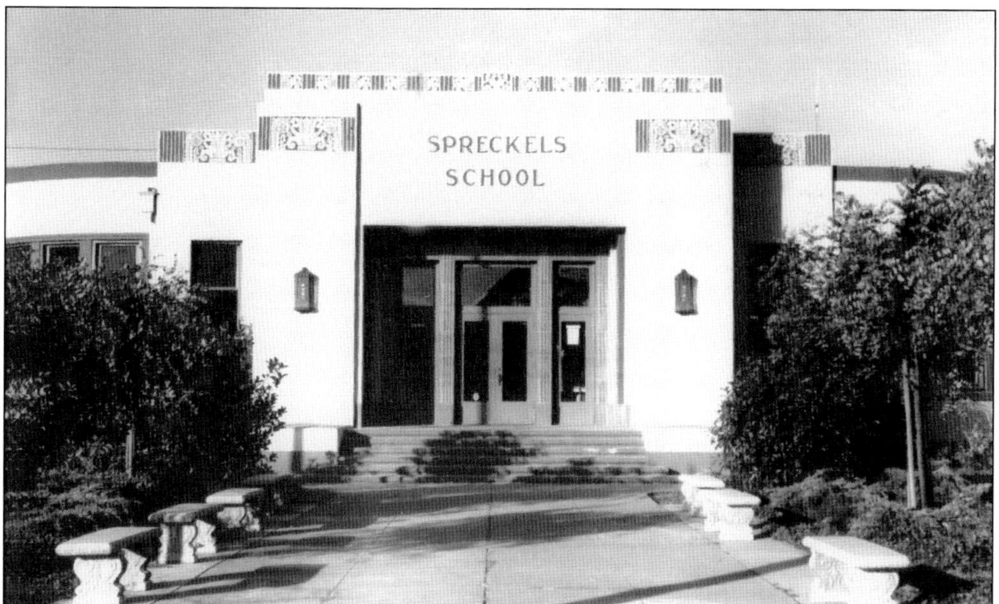

The "new" Spreckels school, with eight classrooms, was built in 1937–1938, replacing the old three-story schoolhouse that was built in 1899 and demolished in 1936. This school still serves the community, and an annex in the same art moderne–style is currently being added.

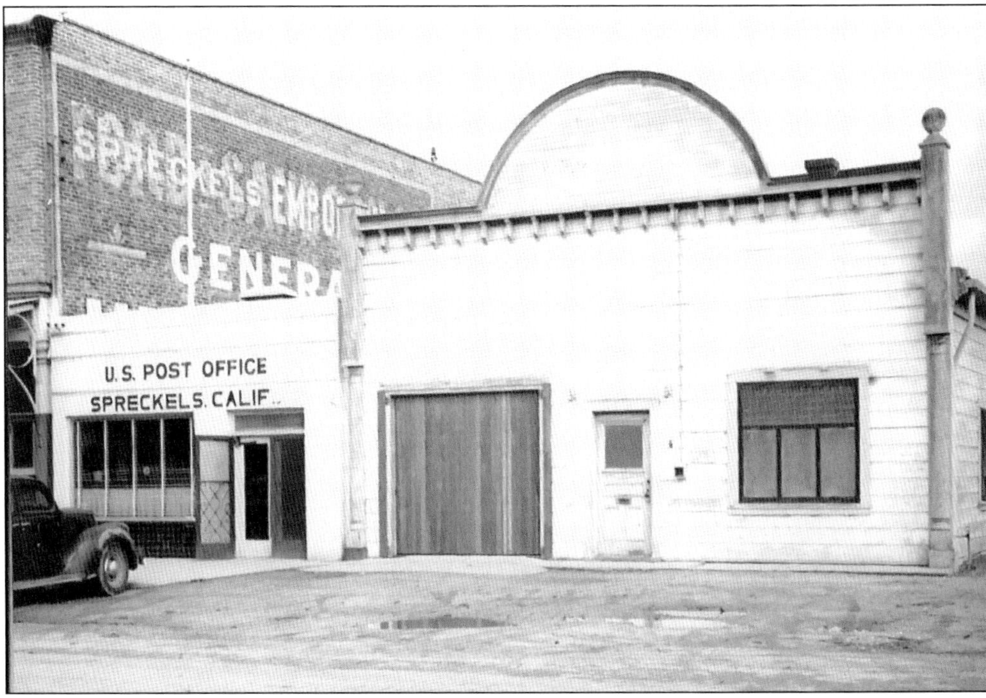

After the Louvre Saloon closed down, the building was occupied by the Spreckels Volunteer Fire Company. The post office moved out of the Emporium into its own building. According to the August/September 1948 *Honey Dew News*, this new post office was begun with W. S. Young as the postmaster. He had two assistants and rented 333 boxes. (Courtesy of Monterey County Agricultural and Rural Life Museum.)

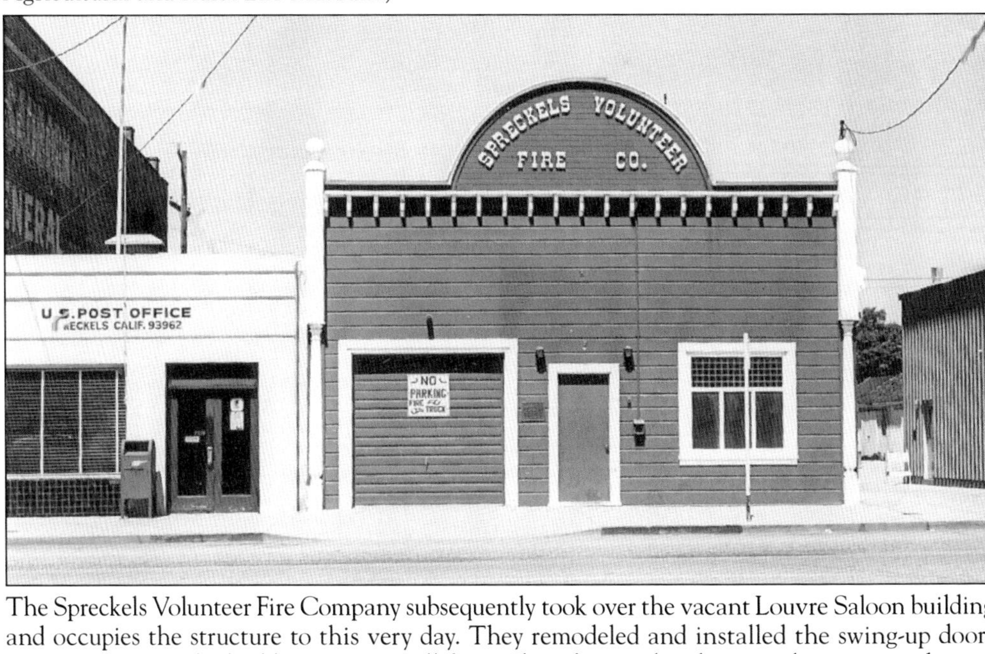

The Spreckels Volunteer Fire Company subsequently took over the vacant Louvre Saloon building and occupies the structure to this very day. They remodeled and installed the swing-up doors in 1948. Because the building is too small for modern fire trucks, those are kept in an adjacent building constructed in 1972.

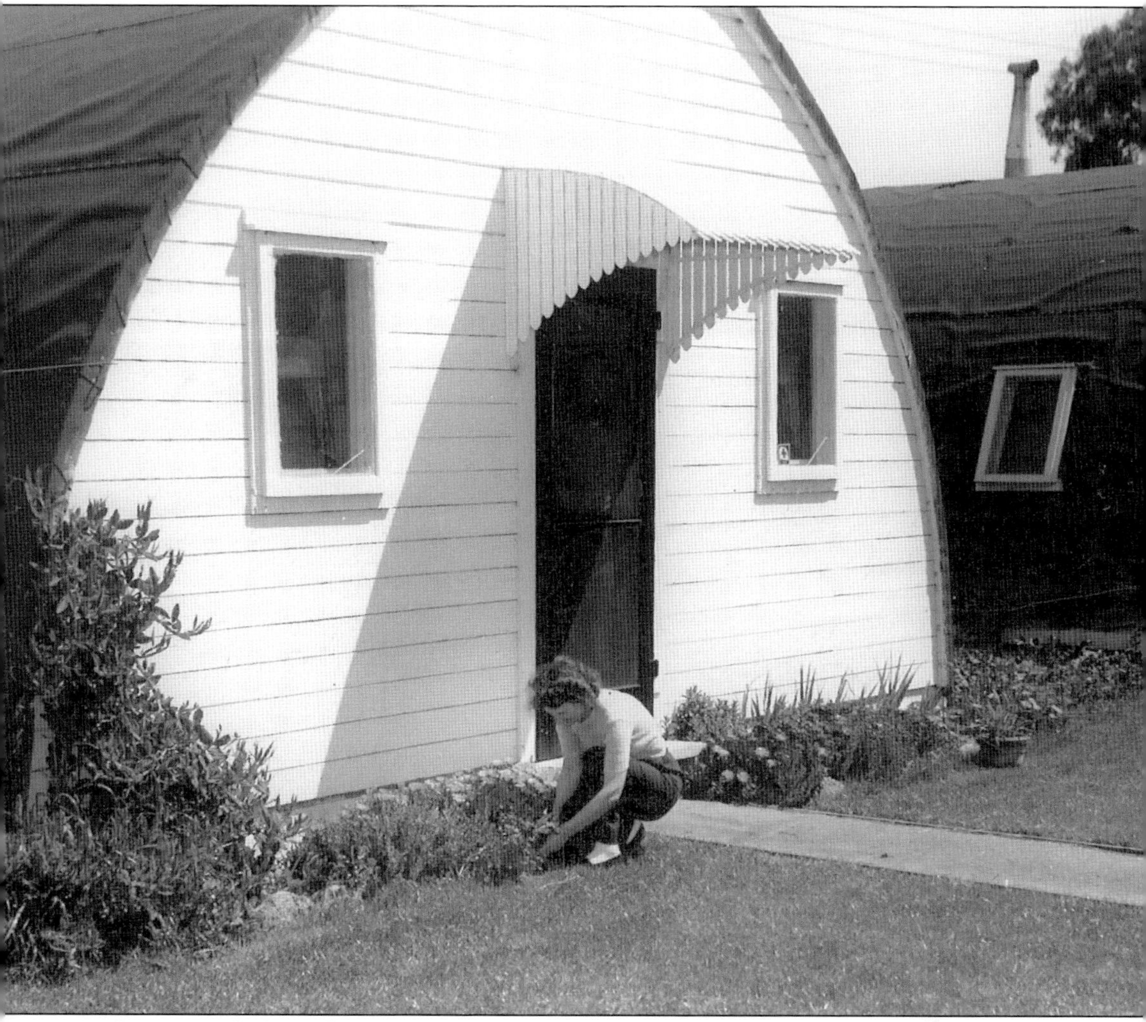

Mrs. Burt Carroll plants flowers in front of one of the World War II–era Quonset huts built as temporary housing on Fifth Street at the northern edge of Spreckels. One account suggests they were designed to house the many gasoline-short workers in the factory, while another report says that these structures were built for women and families whose husbands went to war and worked at the sugar factory. (Courtesy of Monterey County Agricultural and Rural Life Museum.)

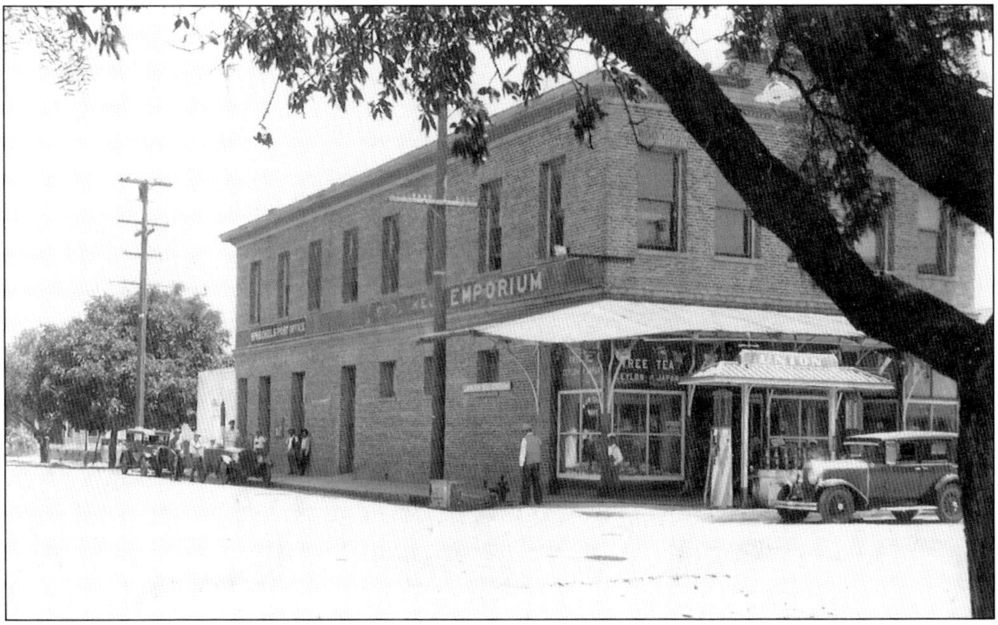

Here is a later view of the Emporium, originally "The Store." The rear of the building at this time contained the United States Post Office, while the front has been converted into a Union gas station.

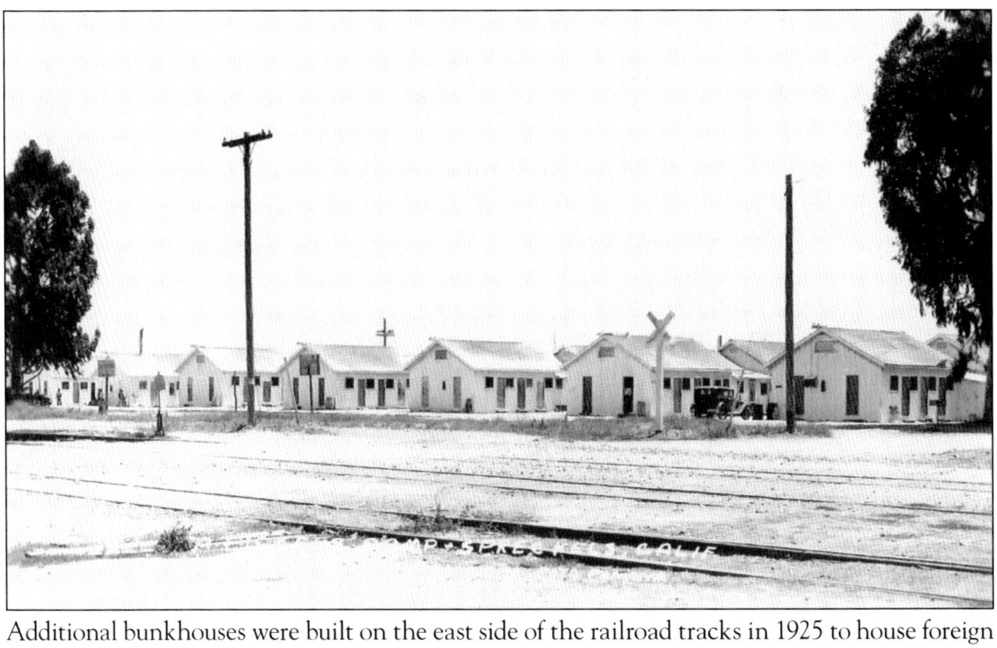

Additional bunkhouses were built on the east side of the railroad tracks in 1925 to house foreign workers. As the factory continued to increase its capacity to process beets, its labor requirements also grew, particularly at harvest time. These bunkhouses were built to shelter some of the temporary workers. They were referred to as "pickers camp" by some.

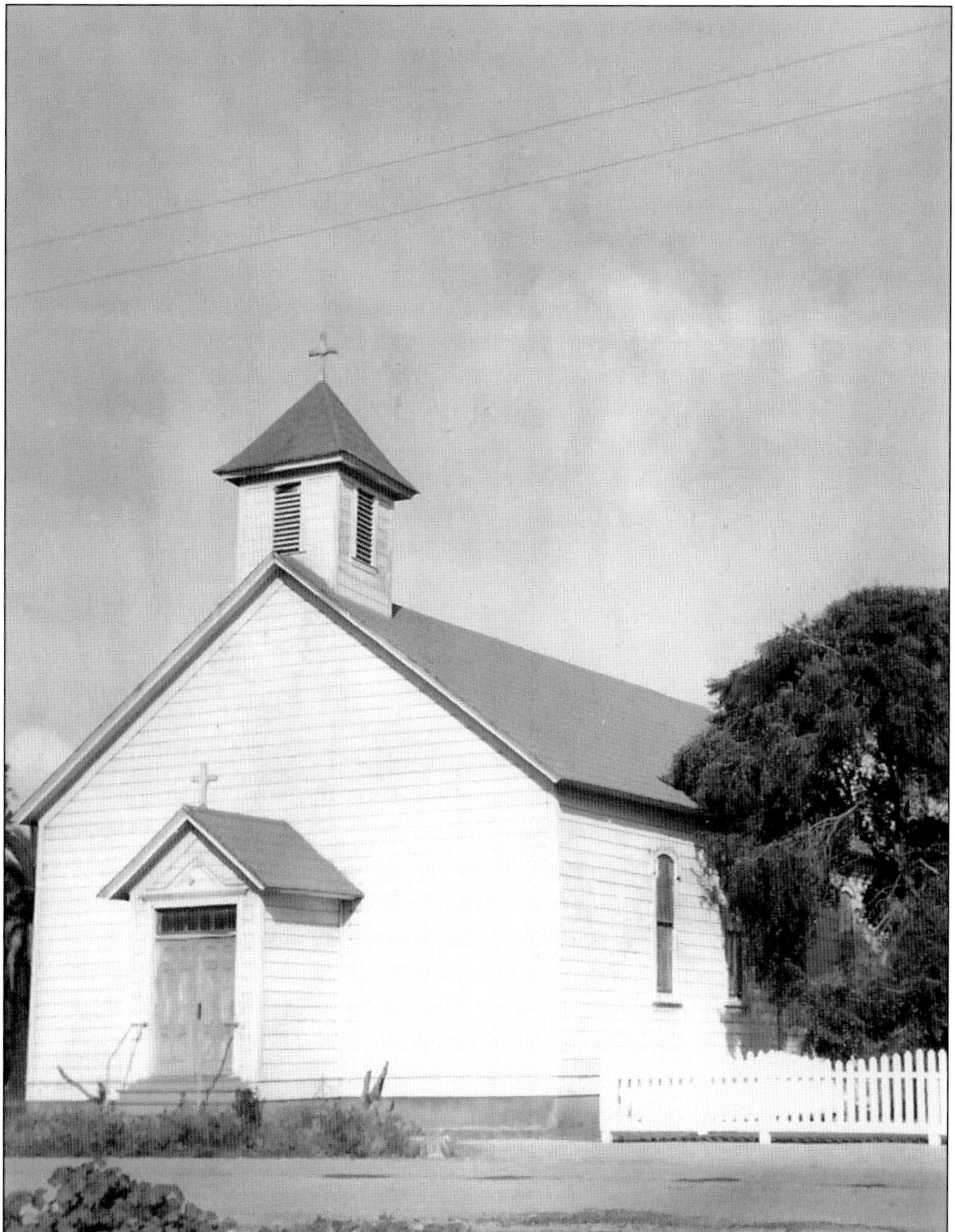

This quaint Catholic church, St. Joseph's, was originally built at the St. Joseph German Colony near the Gavilan foothills. Around 1907, the German colonists faced some rough times, sold their properties, and the small church was moved to Spreckels. Before this, mass was held in the social hall above "The Store." In 1962, the little church was torn down and a larger Catholic church was built where the original Spreckels Hotel once stood. (Courtesy of Monterey County Agricultural and Rural Life Museum.)

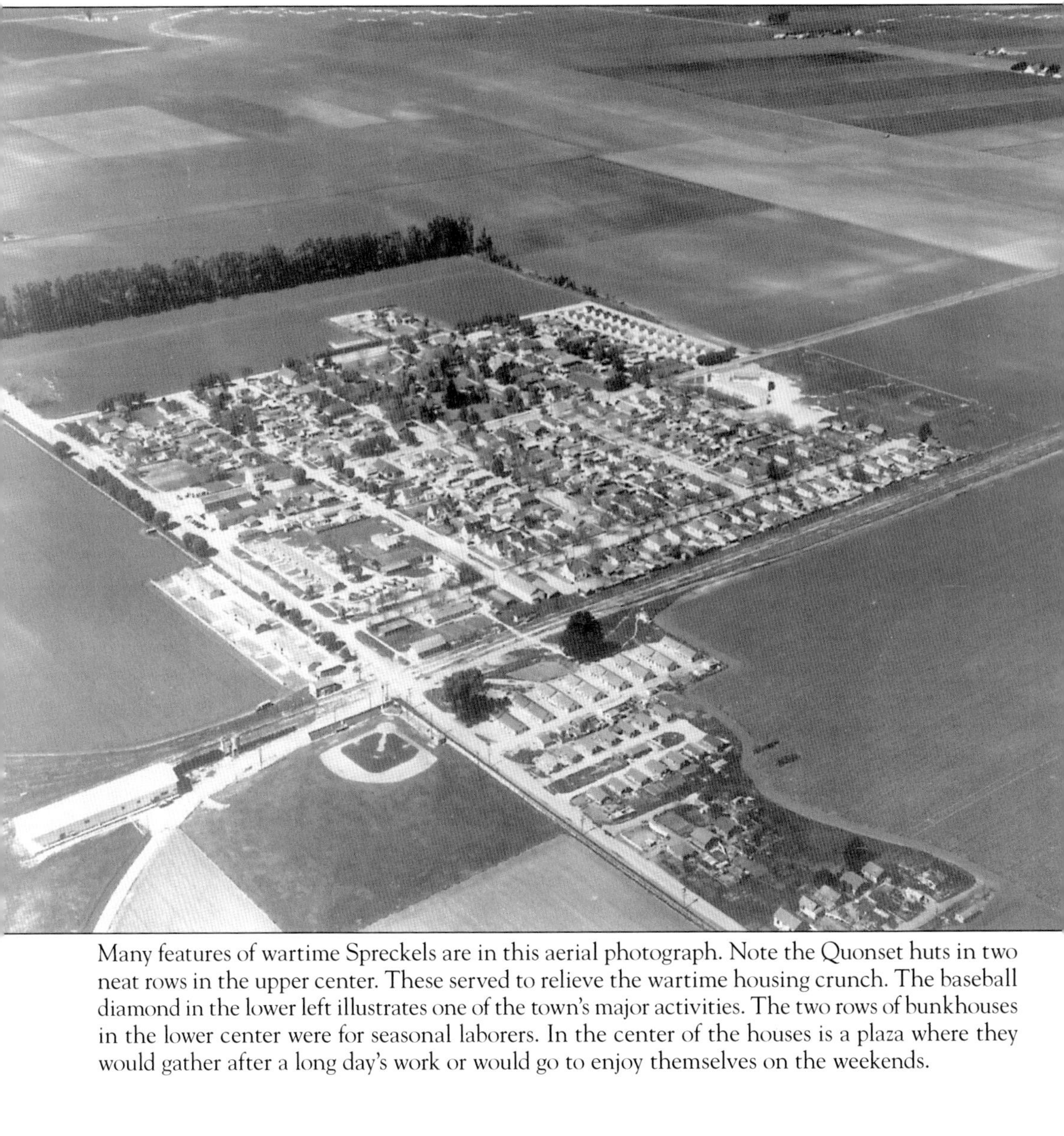

Many features of wartime Spreckels are in this aerial photograph. Note the Quonset huts in two neat rows in the upper center. These served to relieve the wartime housing crunch. The baseball diamond in the lower left illustrates one of the town's major activities. The two rows of bunkhouses in the lower center were for seasonal laborers. In the center of the houses is a plaza where they would gather after a long day's work or would go to enjoy themselves on the weekends.

Four

THE FACTORY

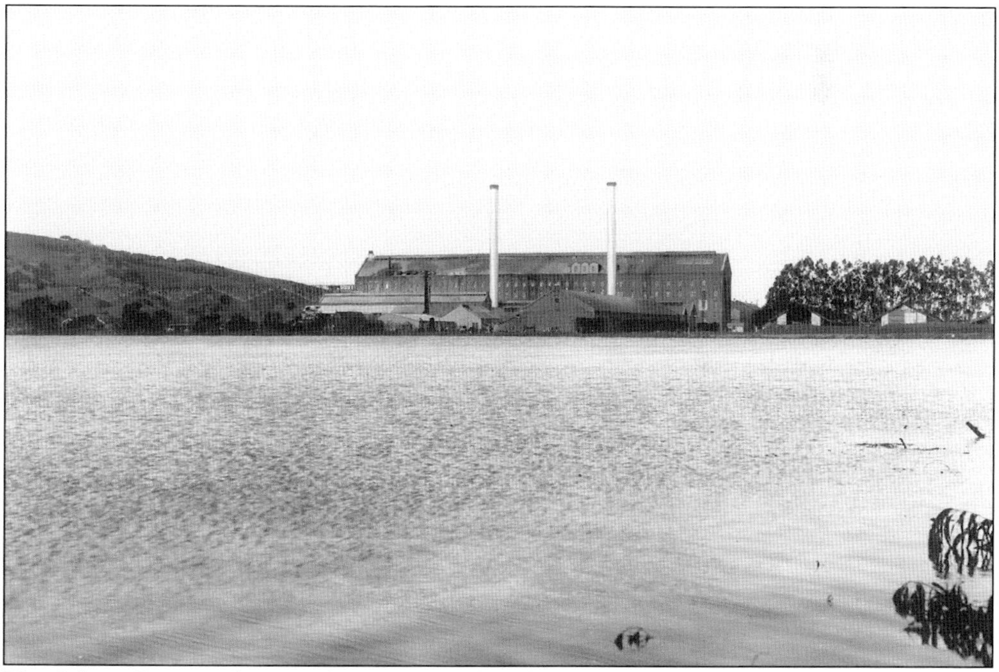

The Salinas River and its aquifer were critical to the sugar factory. The plant itself used a huge amount of water, but beets used even more. Each acre of beets soaked up more than a million gallons of water a year. The Spreckels Sugar Company built a vast network of wells, pumps, ditches, and canals—all to bring water to the beet fields. This irrigation project transformed the dry ranches into fertile farmland. In subsequent years, the irrigation made the switch to row crops possible. In many ways, it was Claus Spreckels who turned the Salinas Valley green.

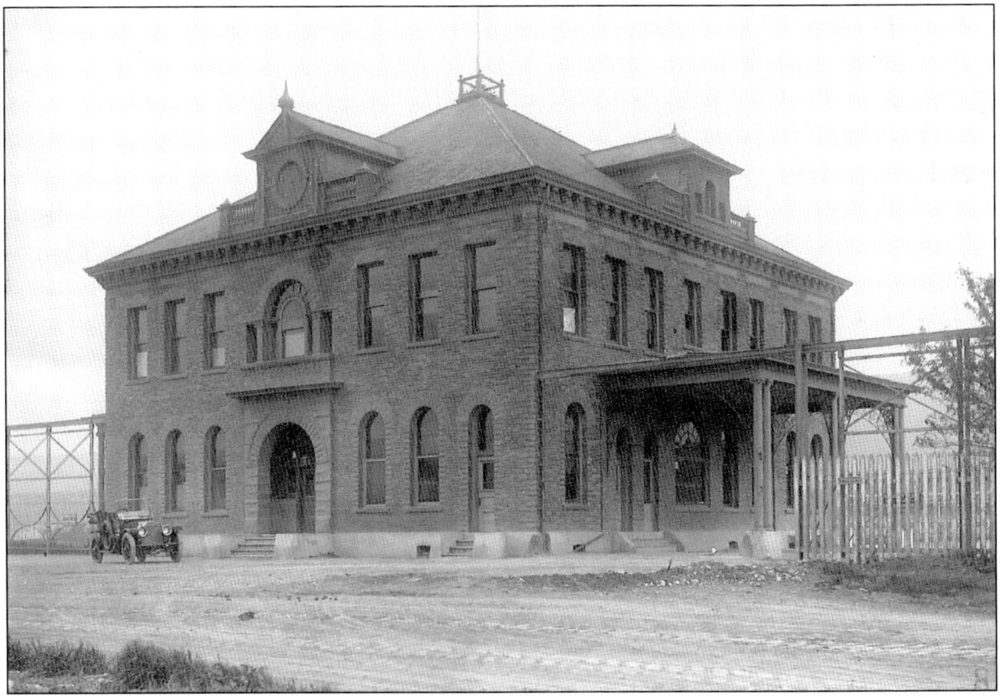

Designed by architect William H. Weeks as one of the original Spreckels buildings, this was the main office housing the agricultural and plant offices. It survived until 1958, when it was replaced by a newer building. The January 23, 1898, edition of the *Salinas Index* stated, "The office-building on which work was commenced twelve weeks ago is rapidly approaching completion. It will be one of the handsomest structures on the site. The building will be 70 by 70 feet, and is constructed on the outside of red pressed brick, trimmed with San Jose sandstone, which makes a pretty combination. . . . The first floor will be devoted to the main or general office, weighing room, timekeeper's offices and private offices. The second floor will be subdivided into 12 elegant offices for the use of the draughtsmen and other branches of work necessary."

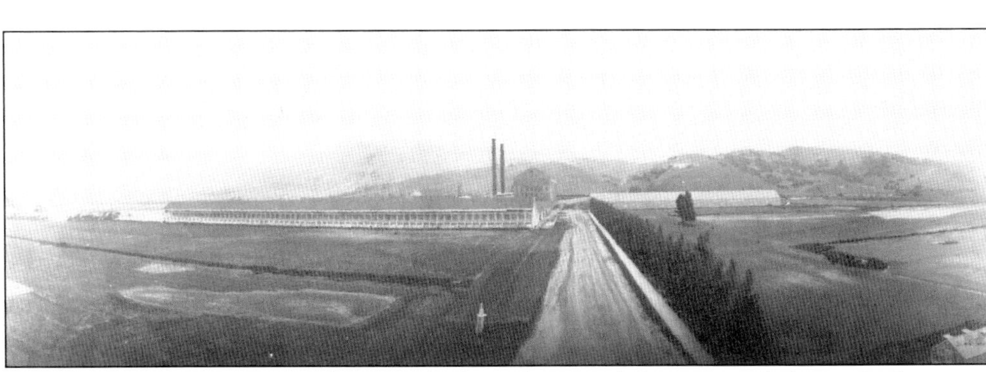

An early and unusual view, looking south along the Spreckels entry road, shows the factory in the background. This photograph was probably taken from the top of the main office building. Note the row of trees along the west side of the road.

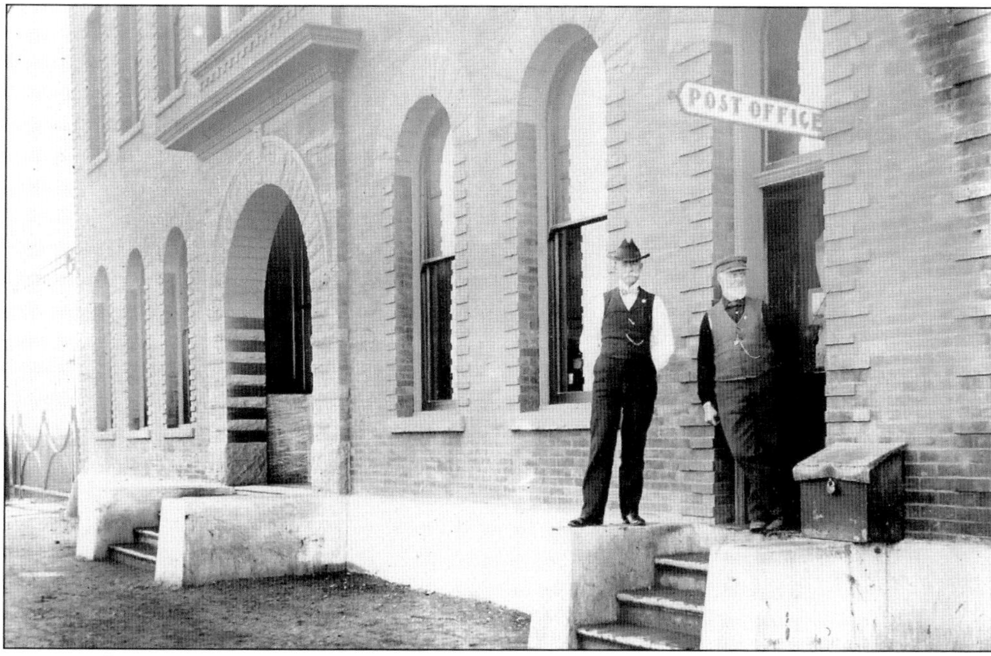

C. Buswell, timekeeper, and Charles Jones, postmaster, stand in front of the first Spreckels Post Office, which was located in the main Spreckels office building. The post office was to see many locations—first at the main office, then to the Moore building, the Emporium, and finally to its current location between the Emporium and the volunteer fireman's building. (Courtesy of Monterey County Agricultural and Rural Life Museum.)

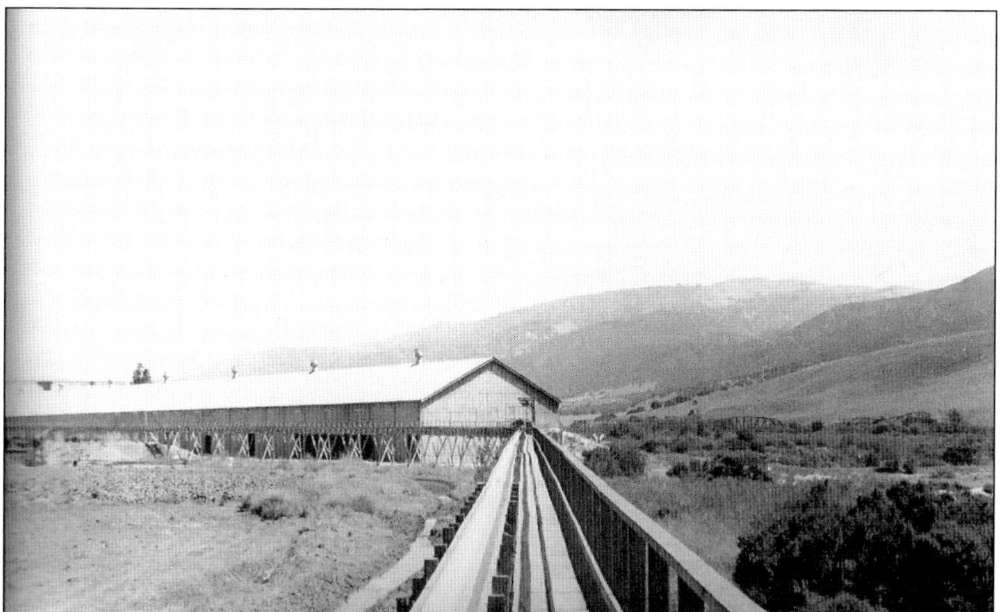

Lime rock was used in beet processing. The waste lime was transported from the factory to settling ponds in these lime flumes and was later reclaimed for use in the agricultural fields. The pulp warehouse is the building in the center of the photograph. It stored bagged, dried beet pulp, which was sold as livestock feed, primarily for cattle.

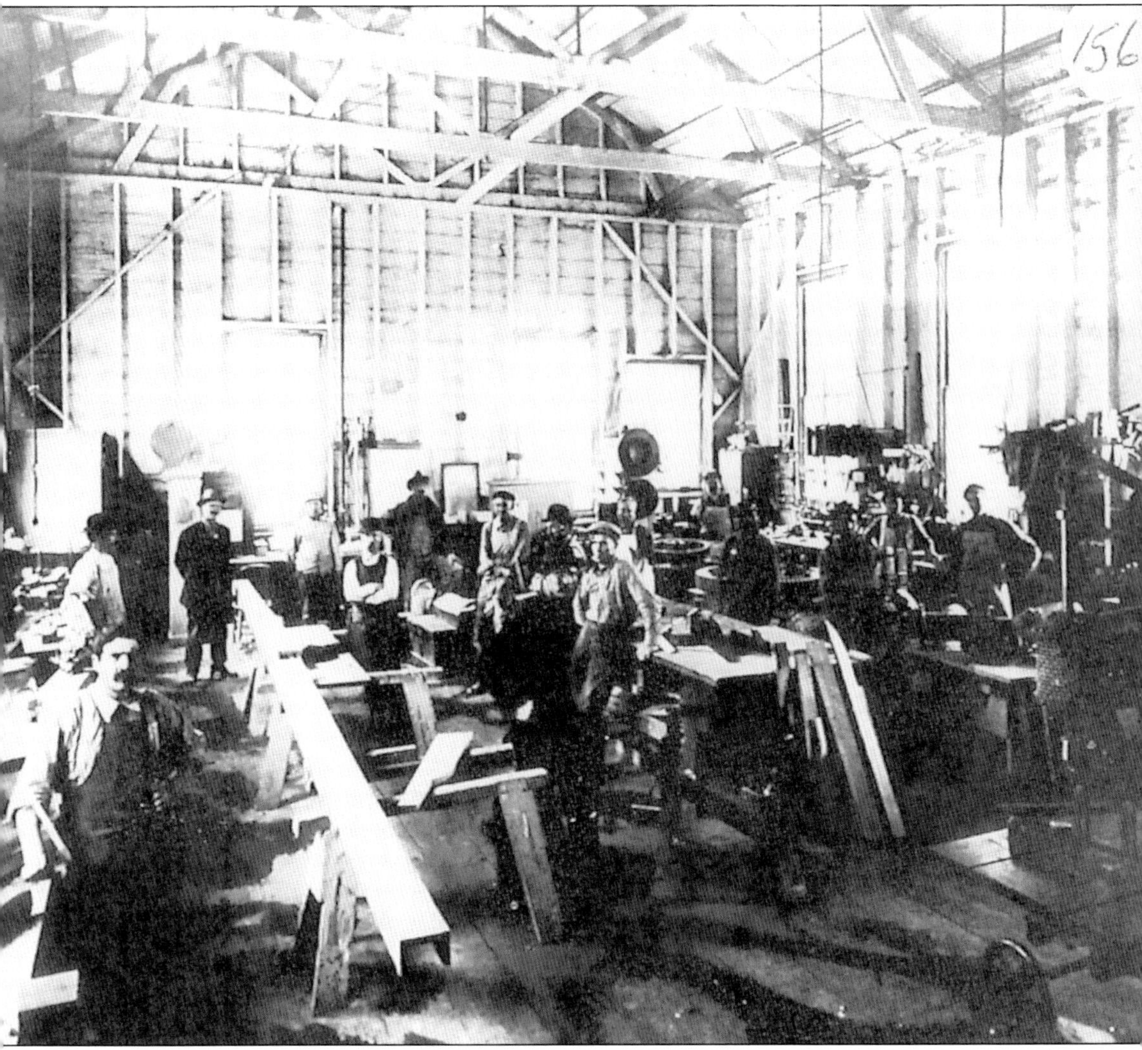

The carpenter shop was one of a series of shops busy fabricating materials needed at the plant. There was also a pipe room, where workers cut and threaded pipe; a blacksmith shop, which repaired broken tools; and a machine shop, which lathed heavy steel bars into needed parts. The machine shop manufactured portions of the 200-horsepower pumping plant designed to draw water from the Salinas River. The names of the men are as follows: U. Ulricksen, now head carpenter on the extreme left; behind him in the dark suit is J. R. Riley, then head carpenter, father of storekeeper Ross Riley; at the back with his hand on his knee is Fred McKee, who was later the blacksmith at Spreckels. The two men in front of McKee are Mr. Bentley and Frank E. Wiley, father of Bill Wiley of Jolon and Frank Wiley of Hawaii. On the other side of the bench, in the white overalls is Mr. Alphonso. Next to him are E. Pucciarelli; John Sheidours, head pattern maker is in the back corner; Frank Crane, second pattern maker; and on the extreme right is Charlie Rice, student pattern maker and future employee of the Salinas Post Office.

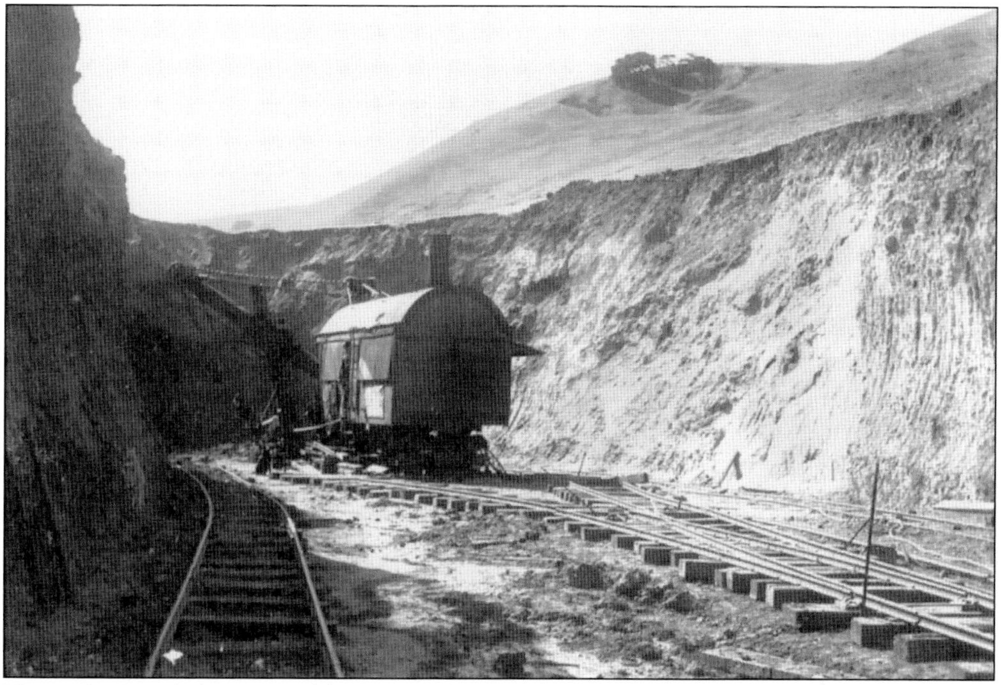

Here is the Spreckels steam paddy in 1897. This quarry area on the hill, across the river to the south from the factory, supplied gravel that was used for multiple purposes during factory construction. This hill was also the site of a reservoir and later a large water tank.

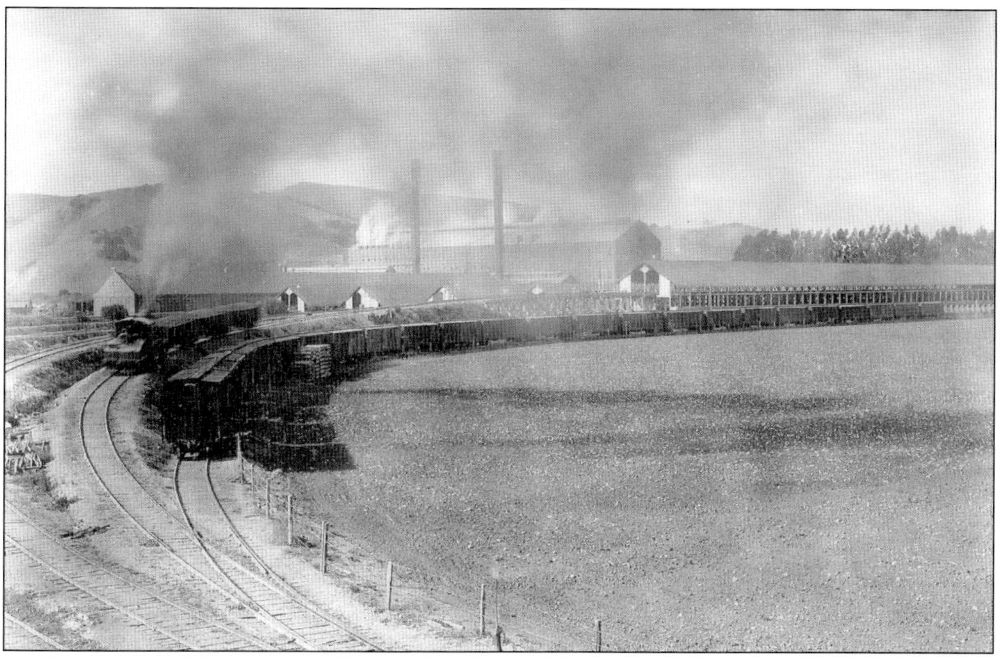

The factory was able to process thousands of tons of beets each day. By 1952, plant capacity had increased from the original 3,000 to nearly 7,000 tons of beets per day—every day—during the annual campaign. This required a major transportation system as other raw materials, such as lime rock, had to be brought in and refined sugar and by-products had to be removed.

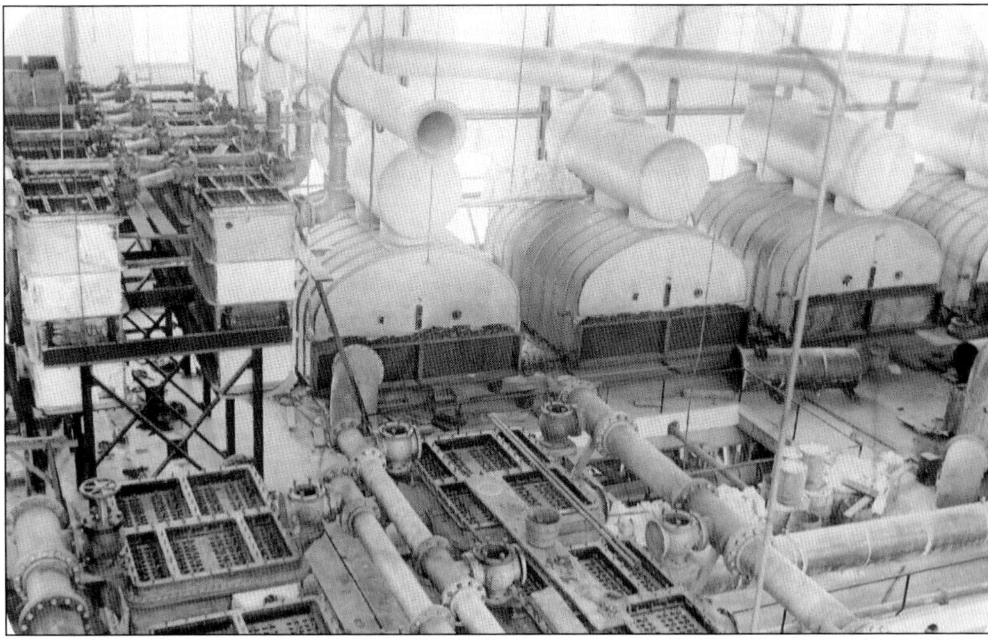

This interior view of the main building shows the enormous number of pipes through which beet juice, water, and other materials were transported during the sugar-making process.

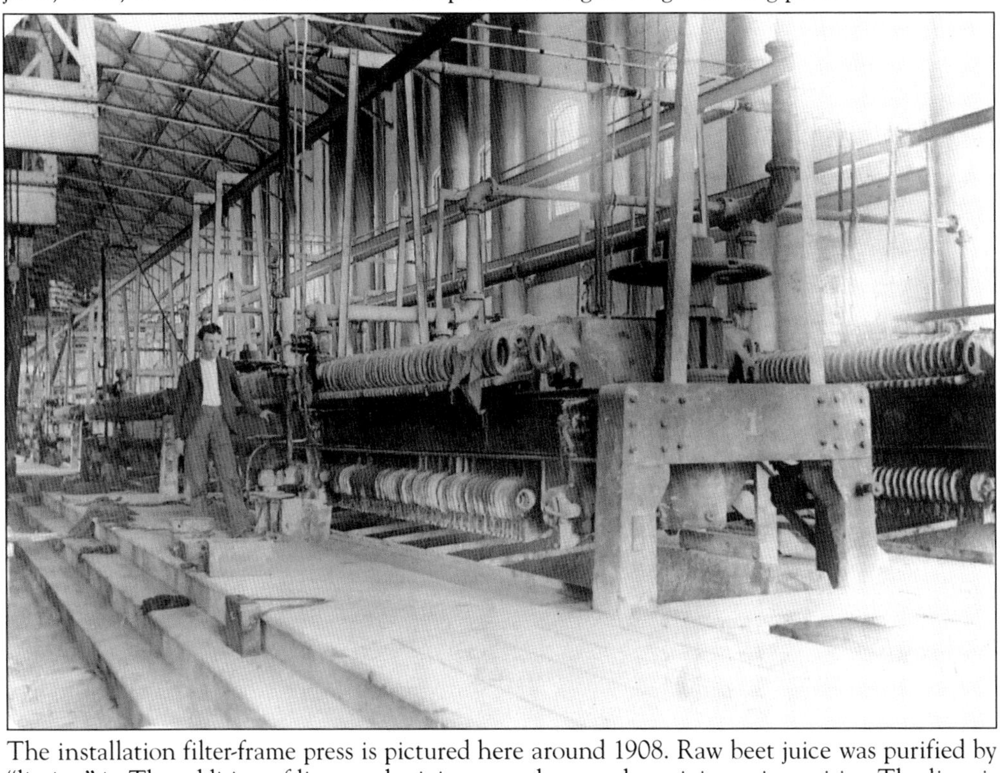

The installation filter-frame press is pictured here around 1908. Raw beet juice was purified by "liming" it. The addition of lime to the juice coagulates and precipitates impurities. The lime is removed by bubbling carbon-dioxide gas through the juice, forming a precipitate, and filtering in pressure filters.

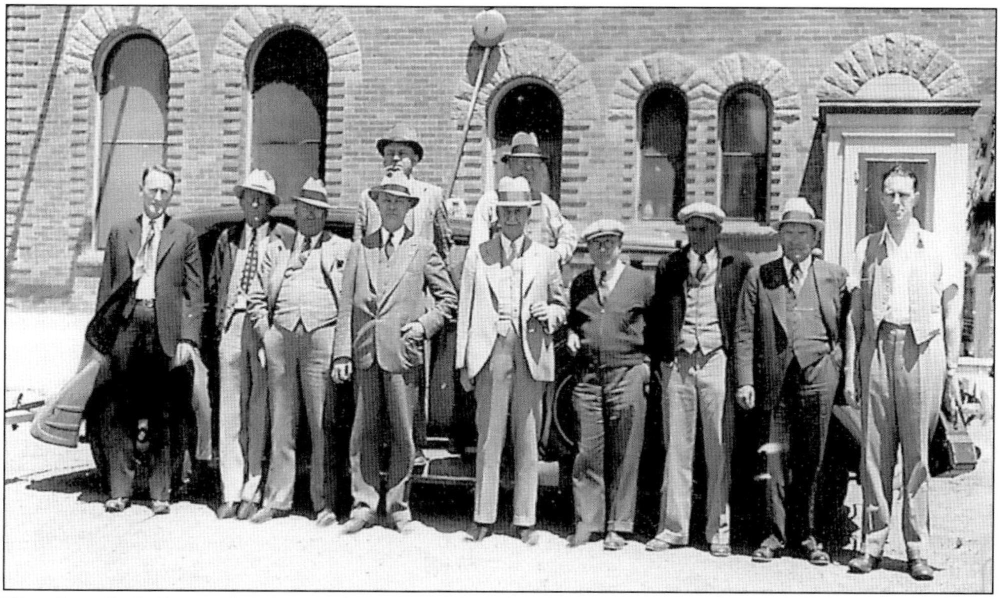

The Spreckels Sugar Company department heads pose for this photograph around 1920. It was not uncommon for Spreckels employees to spend 30, 40, or more years working for the company, often rotating jobs as they moved up the chain of command. (Courtesy of Monterey County Agricultural and Rural Life Museum.)

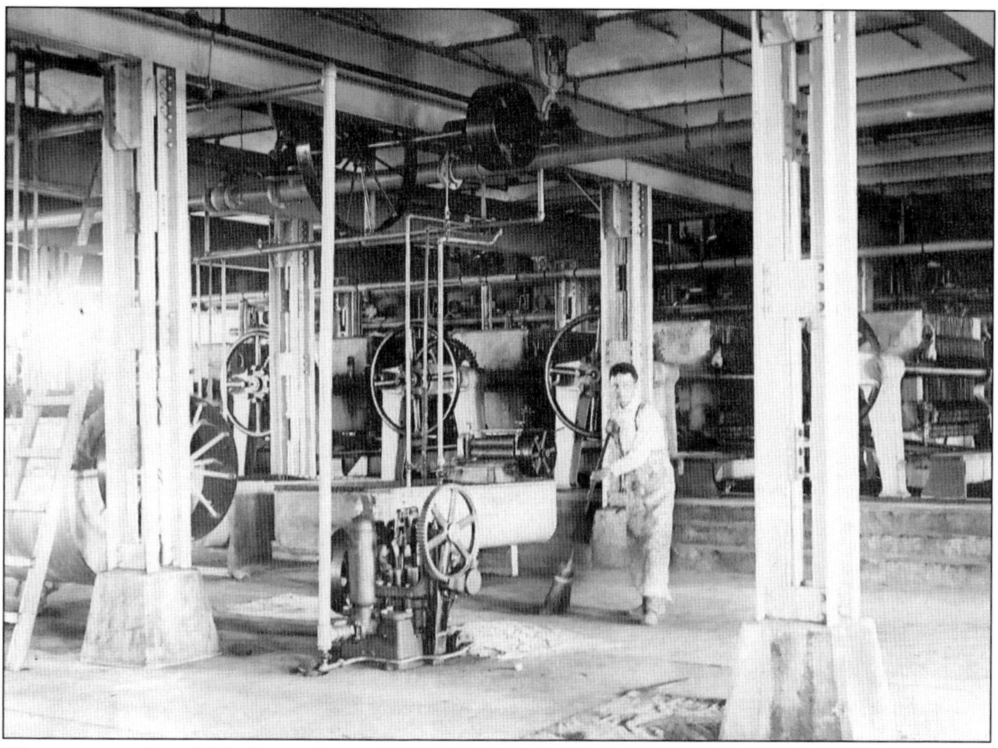

Cleaning up the old-fashioned way, a worker is sweeping up loose sugar with a corn broom. A maintenance ladder reaches into the pipes on the left. Pier blocks support columns, which help support some of the weight of the floor above.

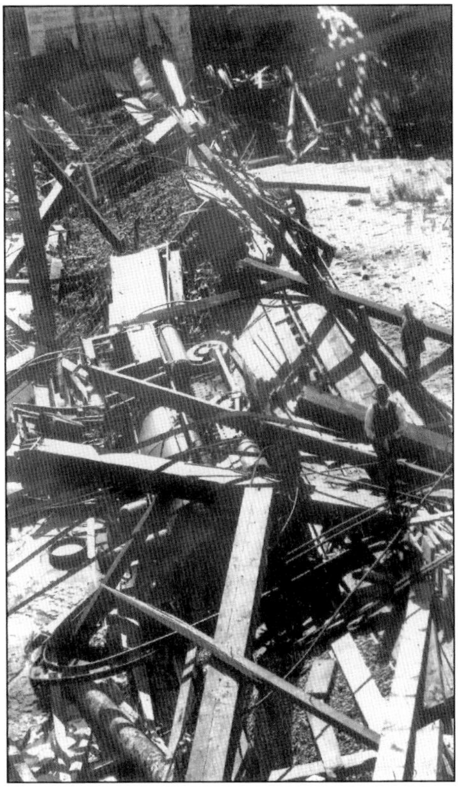

In October 1914, a new four-span wood and steel bridge with trestle approaches had been completed over the Salinas River. As a loaded beet train began crossing the bridge, the span suddenly collapsed, sending the locomotive and six cars to the riverbed. The cause of the collapse was a mystery. That section was replaced with steel, and according to *Sweet Nostalgia*, a company history, it was the only section still standing when the company had the bridge removed.

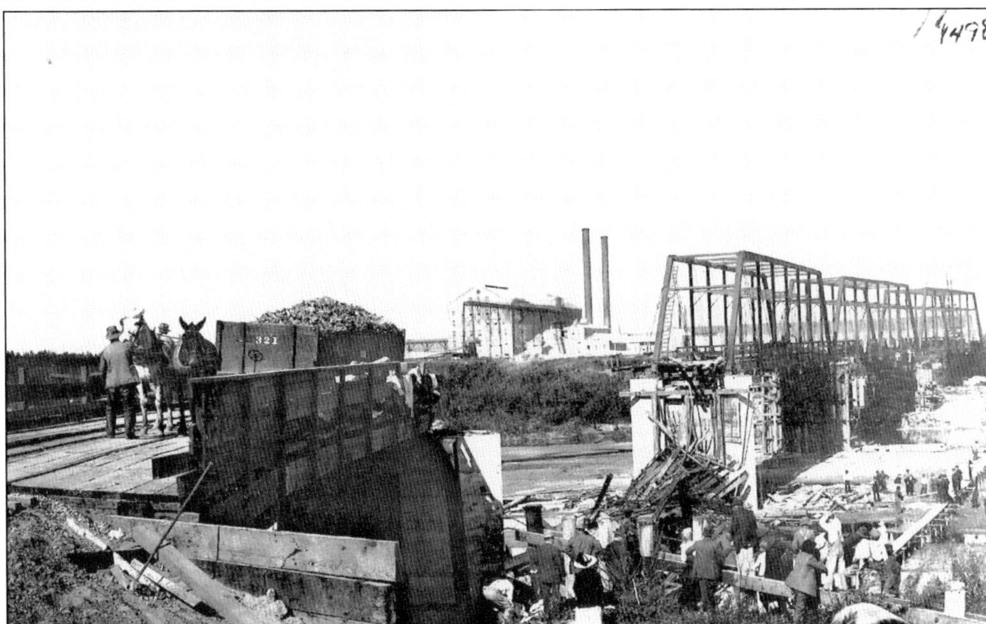

Some of the beets were salvaged from the train wreck. In addition to the train tracks, the bridge also carried the water lines from the reservoir to the sixth story of the factory. When the new water system was installed in 1971, the remaining spans of the old bridge were removed. Note the team being hitched to one of the surviving dump cars to save the load of beets.

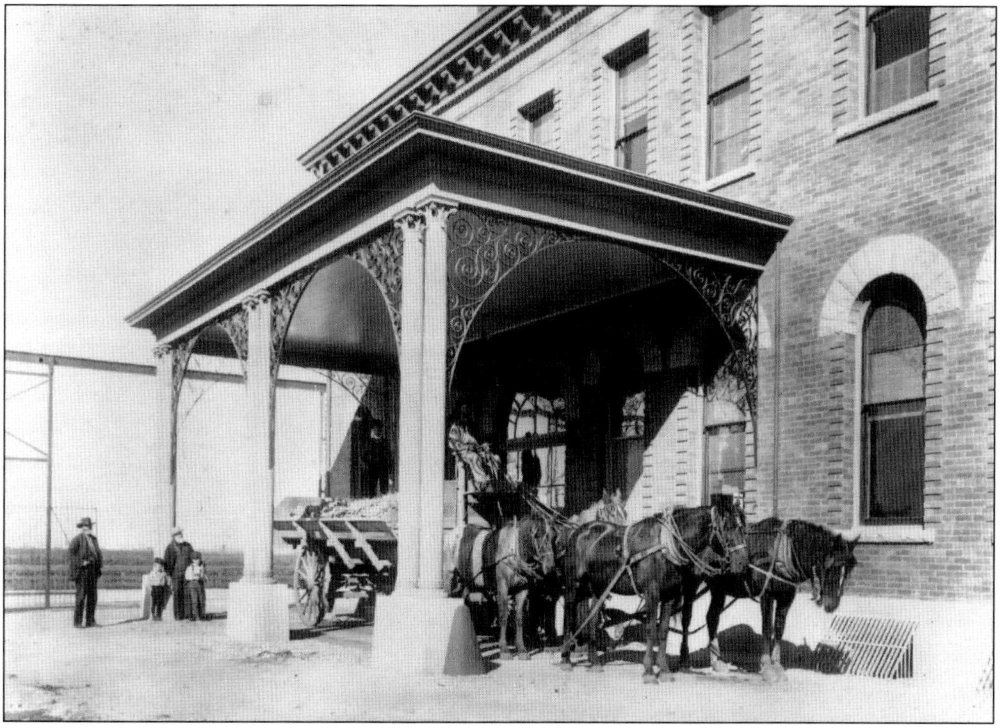

The Spreckels weighing station sat along the side of the office building. These horses are more than ready to rest for a few minutes while the weigh master records the load and takes his samples.

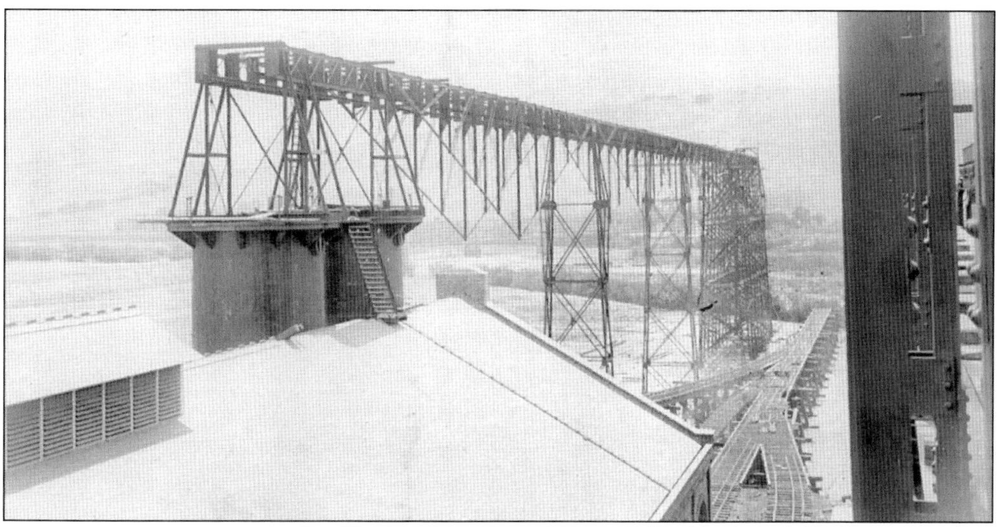

Lime rock was quarried in Alisal Canyon and brought in by railcar. The rock was lifted by bucket hoists and run into the top of the limekiln. There the material was transformed into lime milk, which was used to process the beets. Once used, the waste was transferred via the lime flume to settling ponds.

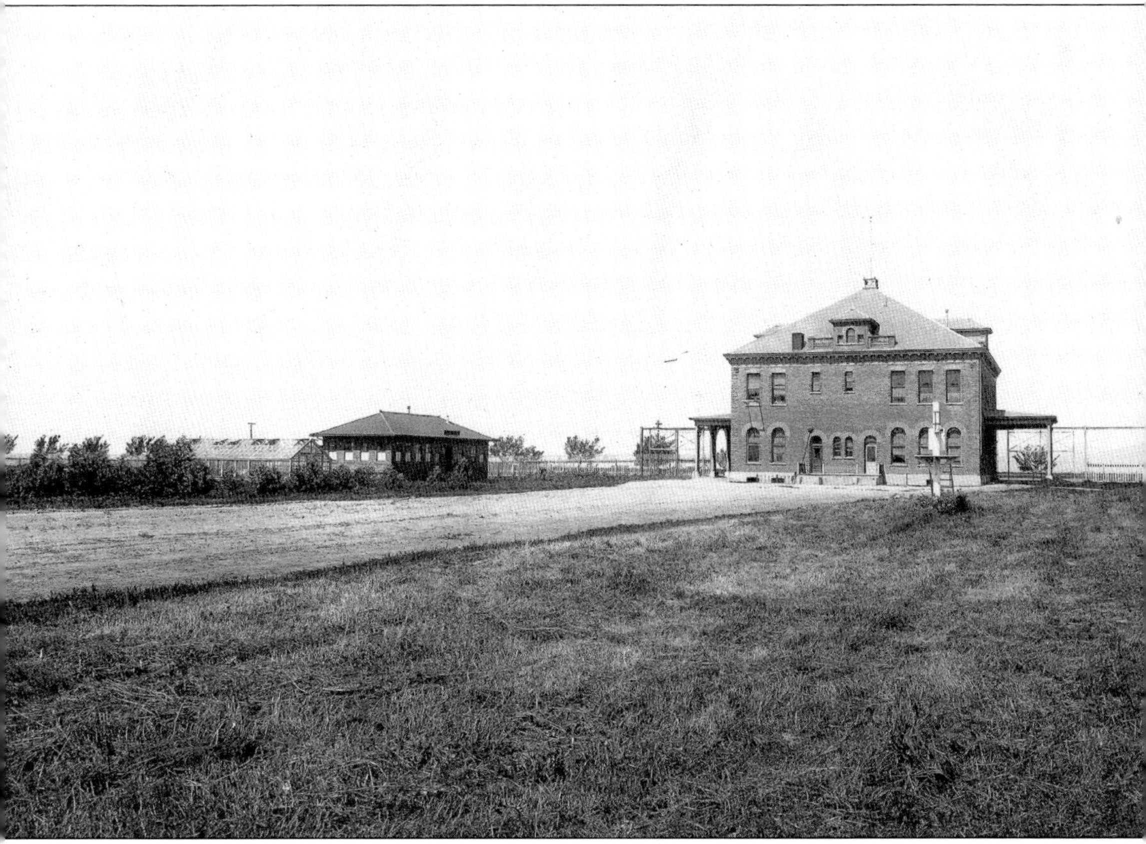

The weighing station and office building are pictured on the right. The smaller building on the left is the research laboratory with associated greenhouses. These fields were eventually used as an experimental plot, which at one time contained over 700 varieties of seed. This represented most of the breeding material that the company used in developing potential commercial varieties. As early as 1899, Percy Morse, the agriculture manager, reported serious crop losses due to a blight disease. Insecticides did not help. Morse had discovered a virus disease, called curly top, which would plague the sugar-beet industry for nearly 35 years. Fewer and fewer beets were planted and even fewer made it to the factory. In 1929, only 197 acres of beets were planted in the area. The town of Spreckels was changed forever as almost all of the businesses closed. Around 1920, Spreckels and other sugar companies pooled their research and gave their data to the U.S. Department of Agriculture. By 1926, the first disease-resistant seeds were developed, and by 1933, they were released to growers. By then, row crops, using the irrigation systems developed for sugar beets, had transformed the Salinas Valley into the "salad bowl of the world."

T. C. Rowe was a civil engineer for Spreckels. His family was provided a home across from the park on the corner of Third and Llano Streets. In a memoir written by his daughter Janet Brazelton, a longtime member of the Monterey County Historical Society, she remembers "the comforting smell of vegetables and fruits from Dad's garden simmering on the wood stove in the kitchen as Mother did her canning." (Courtesy of Monterey County Agricultural and Rural Life Museum.)

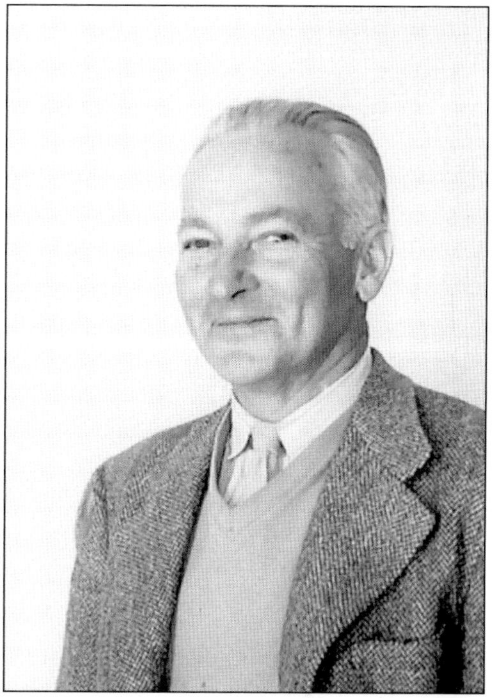

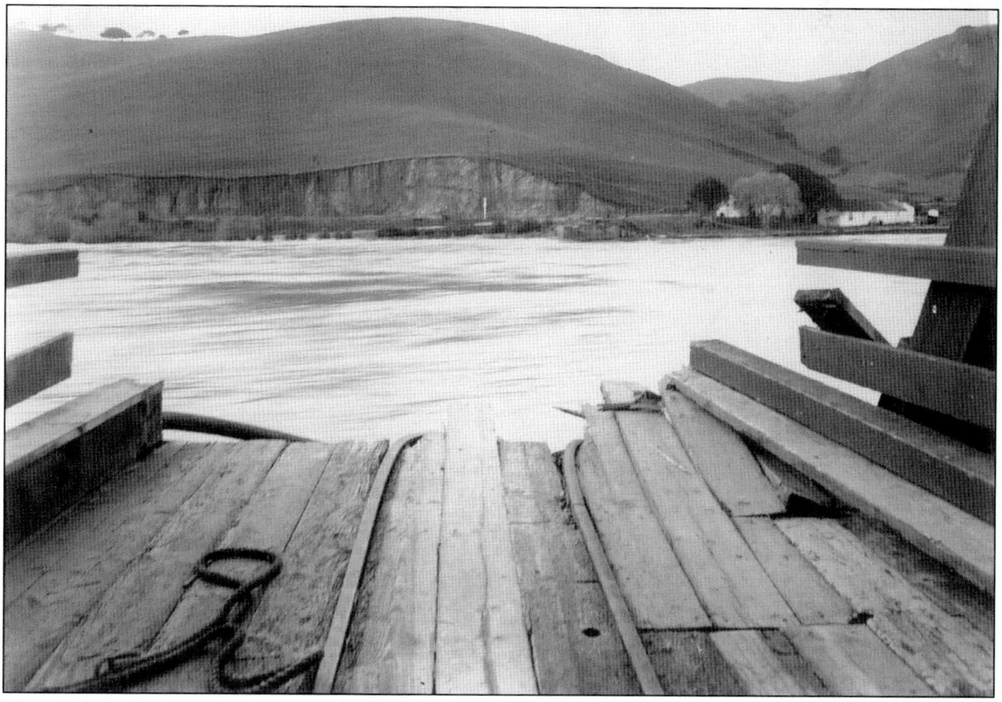

The Salinas River is hard on bridges. The original wooden bridge was destroyed in the flood of 1911. It was replaced with a new structure on concrete piles. After the periodic floods, early newspapers often mentioned all the free wood that had washed up on the coastal beaches. One such early account, in January 1878, describes Hiram Corey's new Hilltown ferry as "fine kindling for the fishermen this summer."

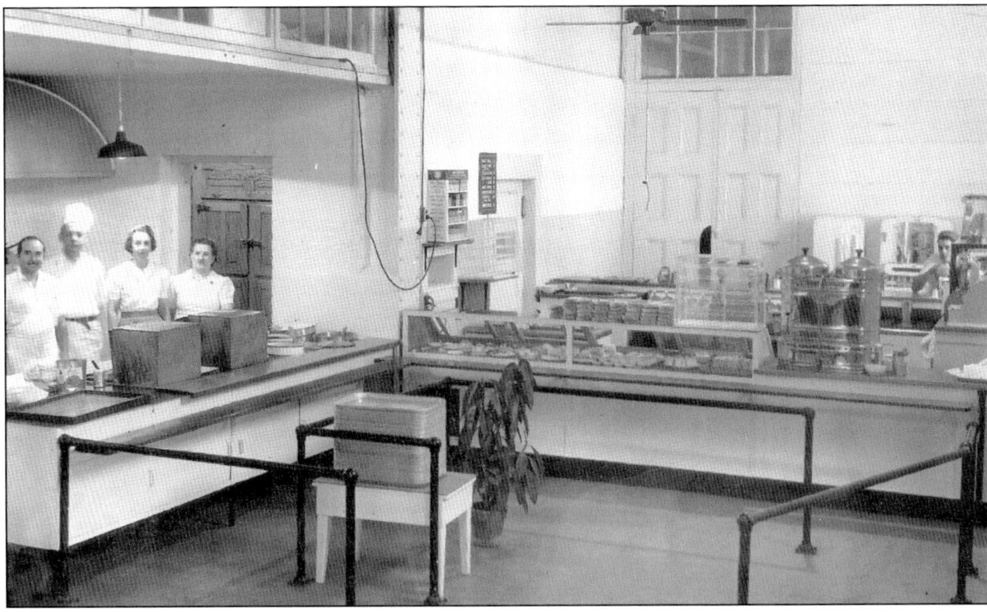

During a campaign (beet harvest), the factory ran 24 hours a day, seven days a week. Many of the workers were single, living either in the hotel or in one of the bunkhouses, and all had to be fed. This is the cafeteria at the factory. (Courtesy of Monterey County Agricultural and Rural Life Museum.)

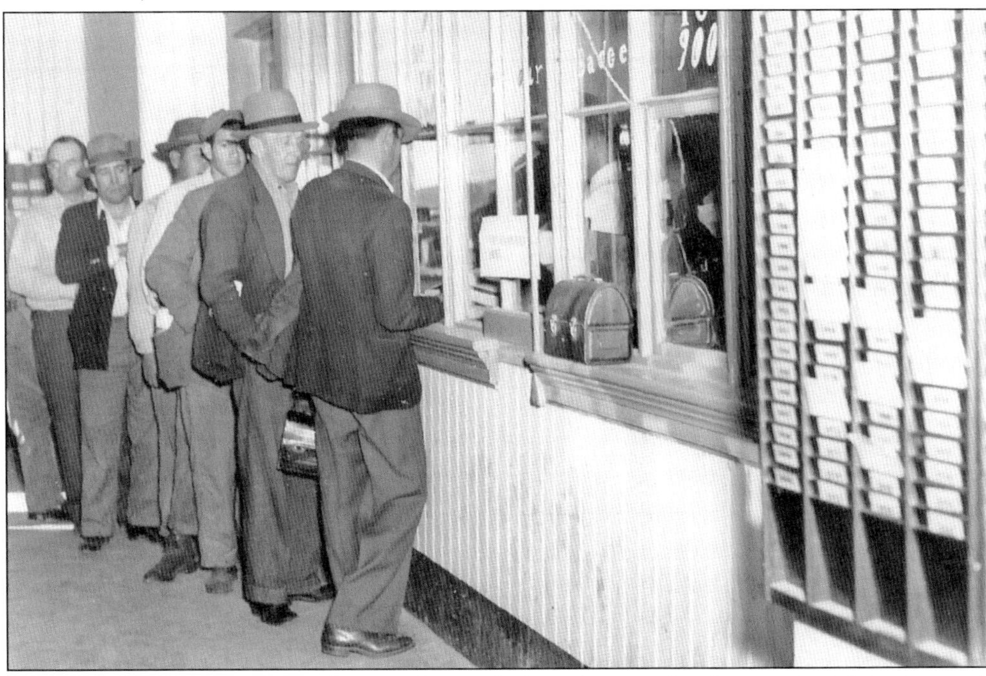

The time office was the place where workers picked up their paychecks, punched their timecards at the beginning and end of each shift, paid their union dues, stocked up on uniforms, or caught up on the latest news. Among the many workers who passed through these offices were novelist John Steinbeck and his father. (Courtesy of Monterey County Agricultural and Rural Life Museum.)

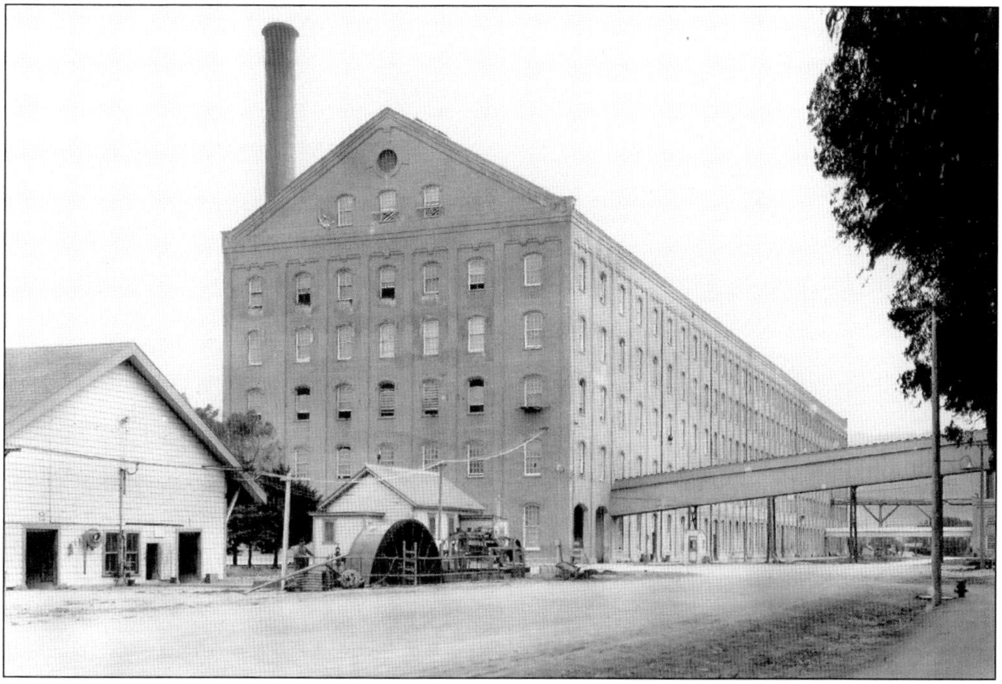

The beet wheel is in front of the main factory building. Beets were transported in an underground flume system, and the beet wheel helped to move them from the beet bins into the factory. The wheels raised the beets from one level to another much like locks in a canal.

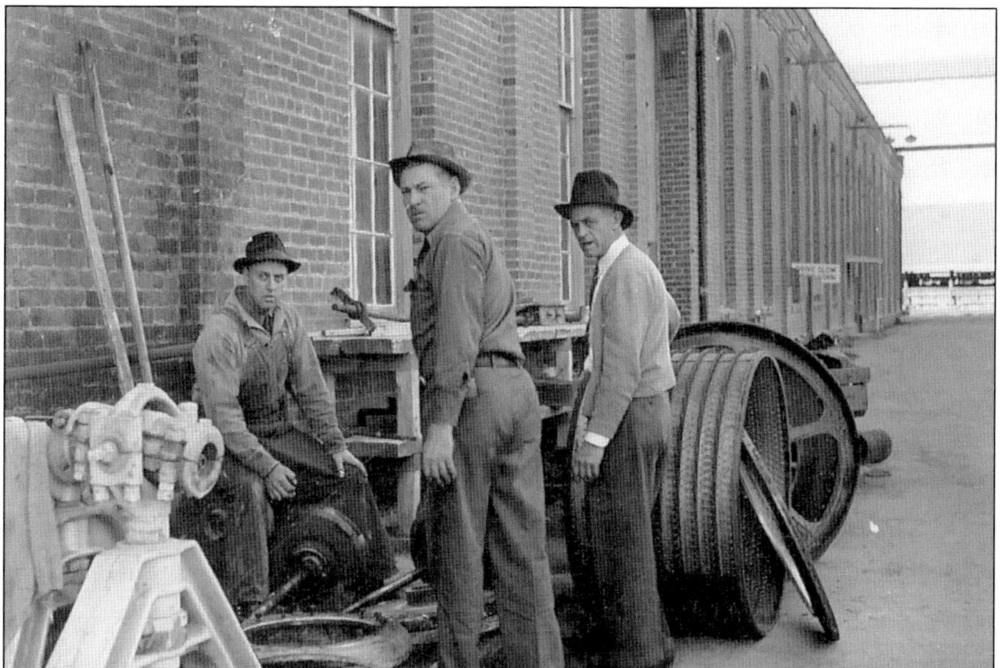

Wallace Greenlaw, Ralph Boyd, and A. J. McKinley of the Mechanical Department inspect a runner on a centrifugal pump outside of the machine shop. The work was tiring, as expressed by Wallace. (Courtesy of Monterey County Agricultural and Rural Life Museum.)

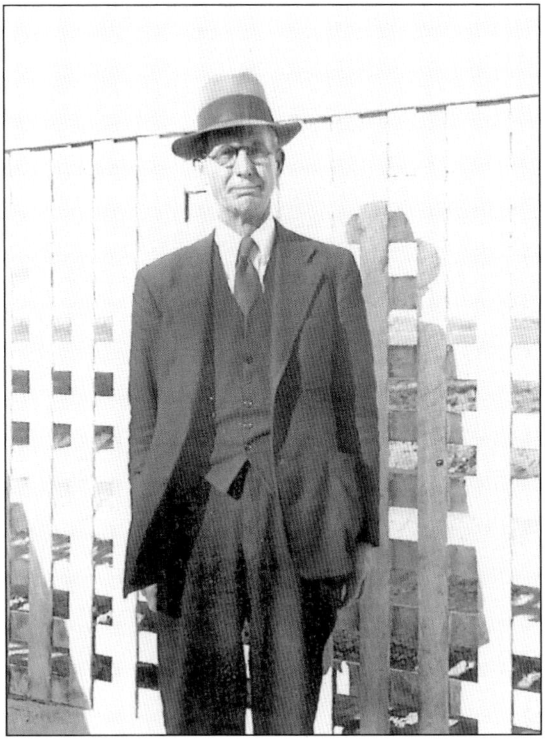

Grover McCandless served as the Spreckels field superintendent until his retirement. His son Ed McCandless, following in his father's footsteps, graduated from UC Berkeley in agriculture and devoted his life as a field representative to the agricultural community. (Courtesy of Monterey County Agricultural and Rural Life Museum.)

This famous photograph, showing tremendous damage to the main building after the 1906 earthquake, may be misleading. According to Ralph Moore, the general manager, repairs were being done to the building at the time of the earthquake, and some bricks had been previously removed to make access easier for the repairs. Other than broken pipes and minor problems, the main damage was a two-foot bulge in the factory wall, concave on the east side and convex on the west side. The bent framework was soon repaired and braced, but the bulge was never entirely removed.

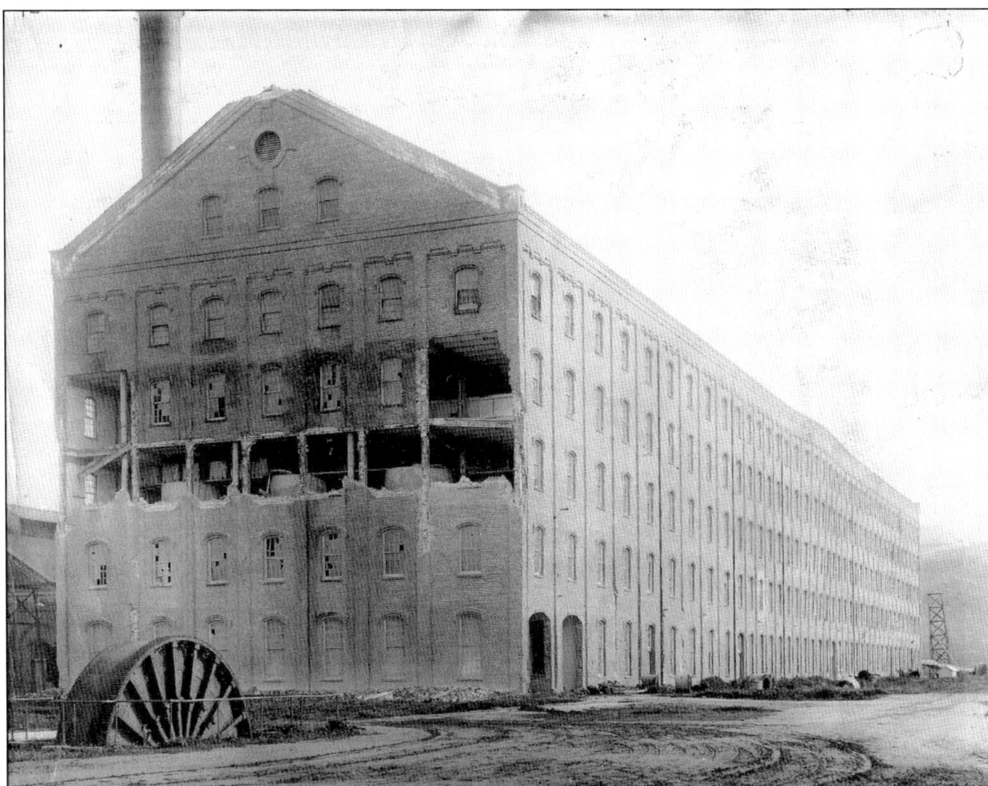

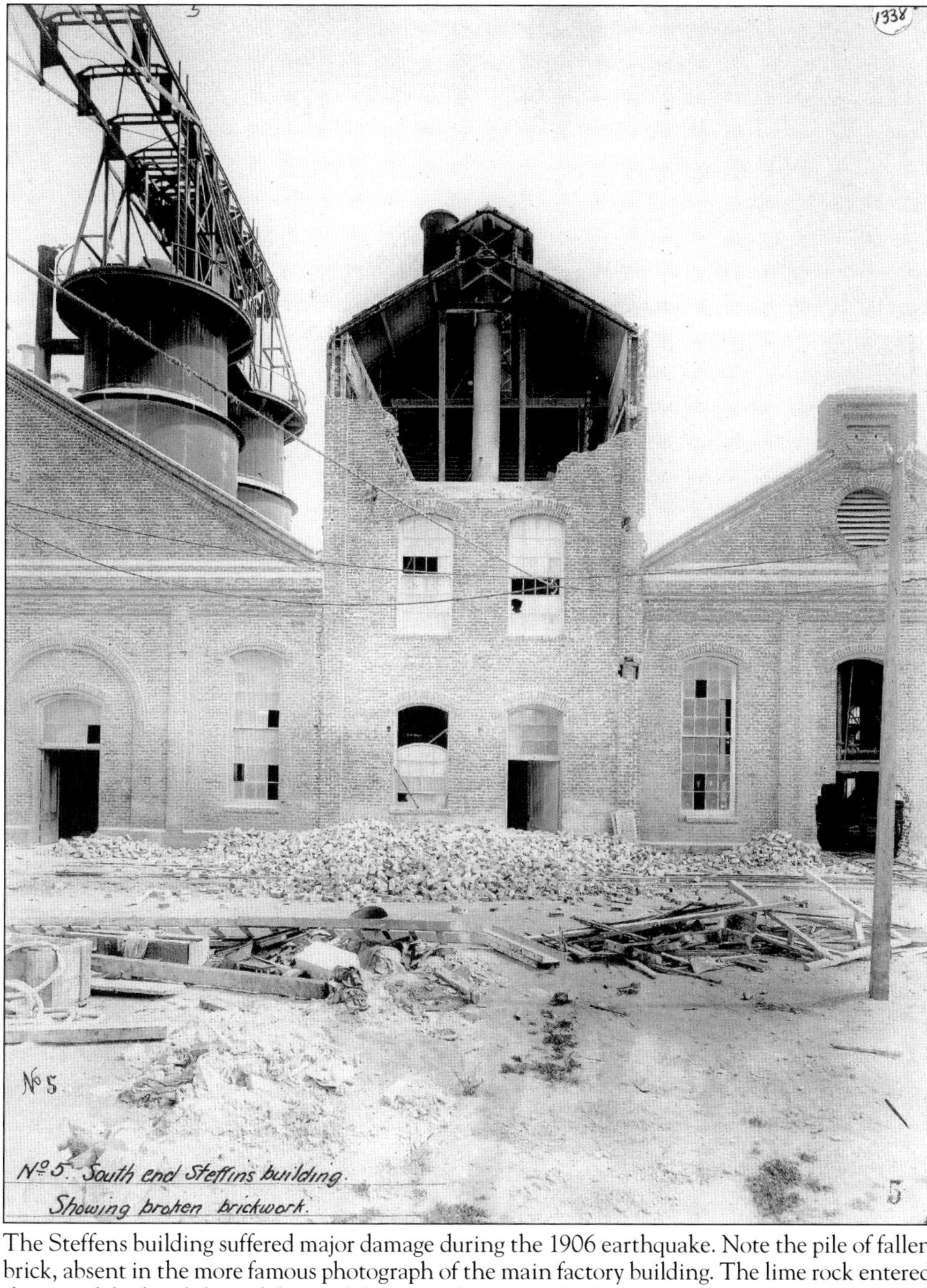

The Steffens building suffered major damage during the 1906 earthquake. Note the pile of fallen brick, absent in the more famous photograph of the main factory building. The lime rock entered the top of the limekiln and dropped down to a hopper at the base. Carbon dioxide was collected from the kiln and sent to a gas washer where it was processed for use in carbonation. The rock passed from the hopper at the base of the kiln onto a conveyor that took it to the crusher, where it was processed into "lime milk" that was used in processing beets. It was then discarded.

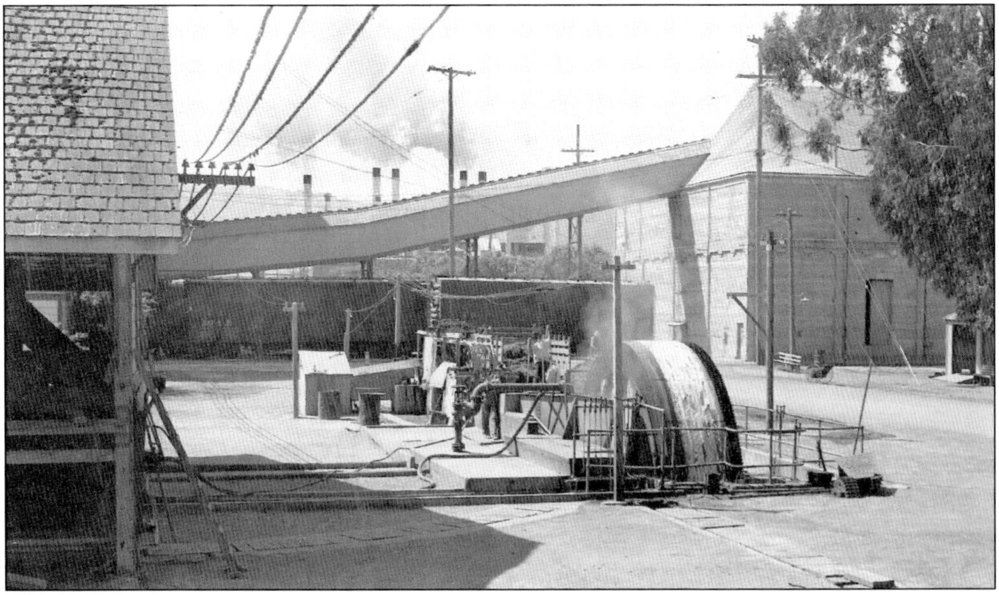

Beet wheels or conveyors were used to transport beets through a water flume to the factory. They passed through a "trash collector," where the clinging debris was removed before entering the beet slicer. (Courtesy of Monterey County Agricultural and Rural Life Museum.)

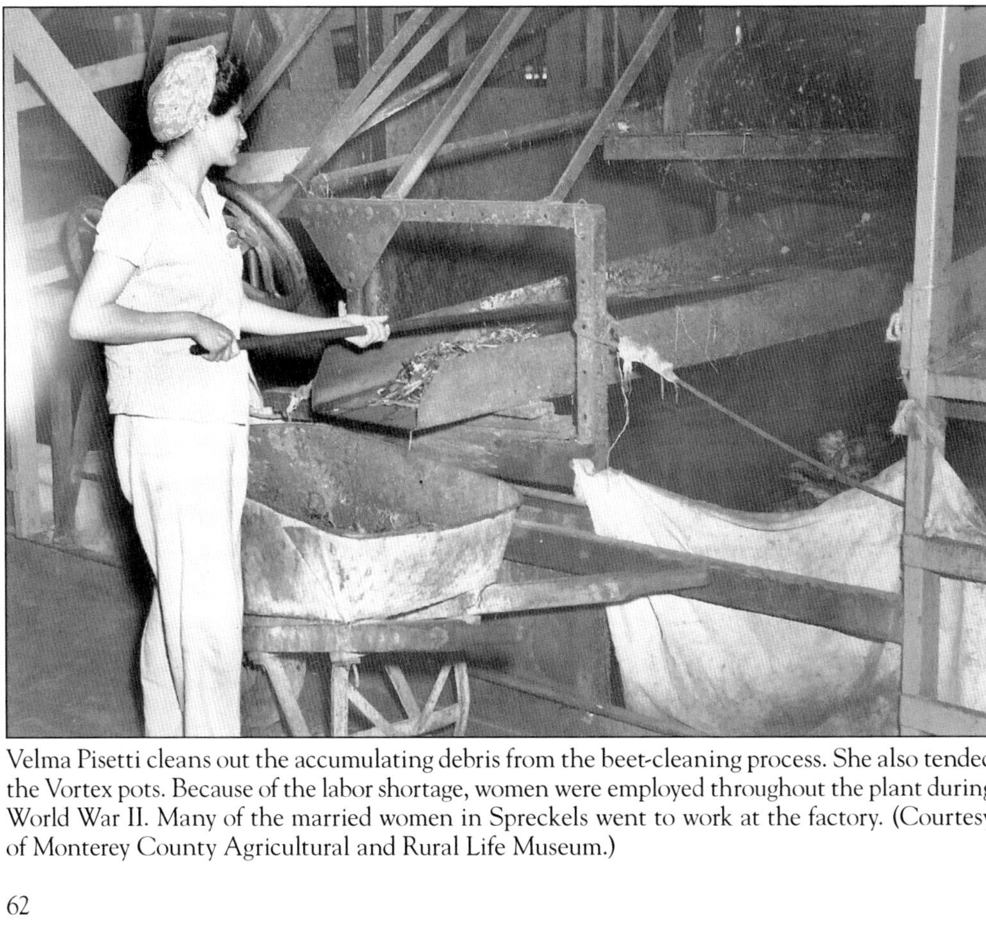

Velma Pisetti cleans out the accumulating debris from the beet-cleaning process. She also tended the Vortex pots. Because of the labor shortage, women were employed throughout the plant during World War II. Many of the married women in Spreckels went to work at the factory. (Courtesy of Monterey County Agricultural and Rural Life Museum.)

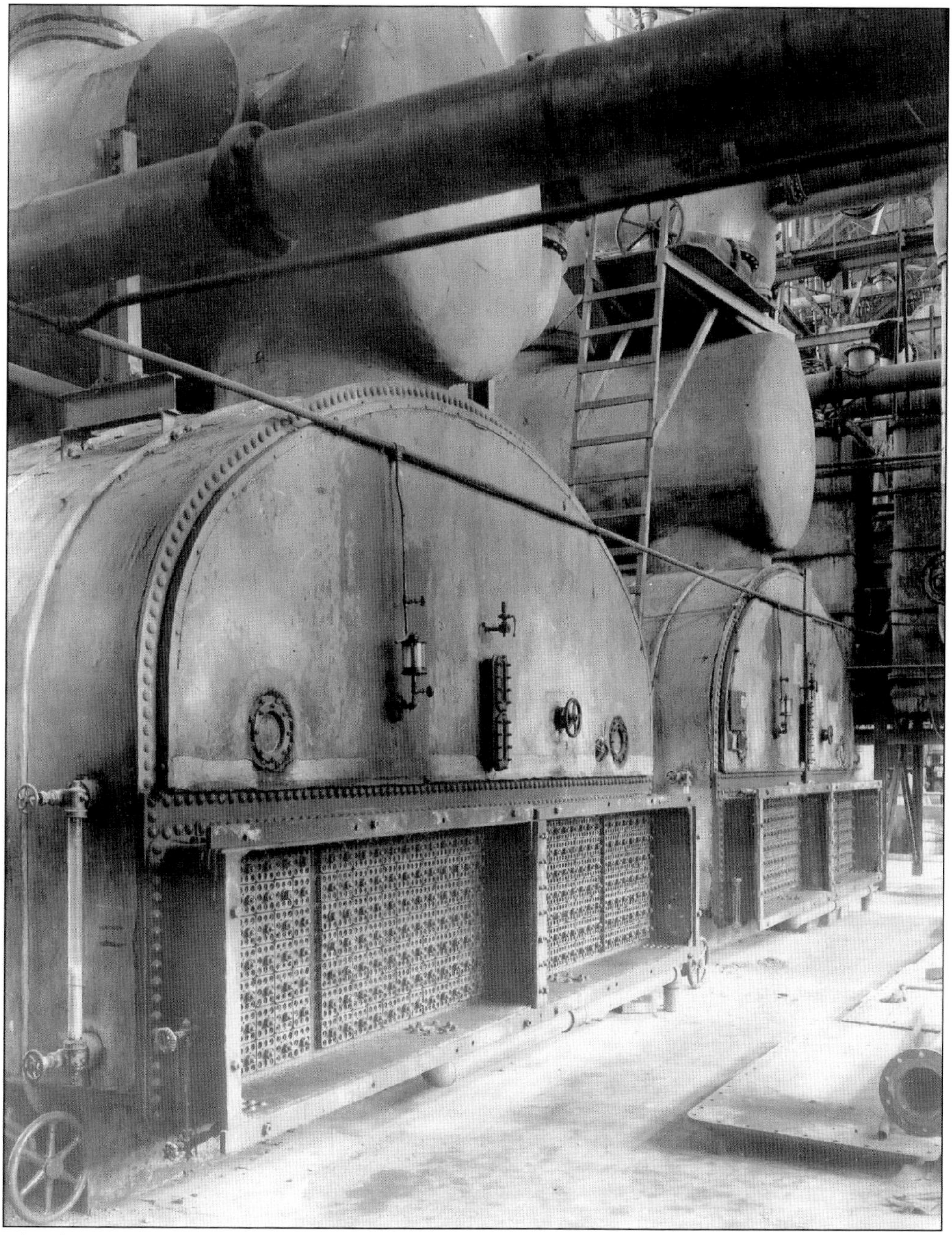

Thin beet juice enters the evaporators where it is converted into thick or concentrated beet juice. That in turn is sent for further reduction in the crystallization section of the plant. With all the steam cast off by this process, nobody wanted to spend much time on the fifth floor of the building, as it was always very hot up there and the workers came down dripping with sweat.

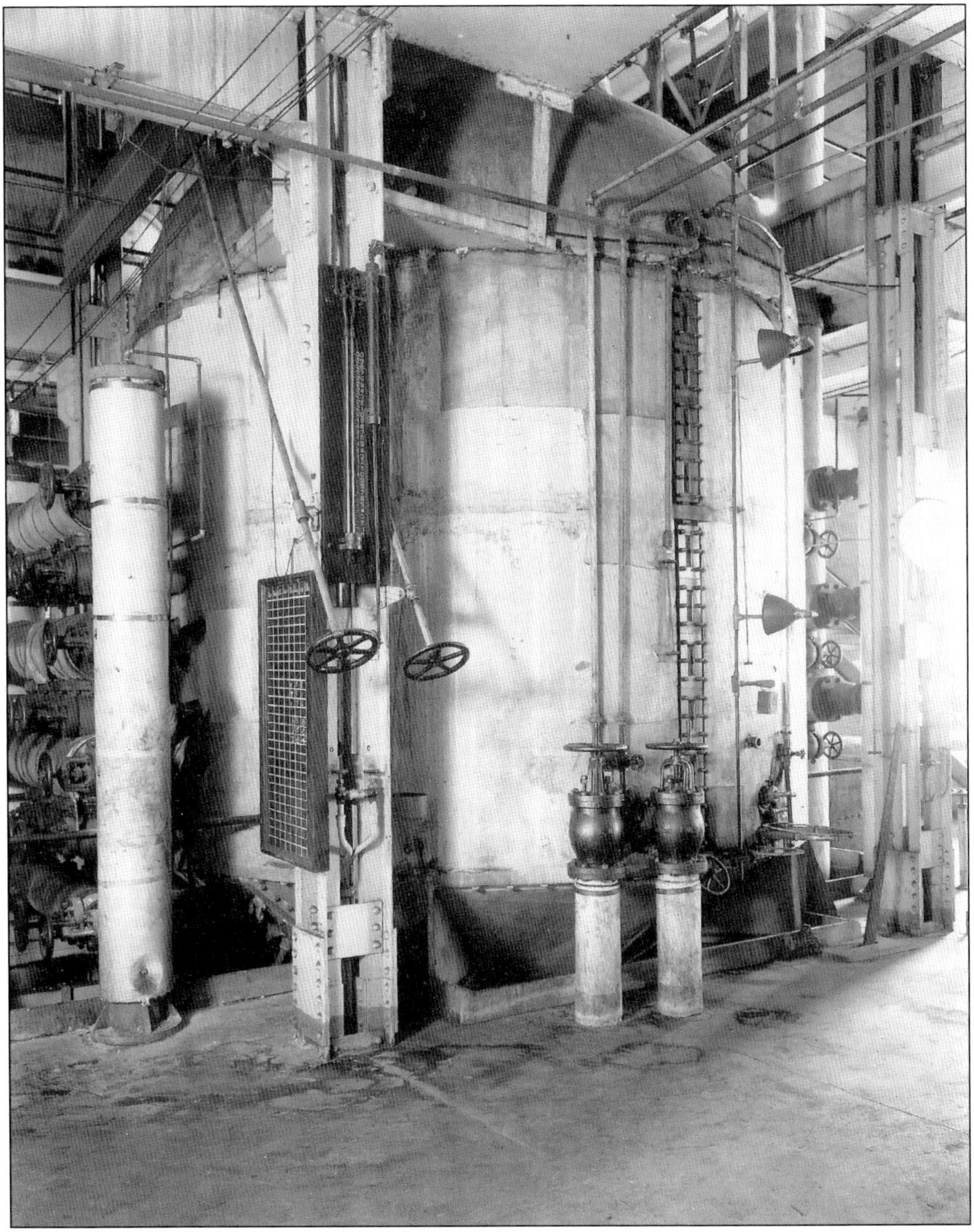

This large vacuum pan was part of the crystallization process. Removing water from the beet juice took place in two stages. First the sugar-laden juice was run through the evaporators, filtered, and put into storage tanks. The thick sugar juice from the evaporators was called "standard liquor." It was then passed on to this vacuum pan, where the crystallization processes began. In the vacuum pan, this liquid was crystallized into white sugar by boiling it under high vacuum and low temperature. This prevented caramelization.

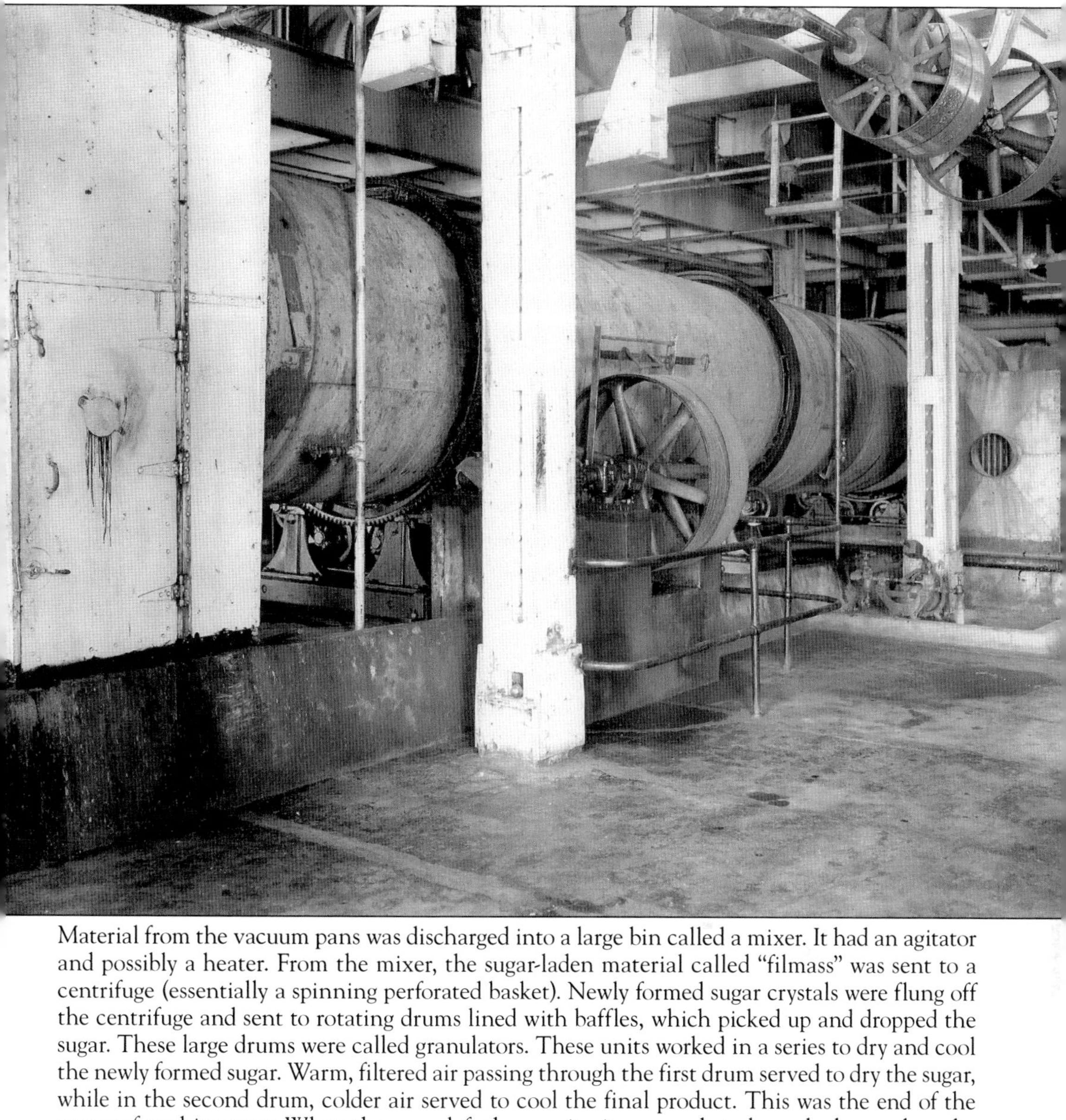

Material from the vacuum pans was discharged into a large bin called a mixer. It had an agitator and possibly a heater. From the mixer, the sugar-laden material called "filmass" was sent to a centrifuge (essentially a spinning perforated basket). Newly formed sugar crystals were flung off the centrifuge and sent to rotating drums lined with baffles, which picked up and dropped the sugar. These large drums were called granulators. These units worked in a series to dry and cool the newly formed sugar. Warm, filtered air passing through the first drum served to dry the sugar, while in the second drum, colder air served to cool the final product. This was the end of the process for white sugar. When the sugar left these units, it was ready to be sacked or packaged.

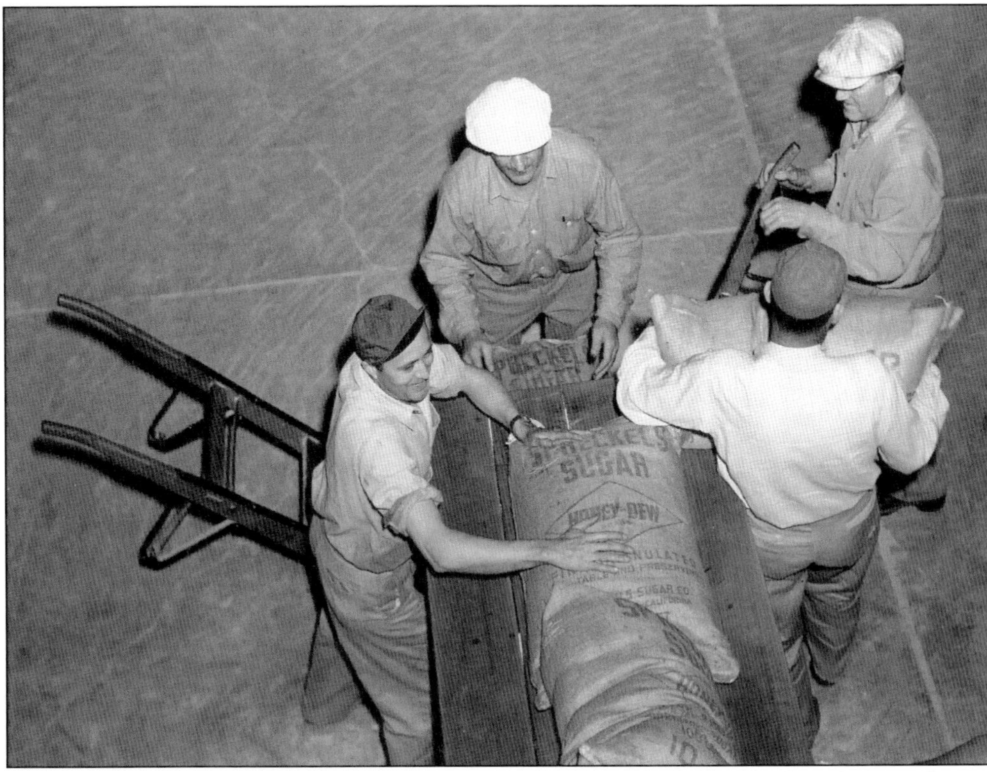

Loading the finished and bagged sugar, from left to right, are Vern Edwards, Joe Shierts, "Whitey" Whitehead, and Vern Nichols. (Courtesy of Monterey County Agricultural and Rural Life Museum.)

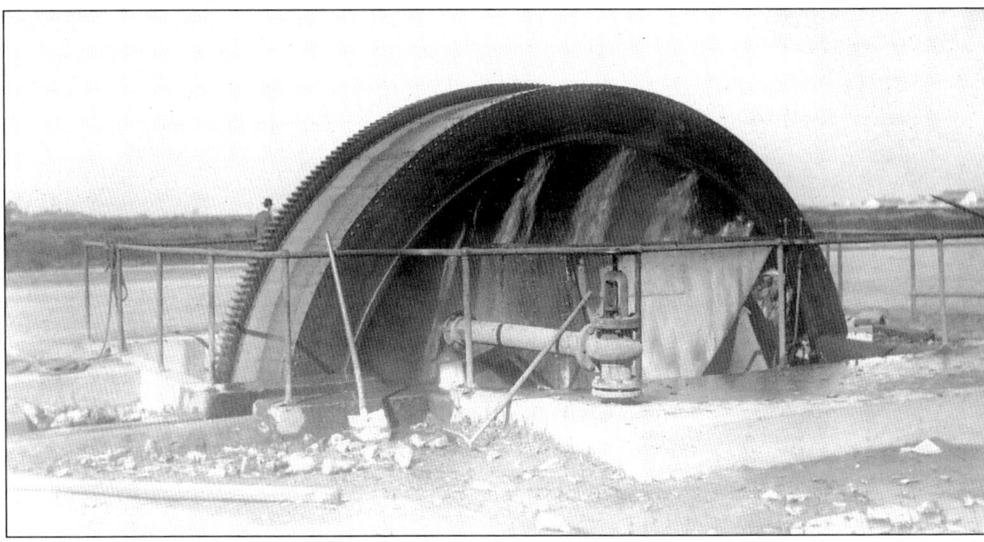

Harvested sugar beets were dumped from railroad cars into beet bins and transferred via water troughs into an underground flume. They were picked up by the conveyor wheel, which continued the washing process. The wheel then lifted the beets to a higher trench at the south end of the factory (the beet end), which was where the processing began. The north end of the factory (the sugar end) was where the final processing of the sugar was completed. Pictured here is a beet wheel.

A long line of steel cable is being pulled from a drum and laid on a pipe or low concrete wall. Nobody is wearing gloves, so this is either a staged photograph or the workers will have many steel splinters. (Courtesy of Monterey County Agricultural and Rural Life Museum.)

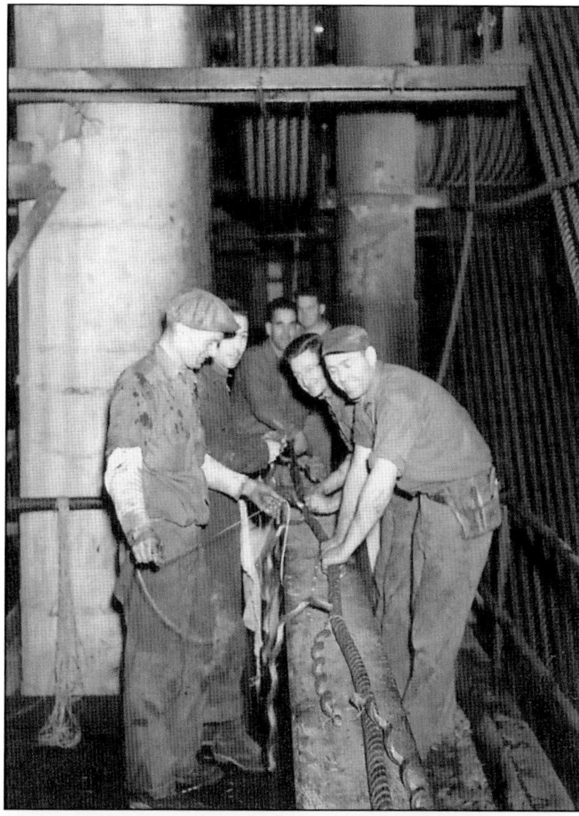

Mrs. Frank Triano oils valves in the machinery, which while running was extremely hazardous. (Courtesy of Monterey County Agricultural and Rural Life Museum.)

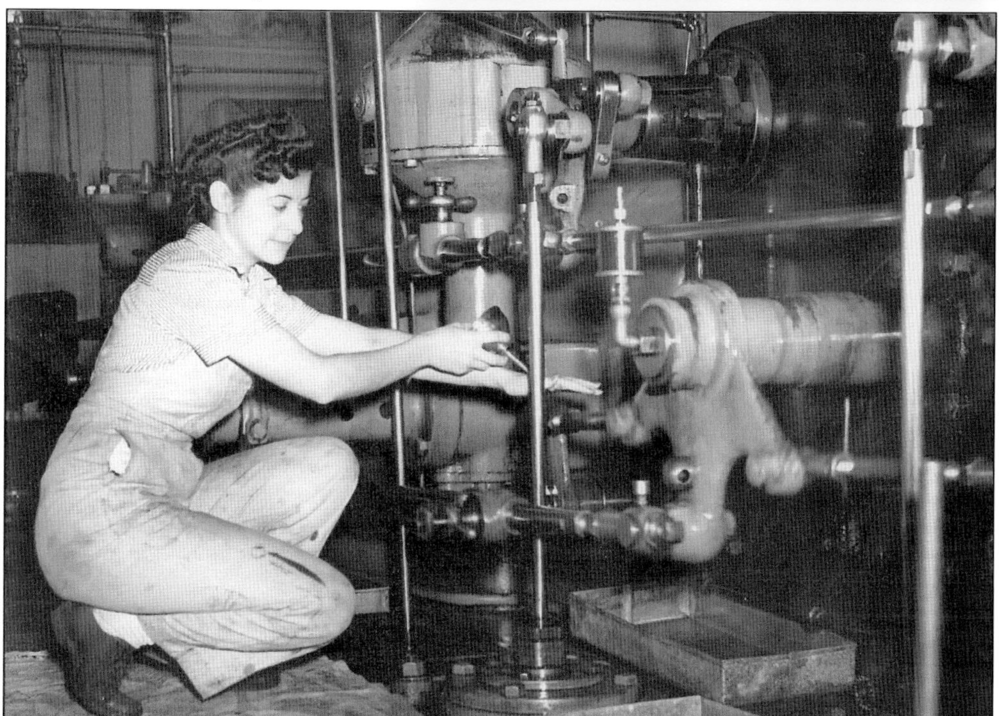

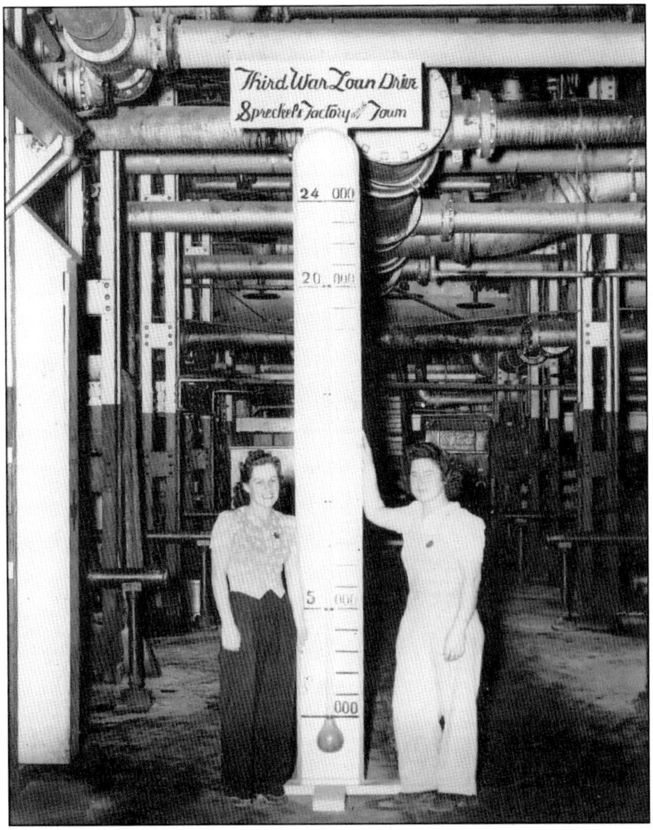

Elva Grantham and Beva Benoit pose with the Third War Loan Drive thermometer for the Spreckels factory and town. (Courtesy of Monterey County Agricultural and Rural Life Museum.)

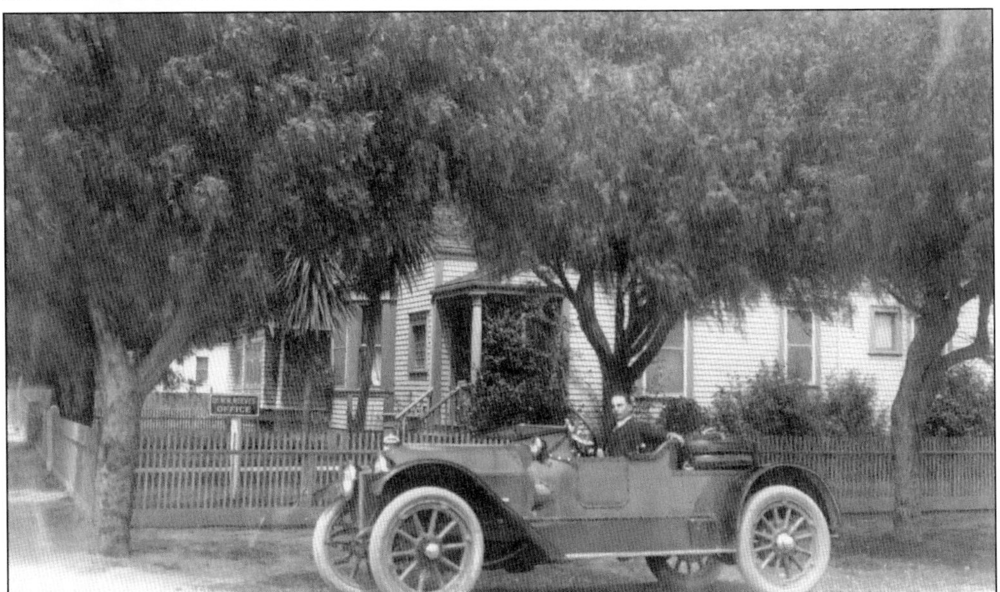

Dr. Rollin Reeves is pictured in front of his Spreckels office in 1942. He is driving a battleship gray Abbott-Detroit roadster. At that time, he was the Spreckels company physician—the first company M.D.

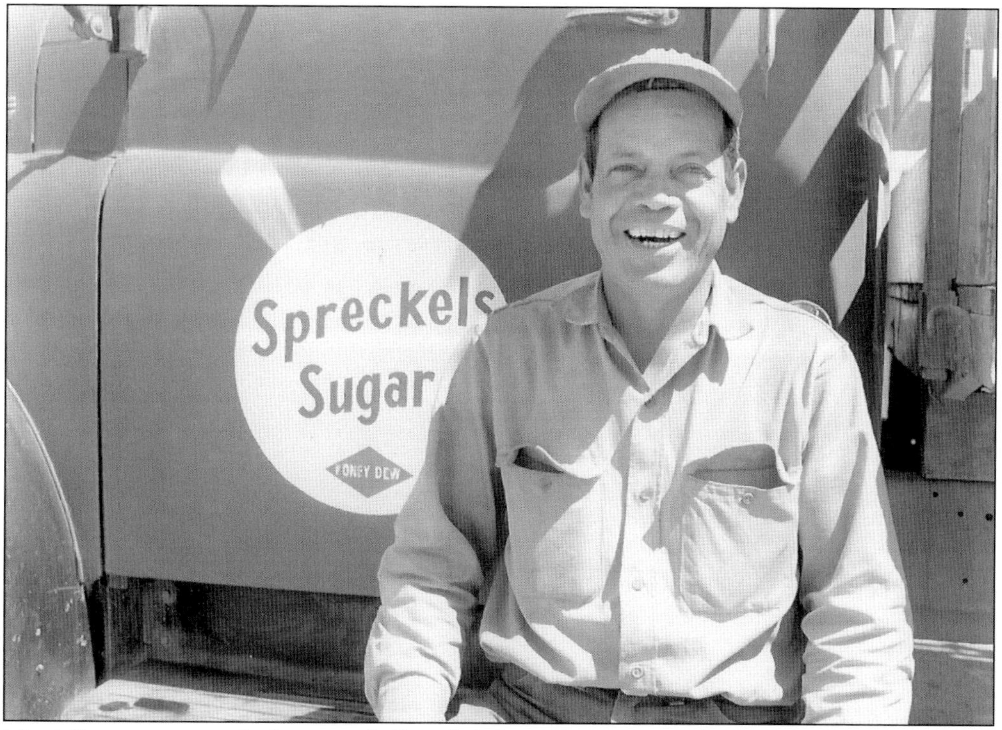

Marci Campos rests on the bumper of a Spreckels Sugar Company truck. He worked for the company for over 30 years. (Courtesy of Monterey County Agricultural and Rural Life Museum.)

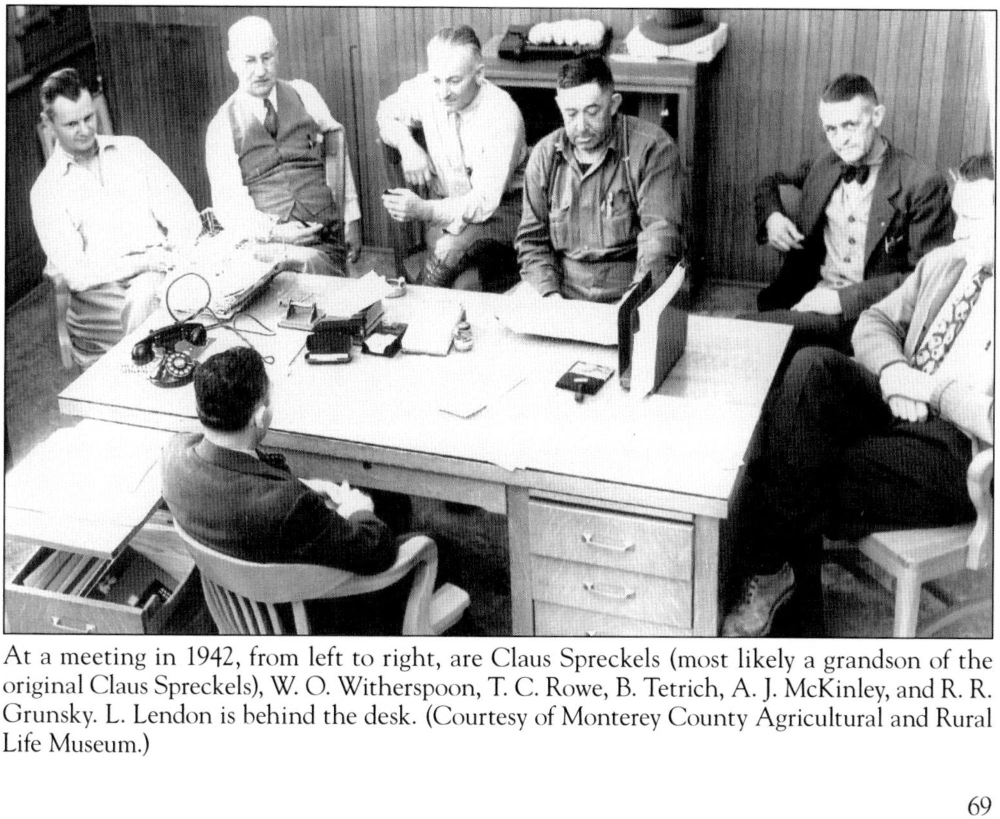

At a meeting in 1942, from left to right, are Claus Spreckels (most likely a grandson of the original Claus Spreckels), W. O. Witherspoon, T. C. Rowe, B. Tetrich, A. J. McKinley, and R. R. Grunsky. L. Lendon is behind the desk. (Courtesy of Monterey County Agricultural and Rural Life Museum.)

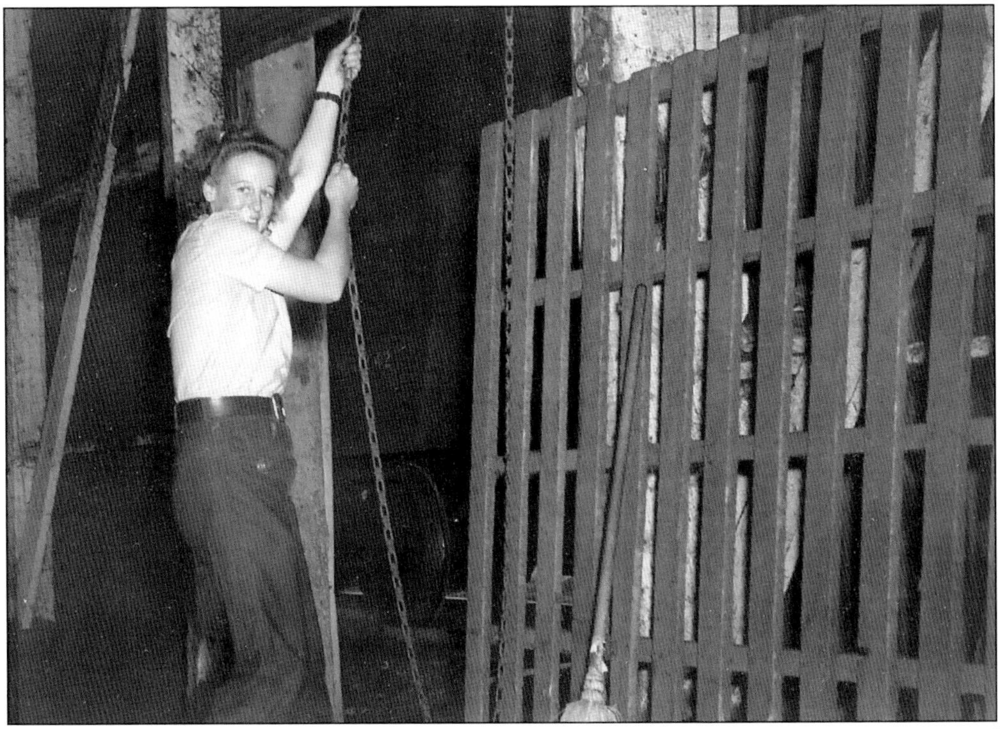

This photograph of Ola Mae Clem opening a gate appeared in the December 1945 edition of the *Honey Dew News*, the company newsletter. (Courtesy of Monterey County Agricultural and Rural Life Museum.)

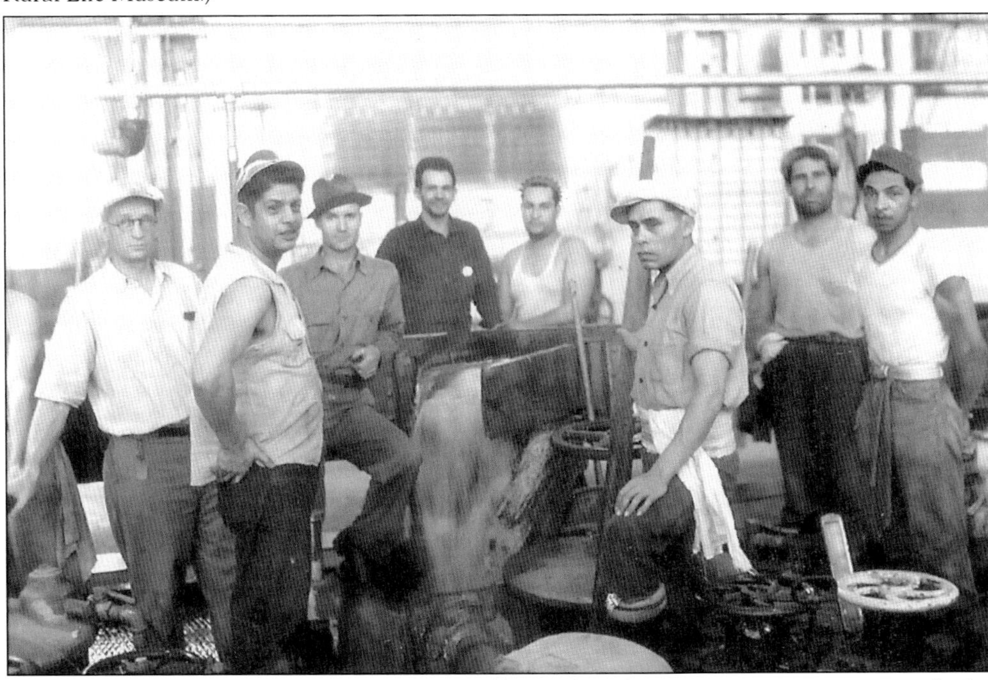

Workers fill the last sugar cell. There is no additional explanation, nor any names, with this photograph. (Courtesy of Monterey County Agricultural and Rural Life Museum.)

Five

The Community

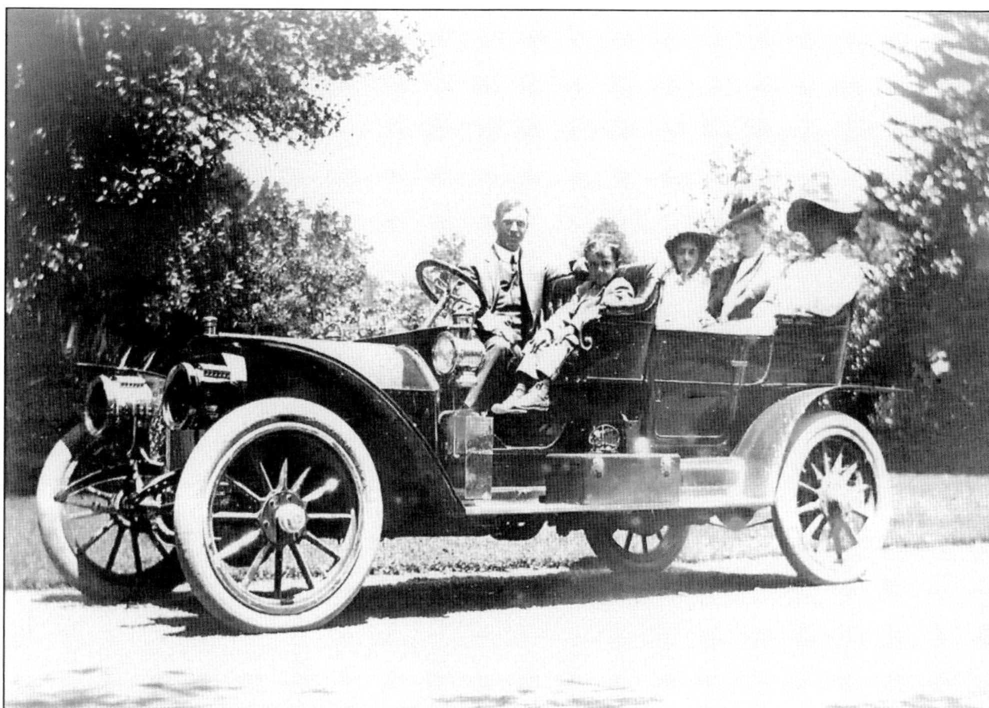

Pictured here in 1909 are Fred Jackson and his son Foster, Louise Bullene, Mrs. Jackson, and Florence (Clem) Tynan. By this date, the horse-drawn carriage is beginning to be replaced by automobiles.

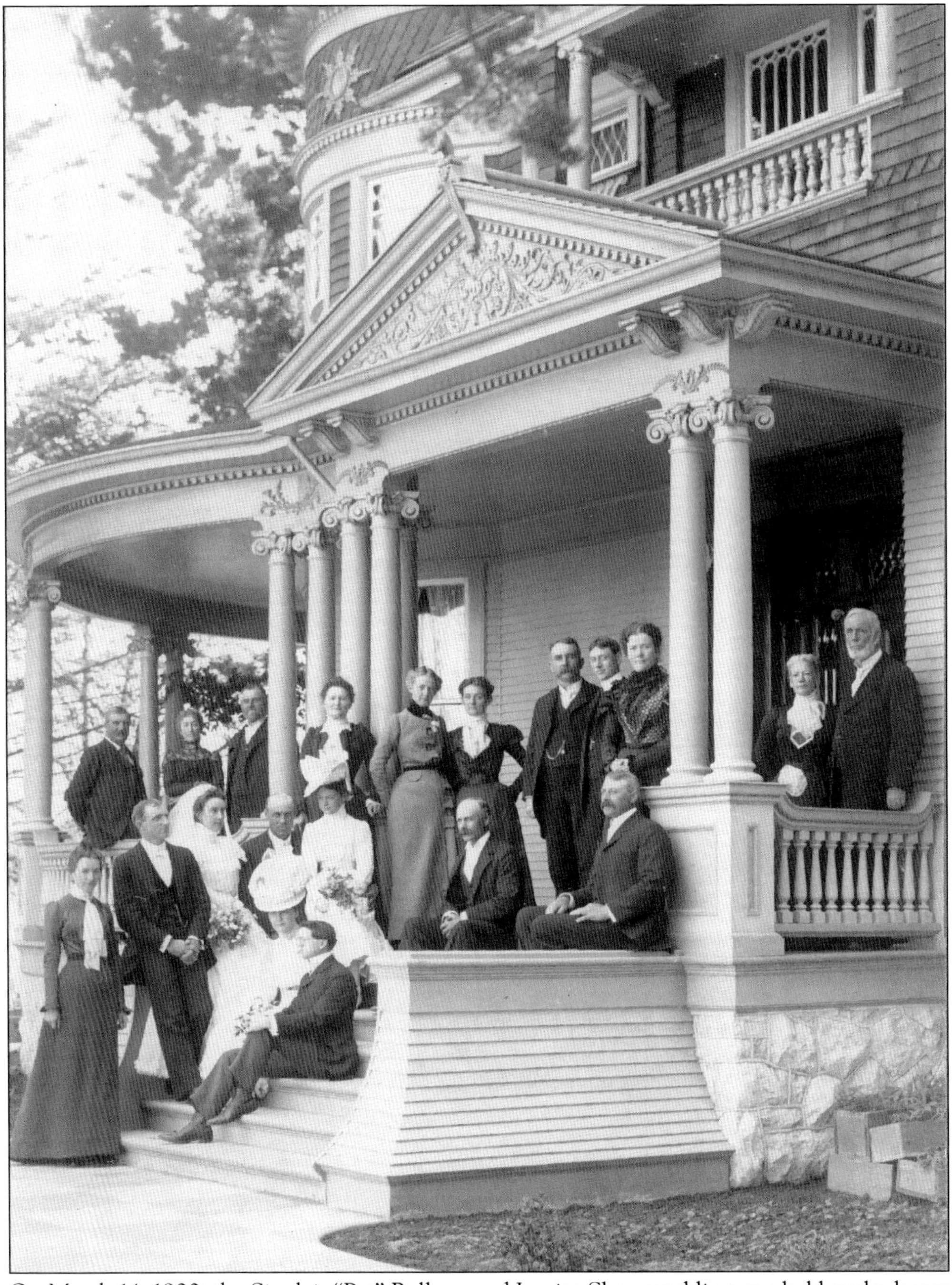

On March 14, 1900, the Sinclair "Pet" Bullene and Louise Shaw wedding was held at the home of the Spreckels sugar-factory superintendent in Spreckels. Pictured here, from left to right, are (standing on porch) Mr. O'Cayer, Mrs. Huff, Mr. Waters, Mrs. Baker, Mrs. Sanford, Mrs. O. H. Bullene, Mr. Huff, Rev. Sanford, Mrs. Frank Bullene, Mrs. Waters, and Mr. Hatch; (on walk and steps) unidentified, Alec Andrews, Mrs. ? Bullene, Mr. Bullene, Olive Waters, Mr. O. H. Bullene, Mr. Frank Bullene; and (seated on steps) Hazel Baker, Louis Waters. "Pet" Bullene appears as a minor character in John Steinbeck's *East of Eden*.

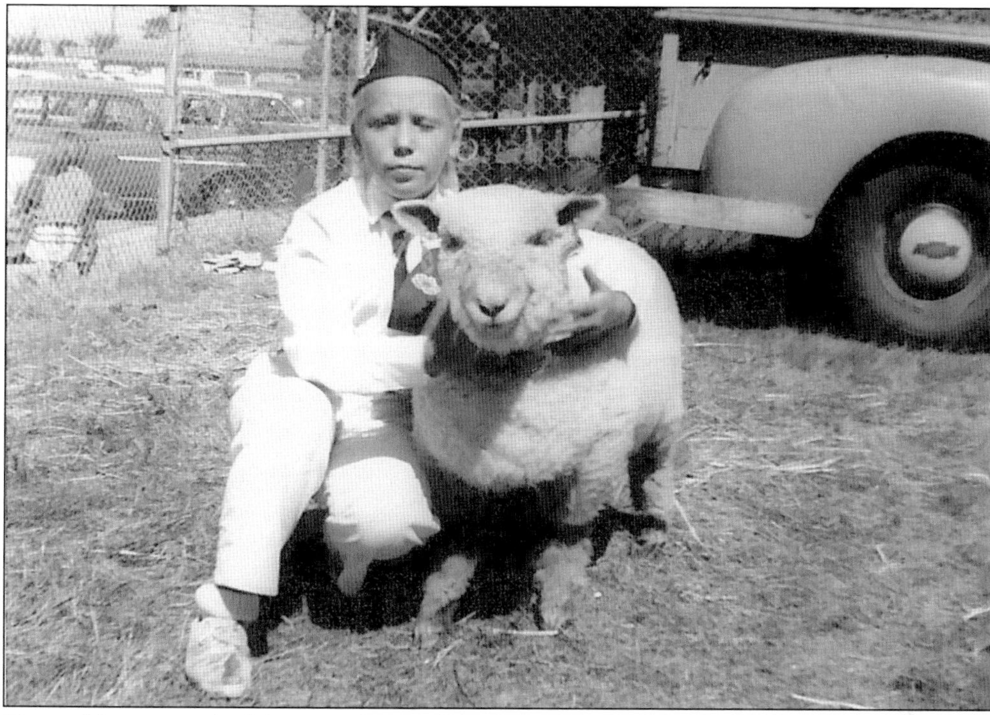

Sharon Vosti visits the Monterey County Fair. (Courtesy of Monterey County Agricultural and Rural Life Museum.)

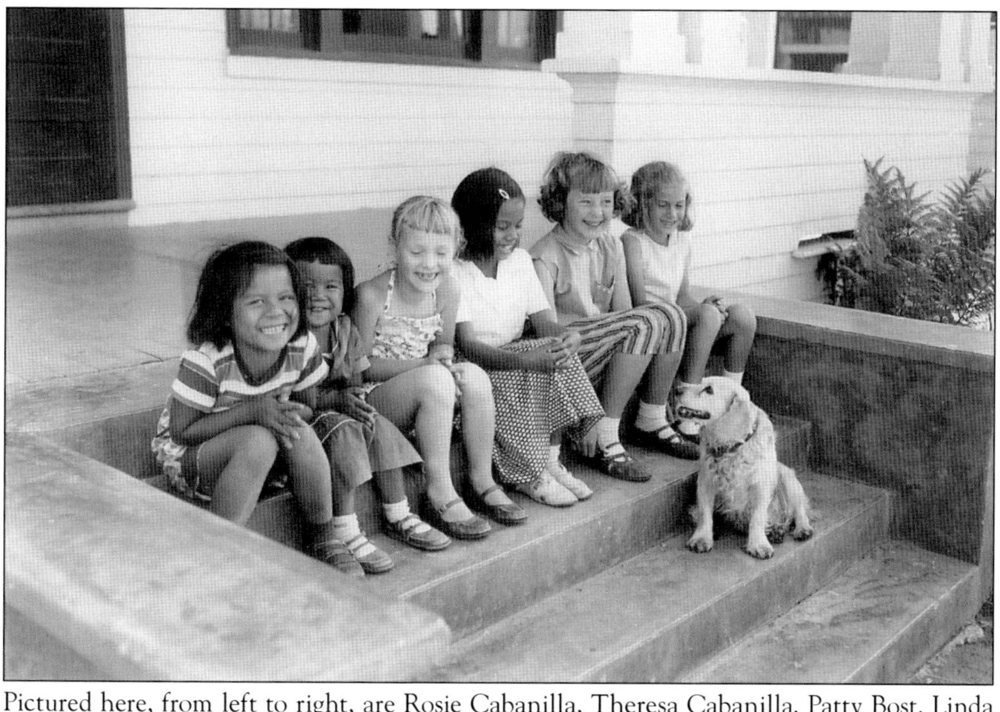

Pictured here, from left to right, are Rosie Cabanilla, Theresa Cabanilla, Patty Bost, Linda Cabanilla, Shirley Means, and Judy Hampton. (Courtesy of Monterey County Agricultural and Rural Life Museum.)

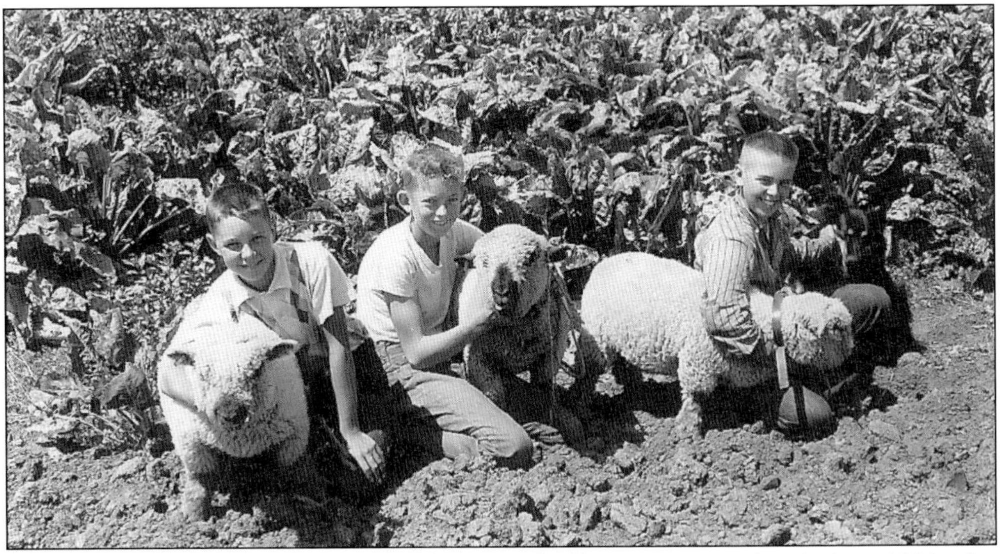

From left to right, Brian Bost, Larry Williams, and Billy Pi are pictured with their 4-H lambs. The 4-H Club was an important part of rural life in Spreckels and helped encourage the next generation of farmers and ranchers. (Courtesy of Monterey County Agricultural and Rural Life Museum.)

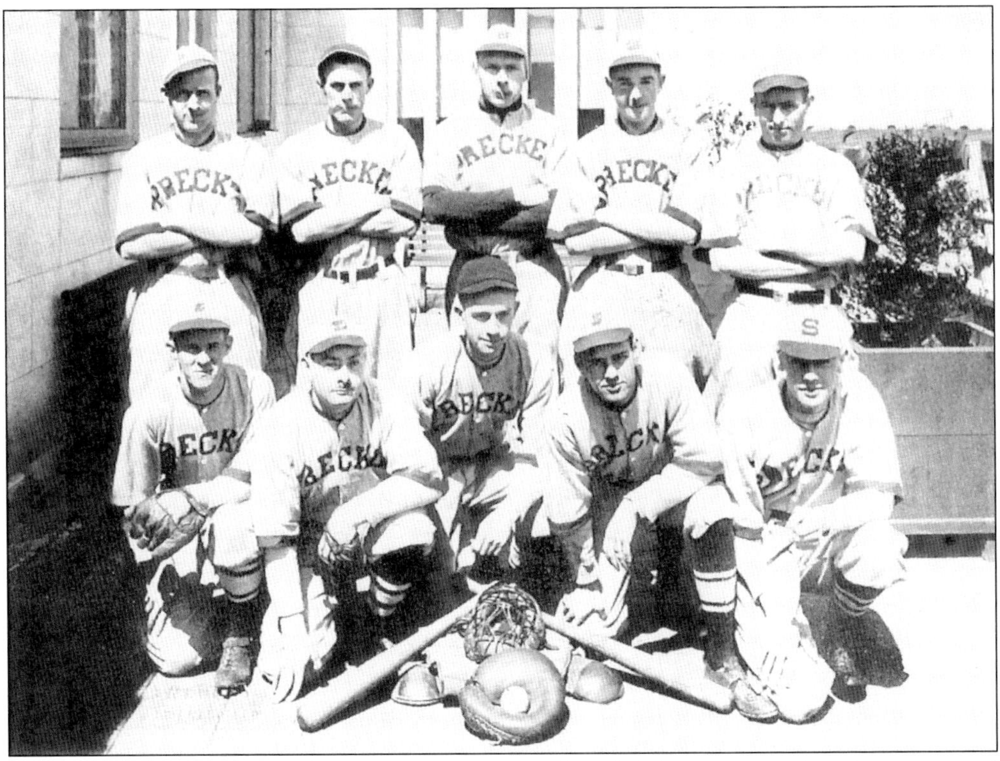

Spreckels saw its first baseball team suit up in 1907. They did the town proud as they competed with other cities throughout the county. The sport was so popular with the people of Spreckels that everywhere one looked there were baseball diamonds. (Courtesy of Monterey County Agricultural and Rural Life Museum.)

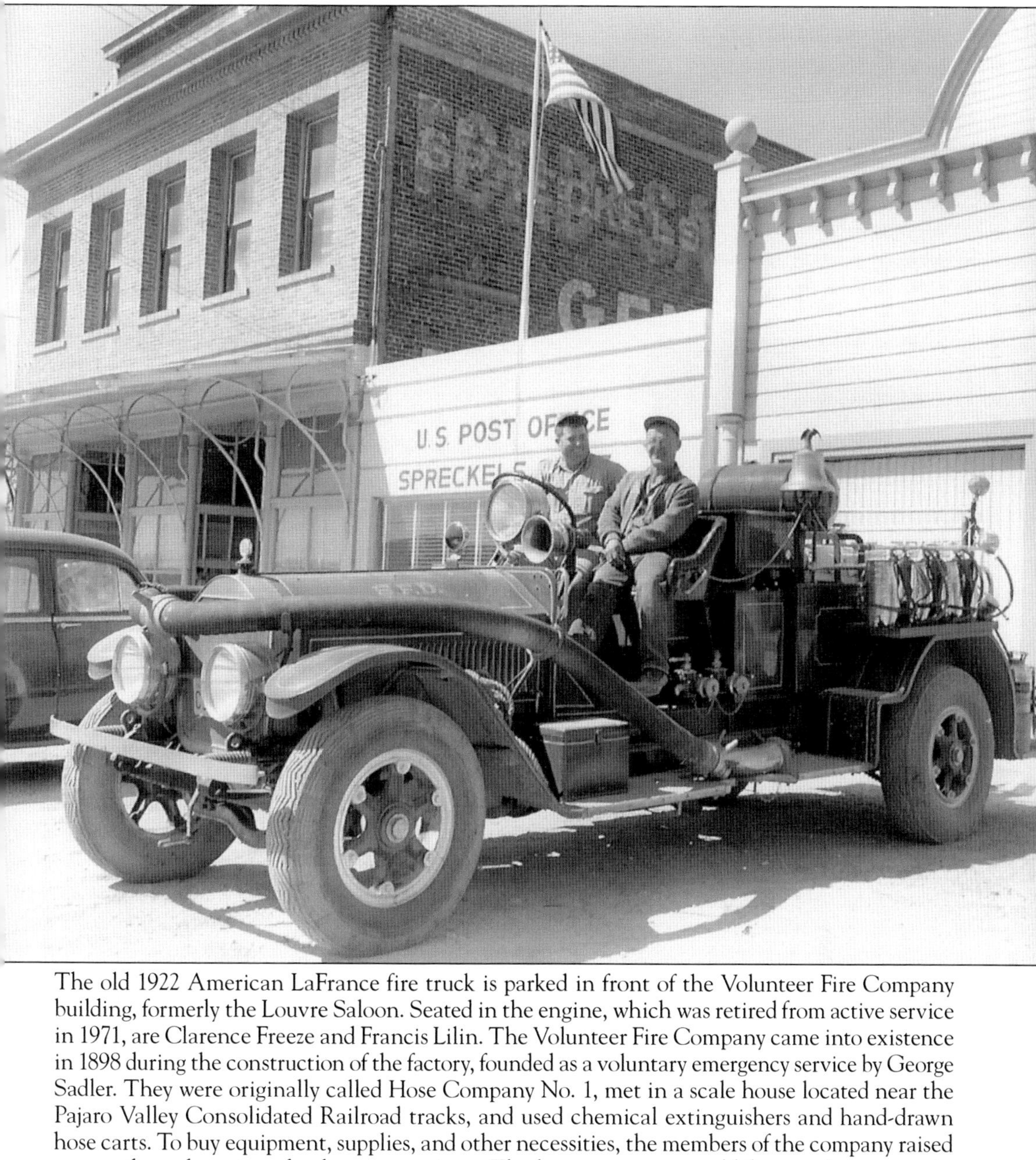

The old 1922 American LaFrance fire truck is parked in front of the Volunteer Fire Company building, formerly the Louvre Saloon. Seated in the engine, which was retired from active service in 1971, are Clarence Freeze and Francis Lilin. The Volunteer Fire Company came into existence in 1898 during the construction of the factory, founded as a voluntary emergency service by George Sadler. They were originally called Hose Company No. 1, met in a scale house located near the Pajaro Valley Consolidated Railroad tracks, and used chemical extinguishers and hand-drawn hose carts. To buy equipment, supplies, and other necessities, the members of the company raised money through various fund-raising projects. The hose company would frequently compete in races with the Salinas hose company or other firemen. (Courtesy of Monterey County Agricultural and Rural Life Museum.)

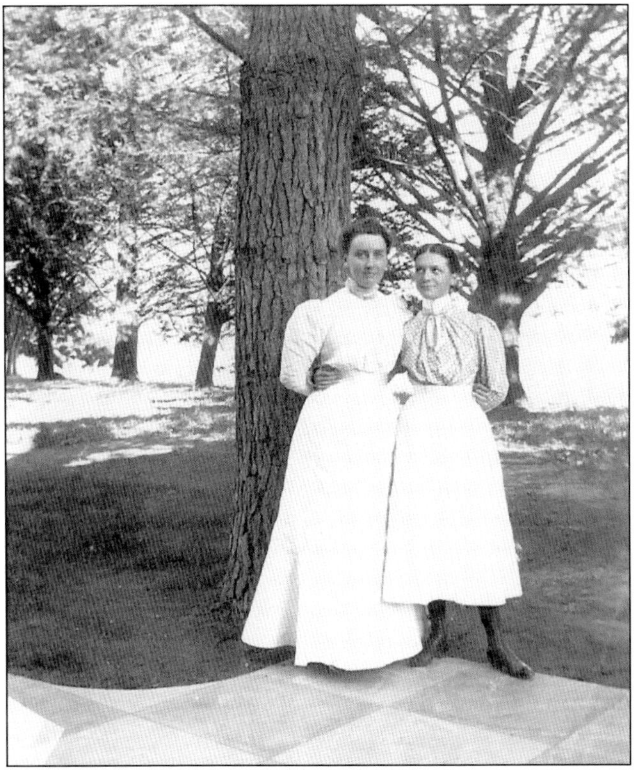

This photograph of Louise Bullene and her cousin Olive Waters, daughter of Spreckels superintendent Waters, was taken at the Waters's home in Spreckels around 1899.

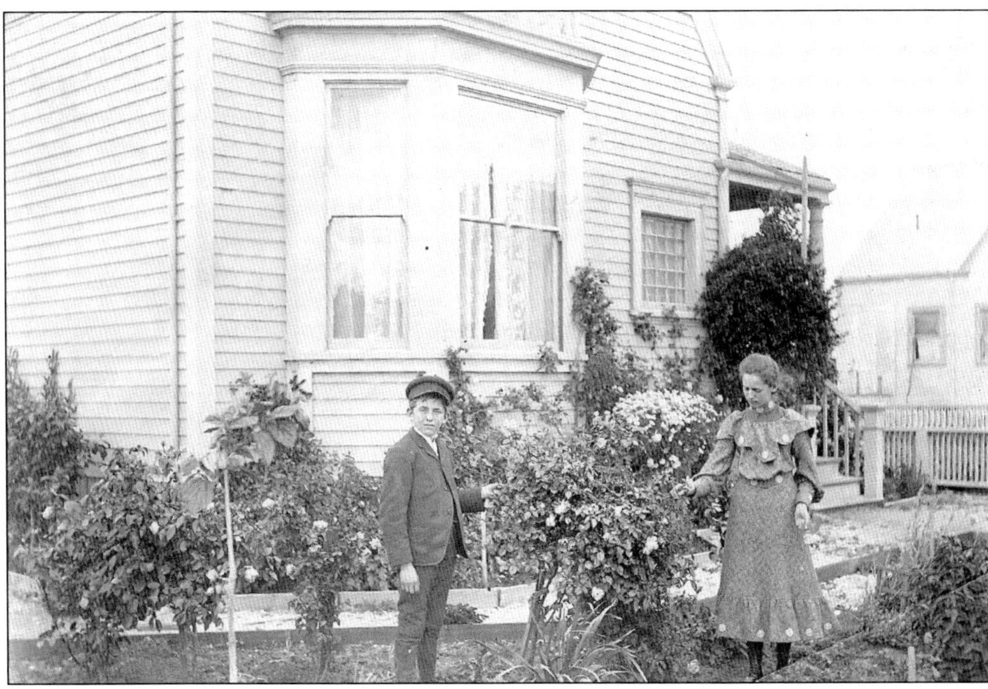

Rose Rhyner and her brother William "Willy" Rhyner stand in the front yard of their Spreckels home. Their father was one of the early employees at the factory, and both children subsequently went to work for the company.

The wedding of Mr. and Mrs. Elmer Lanini is pictured here. Weddings were frequently reported in the *Honey Dew News*, as many local residents worked at the factory, and many couples met while at work. (Courtesy of Monterey County Agricultural and Rural Life Museum.)

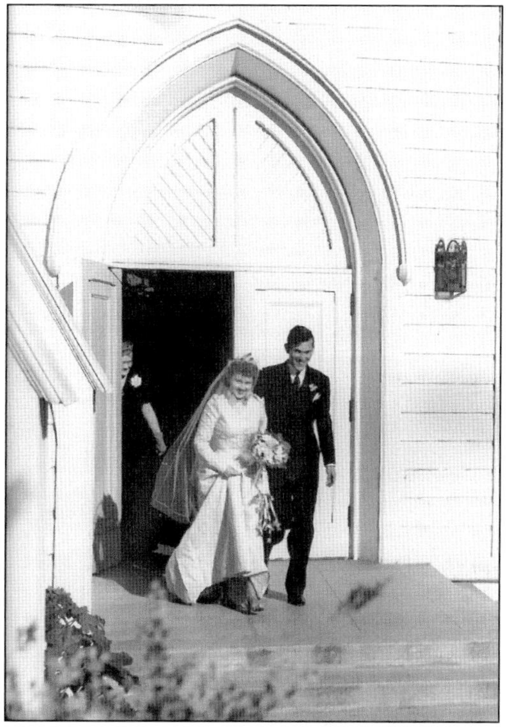

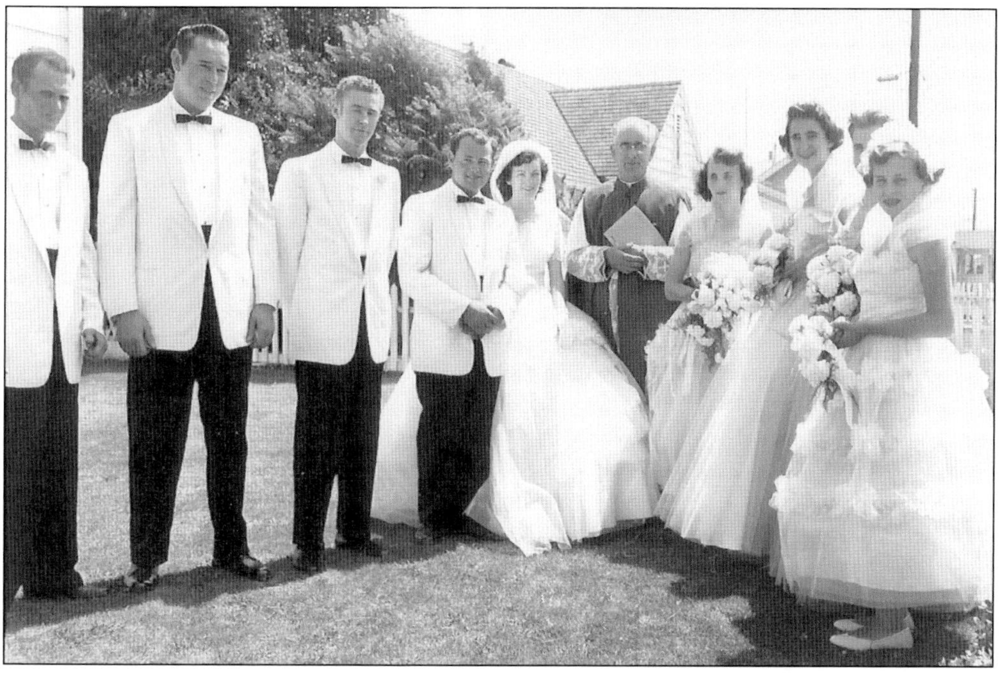

Some of the wedding guests at Jean Williams's and Jerry Campos's wedding, from left to right, are Gerald Lawson, Bob Meeks, Jerry Horton, Jerry Campos, Jean Campos (nee Williams), Msgr. Thomas J. Earley, matron of honor Mrs. W. E. Corlis, Miss Jo Ellen Fontes, Miss Everileen Fontes, and Miss Judy Williams. The wedding was held at the St. Joseph's Catholic Church in Spreckels in early August 1957.

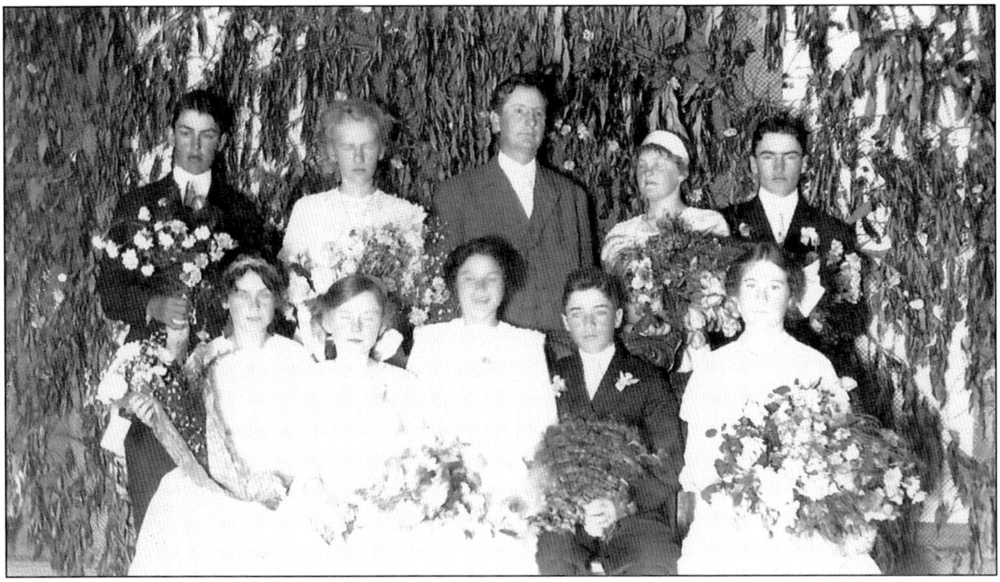

The Spreckels school held its eighth-grade graduation in June 1913. Pictured, from left to right, are (first row) Nona Beck, Ara Mae Wilson, Mabel Richey, Harold Richie, and Bessie Riley; (second row) Haro Walter Phillips, Adele Bremer, principal Mr. Ginn, Hazel Schmidt, and unidentified. (Courtesy of James Ross Riley III.)

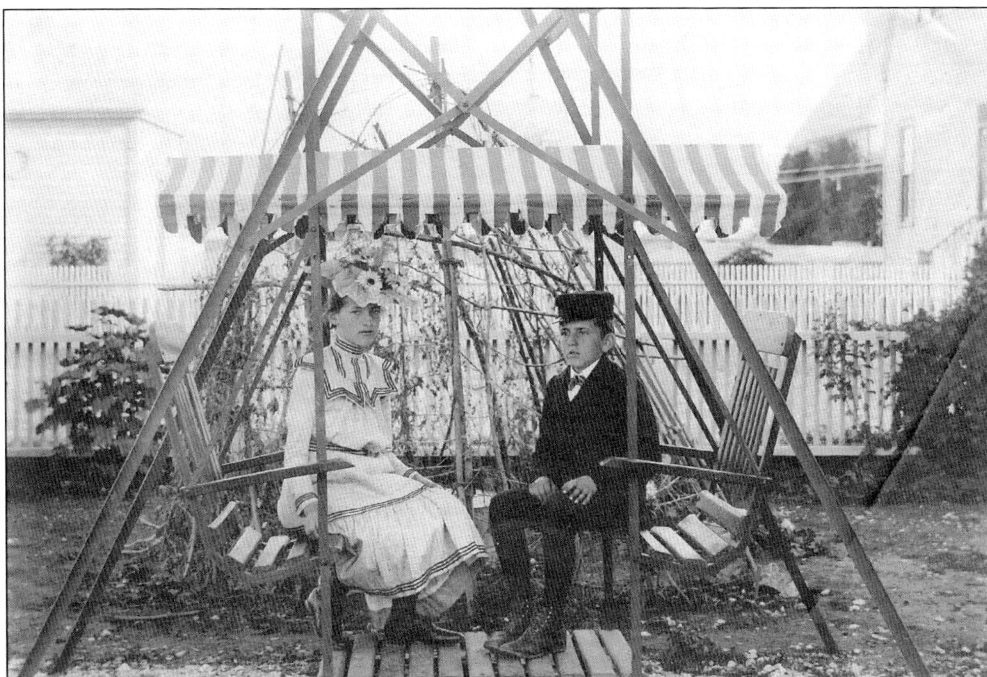

Rose Rhyner and her brother Willy grew up in Spreckels. Their father, Joseph Rhyner, was one of the first residents of the new town, as he was already working for Claus Spreckels. Rose and Willy both became long-term company employees. Rose became the editor of the *Honey Dew News*, the company newsletter, from which some of the information in this book was gleaned.

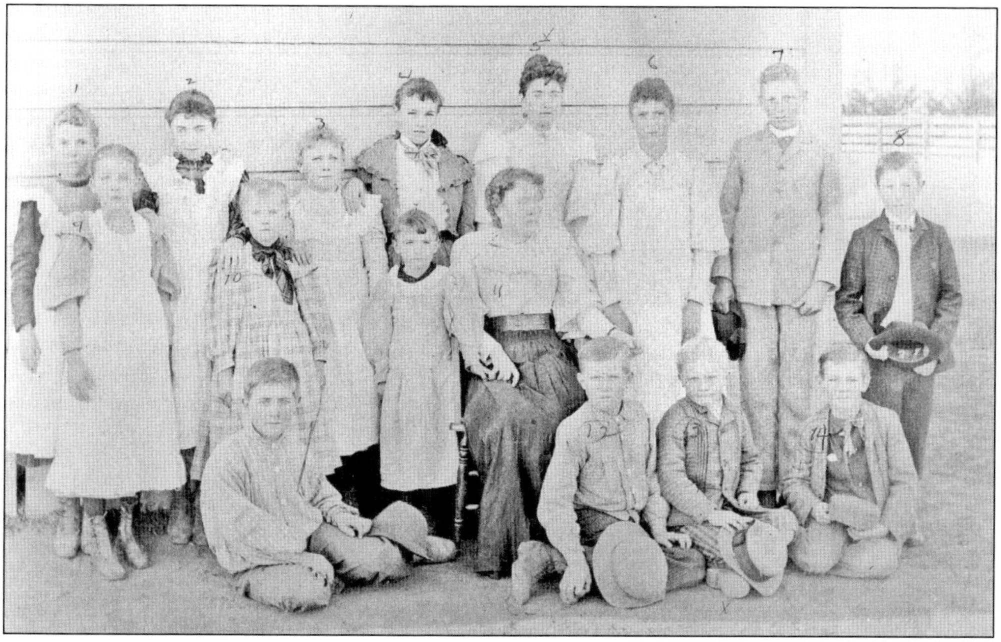

The Llanos School District supported an early school in the Spreckels area. Pictured here, from left to right, are (center) Mary Tavernetti holding teacher Christina Keith's (Hill) hand; (sitting) Paul Tavernetti, John Grau, Jeppe Grau, and Elton Hebbron; (standing) Mable Harris, Madge Harkins, Edna Harris, Mabel Hebbron, Mamie Harkins, Dave Thompson, Mabel Williamson, Christina Grau, Richard Harkins, and Euewl Logwood.

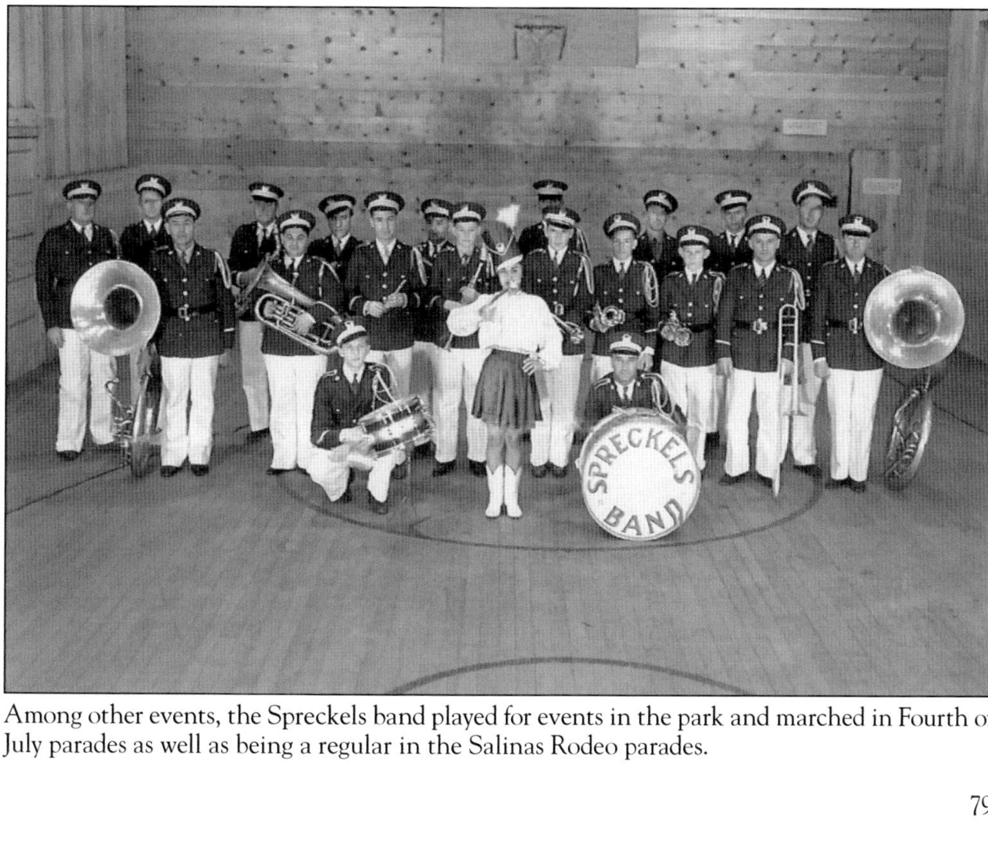

Among other events, the Spreckels band played for events in the park and marched in Fourth of July parades as well as being a regular in the Salinas Rodeo parades.

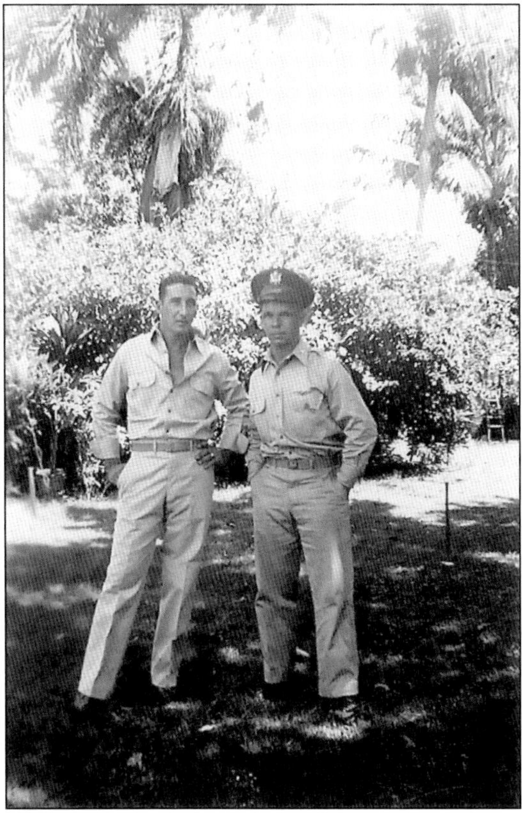

Karl Phillips and Kenny Cox, here in 1941, were two of the many Spreckels workers who joined the service. On the back of the photograph it is written, "We would certainly like to be working for you this year." Local servicemen were sent copies of the *Honey Dew News*, and letters from them to the folks back home were frequently printed in the newsletter. (Courtesy of Monterey County Agricultural and Rural Life Museum.)

A Victorian "tea party" was held at the Rhyner home around 1898.

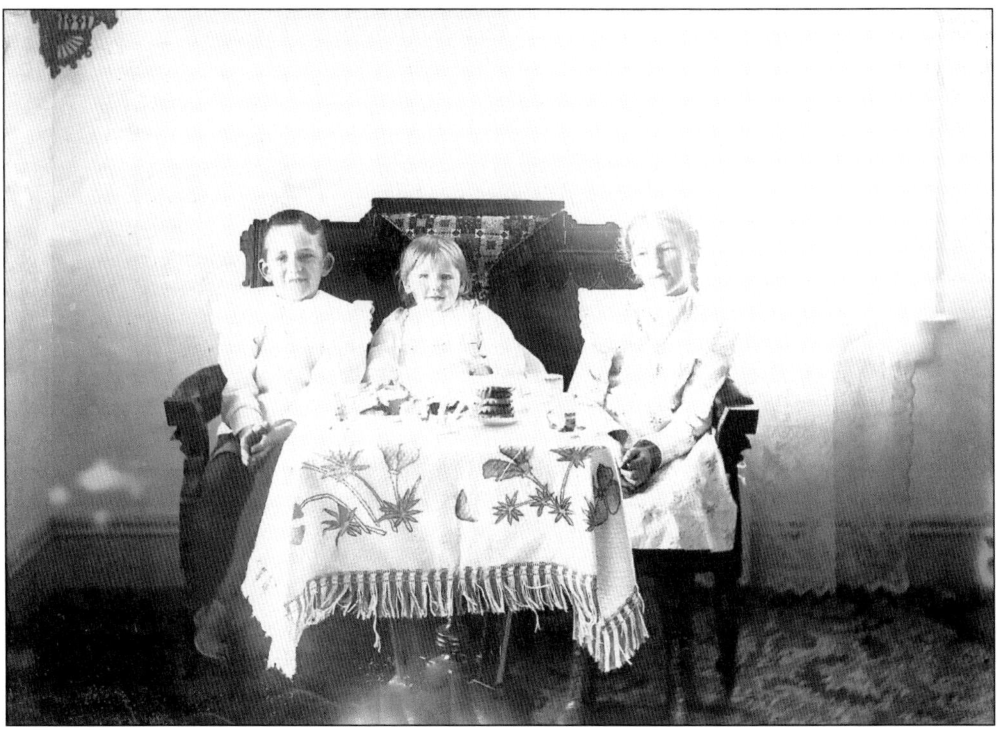

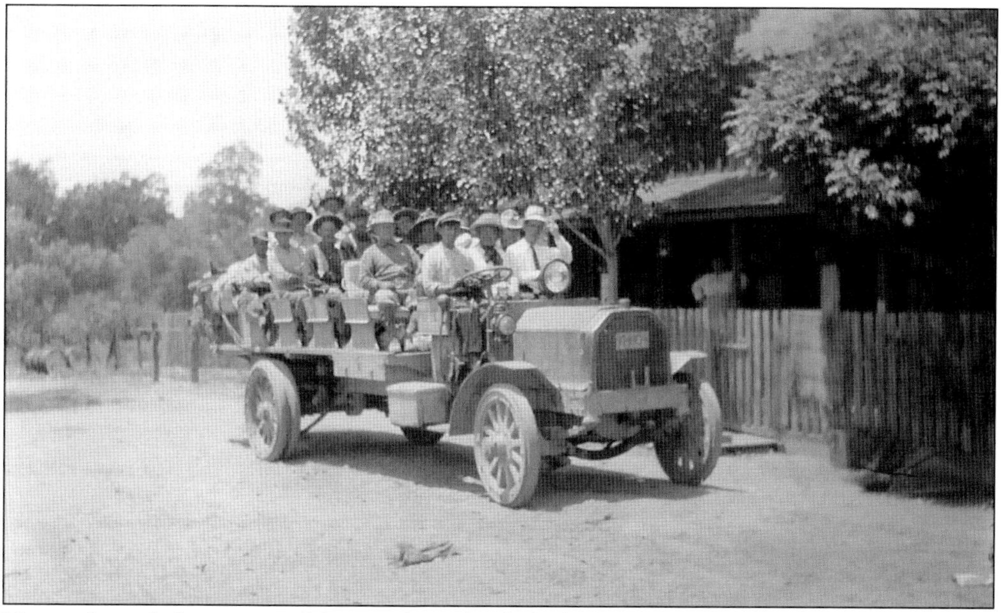

Here is the early forerunner of the tour bus. The flatbed of this vehicle has been fitted with bench seats for the "comfort" of its passengers; solid tires would not have afforded much cushion. Note that at the rear wheel, the differential leads to an axle that drives a sprocket and chain assembly, which drives the wheel.

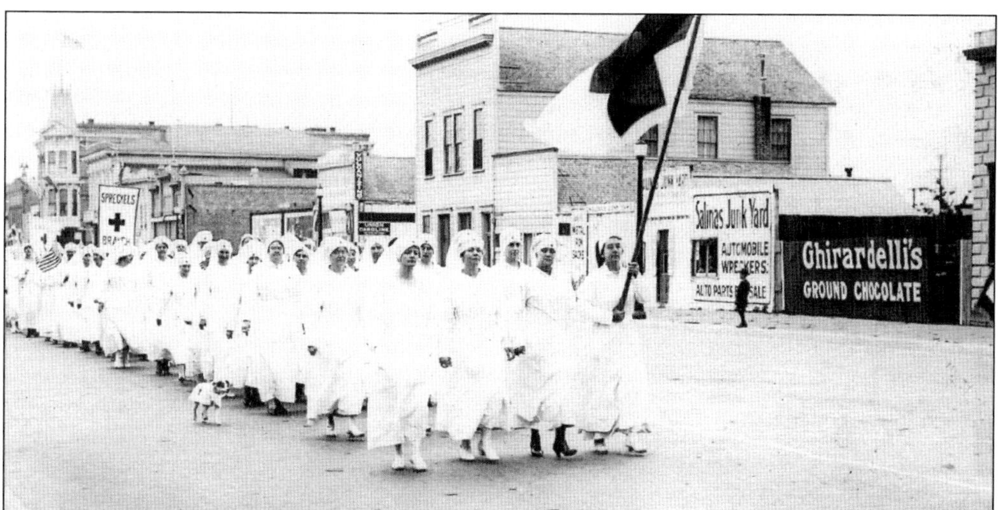

Members of the Spreckels branch of the Red Cross march in Salinas during World War I in support of war bonds.

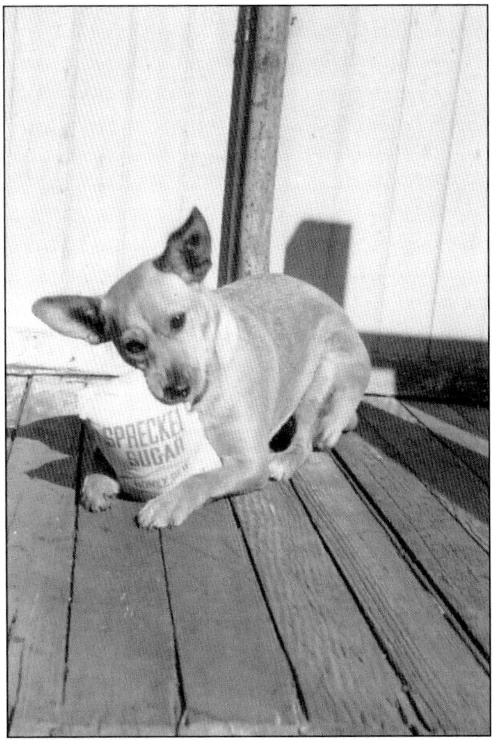

Windy chews her Spreckels "chew toy." Windy's owner was Jean Schaar, who worked in the sales department. (Courtesy of Monterey County Agricultural and Rural Life Museum.)

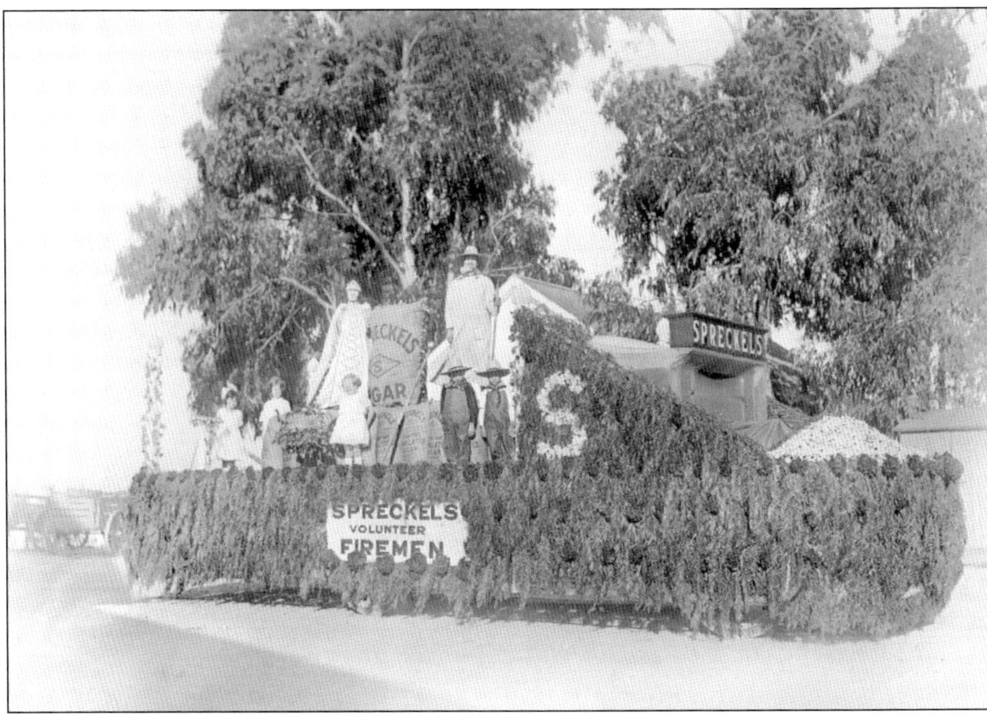

The Spreckels Volunteer Fire Company was formed in 1898 and did a lot more than put out fires. They sponsored barbecues and held other social events, hosted the Fireman's Ball, and regularly turned out in full uniform for a variety of functions.

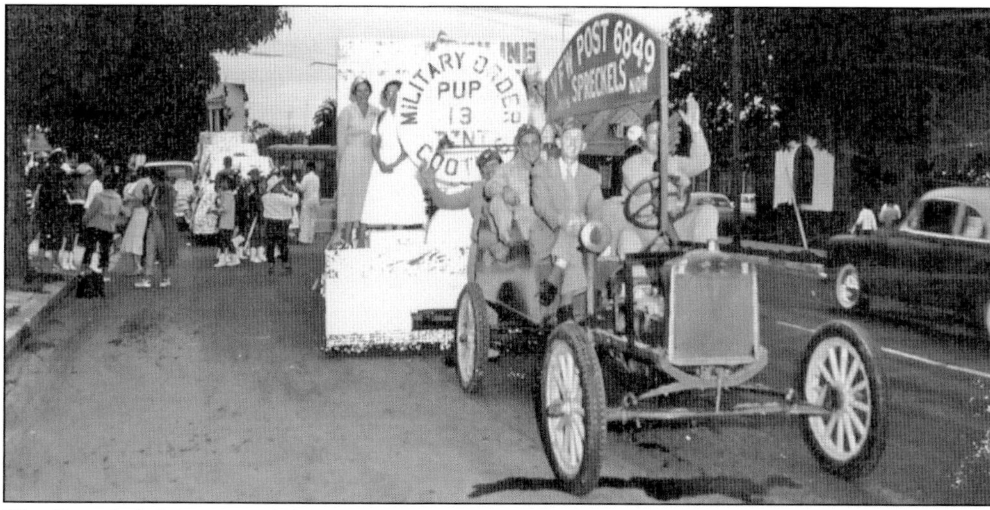

The Spreckels Veterans of Foreign Wars participated in the Fourth of July parade as well as the Salinas Rodeo parade. Spreckels formed a memorial district in 1947, and in 1955, a veteran's building was constructed at the corner of Fifth and Llano Streets on the site of 30 Quonset huts erected during World War II. (Courtesy of Monterey County Agricultural and Rural Life Museum.)

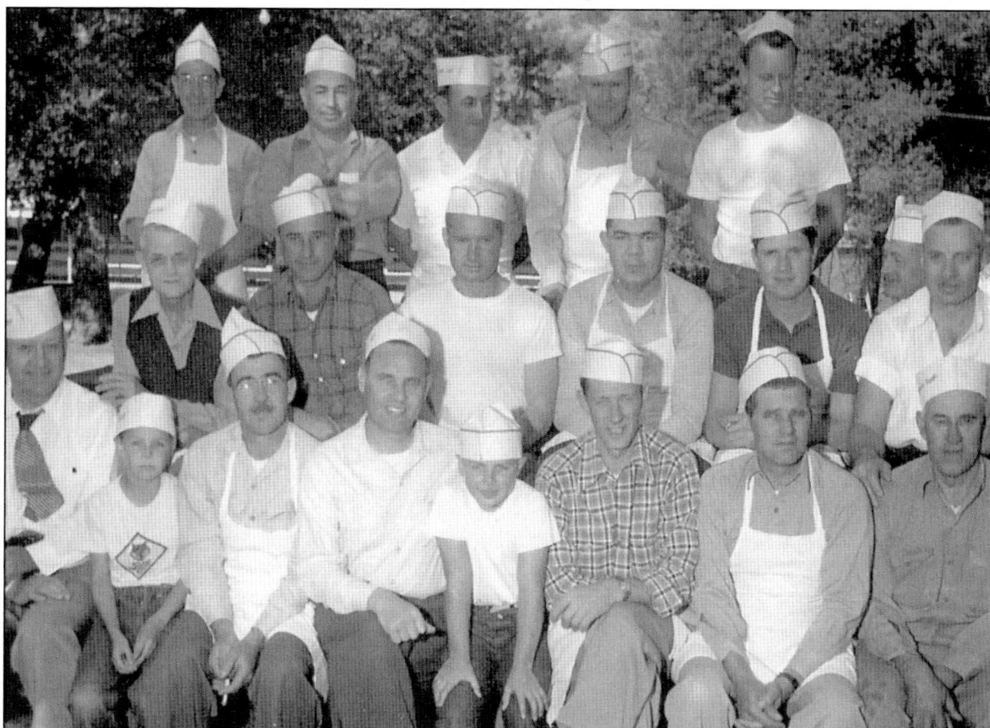

Pictured here, from left to right, are (first row) E. W. Mitchell, Buddy Bost, Jack Meyer, Harold Dios, Billy Pierce, W. D. Bost, Merton Elliott, and Virgil Wallace; (second row) A. J. McKinley, William King, E. Mattart, L. Frasier, J. Jones, H. Means, and Arnold Conley; (third row) Bob Locke, Al Pierce, Barney Freire, H. J. McCann, and Don Deiss. The image shows just a few of the workers at the annual Company-Union picnic held at Bolado Park. (Courtesy of Monterey County Agricultural and Rural Life Museum.)

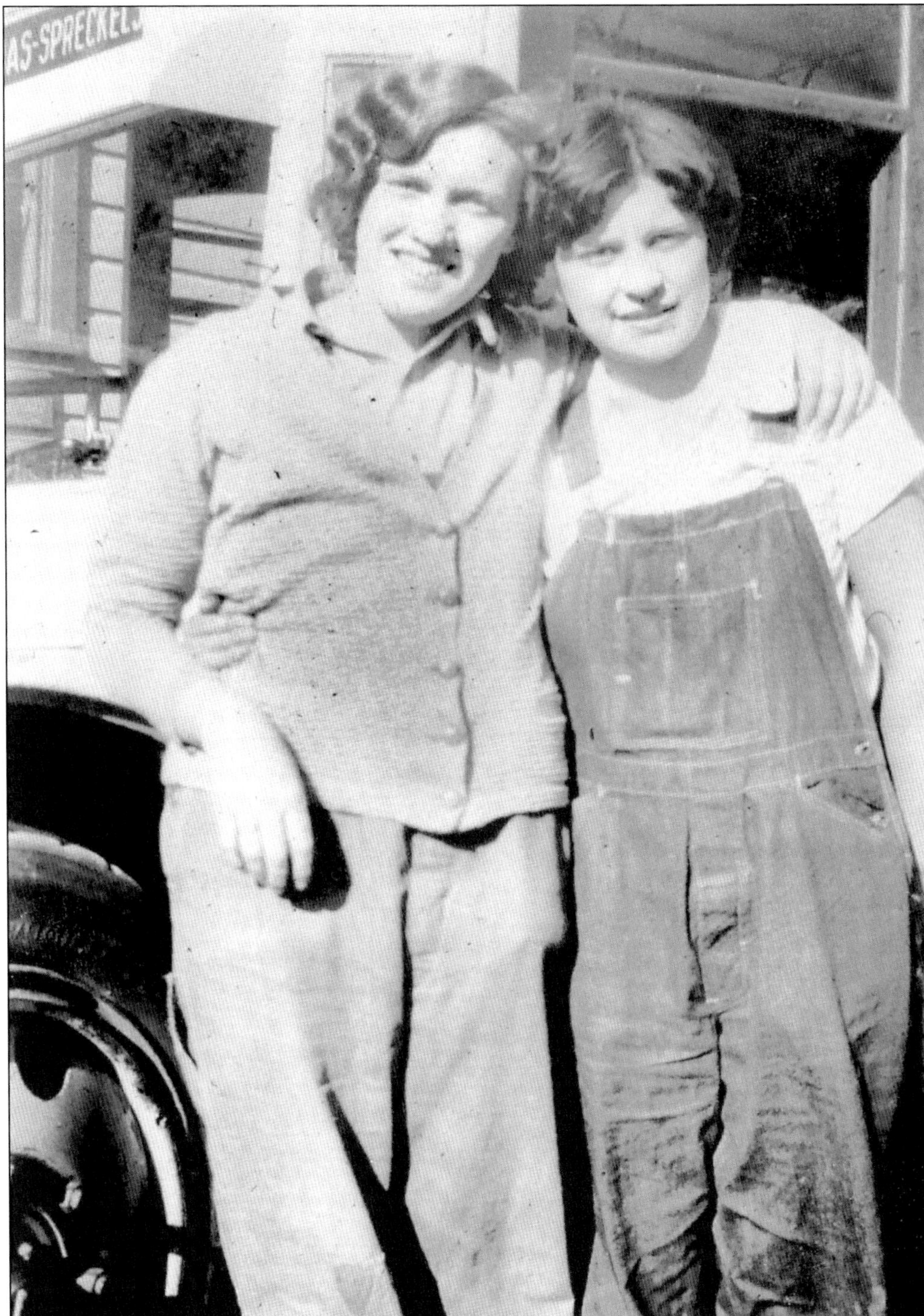

Lillie Callahan, left, worked for 49 years in the Spreckels factory sewing room. When she retired, company officials informed her she did not qualify for a pension. Lillie sued the company with the help of the union and eventually received her pension. The company also agreed to fill more factory jobs with women. (Courtesy of Monterey County Agricultural and Rural Museum.)

Six

Trains and Transportation

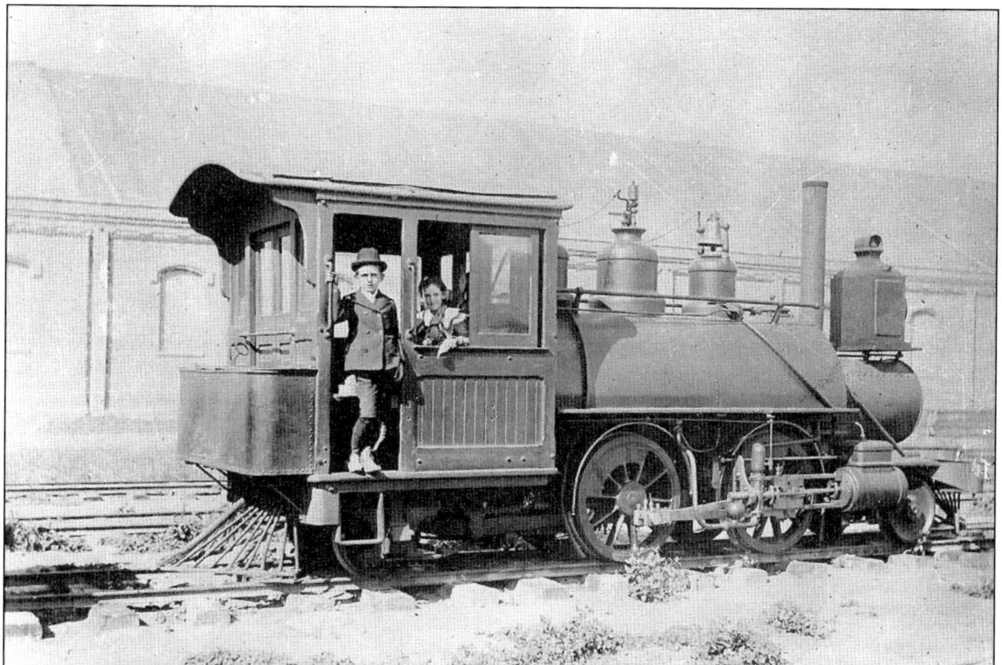

Willy and Rose Rhyner ride on the Dinky Line's engine. Although this may appear to be a toy train, this engine was one of the workhorses of the narrow-gauge railway. The name Dinky Line in fact came from the small size of the engines. The Pajaro Valley Consolidated Railroad was also known as "The Dead Beet Railroad."

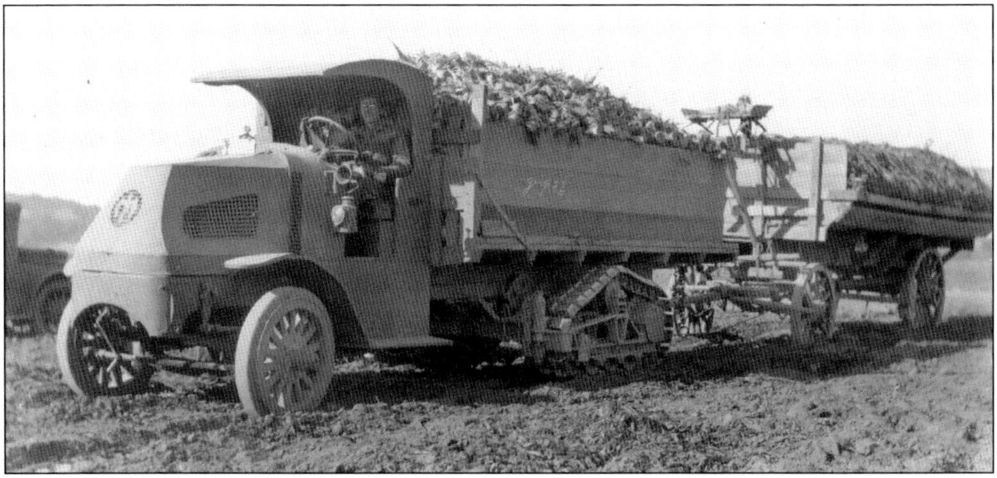

Pictured here are Spreckels's beets being hauled off from the filed in 1920. Note the switch from horse teams to trucks. The horse-drawn wagon behind the truck has been converted into a "trailer."

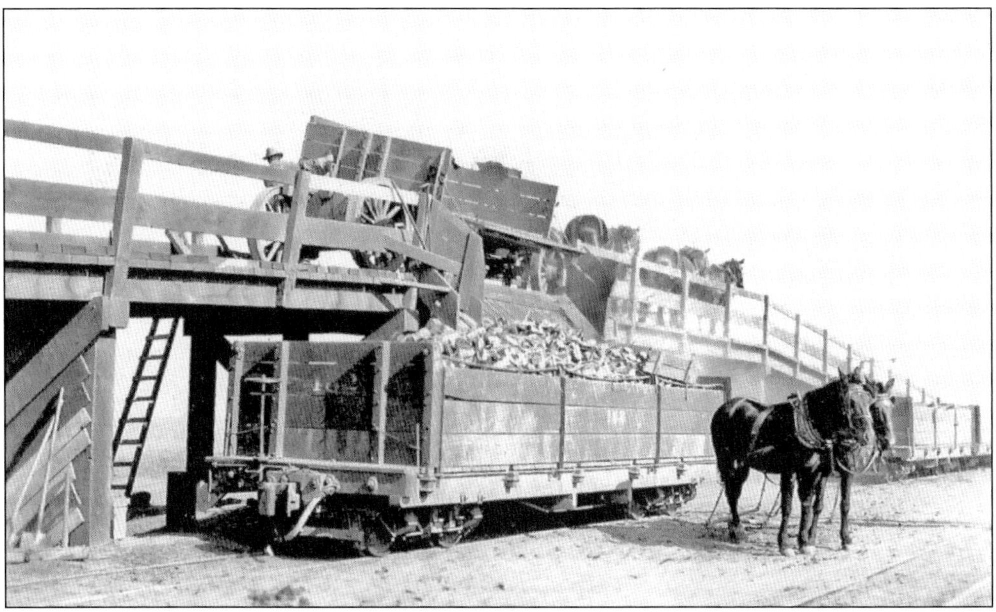

Workers are loading beets into railroad cars on Ranch No. 1 in Spreckels. Here wagons are dumping their loads into a chute, which funnels the beets into the waiting railcars. The sides of the wagons dropped to release the beets. This is but one of many ways invented to get beets to the factory.

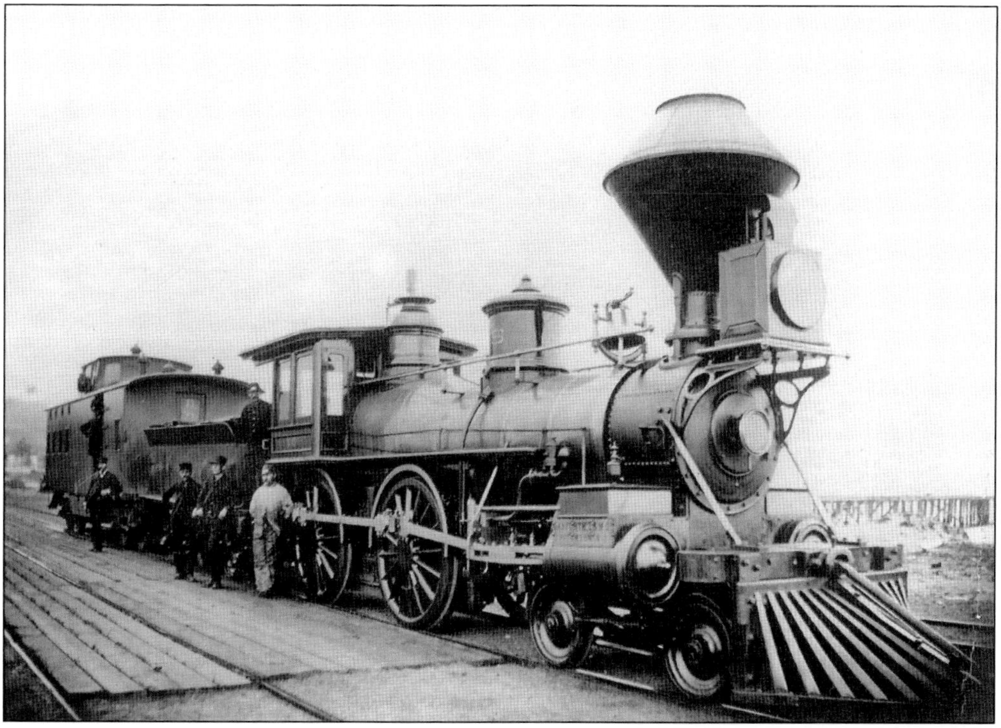

The original Spreckels train was known as the Pajaro Valley Railroad, but the name was changed to the Pajaro Valley Consolidated Railroad when it joined with the Salinas-area branches. The railroad was always known locally as the Dinky Line because of its tiny engines. Branch lines extended south over the river bridge to Buena Vista, where beets were grown, and to the north, passing east of Salinas near the present airport terminal, to Alisal Canyon, where Spreckels obtained lime rock.

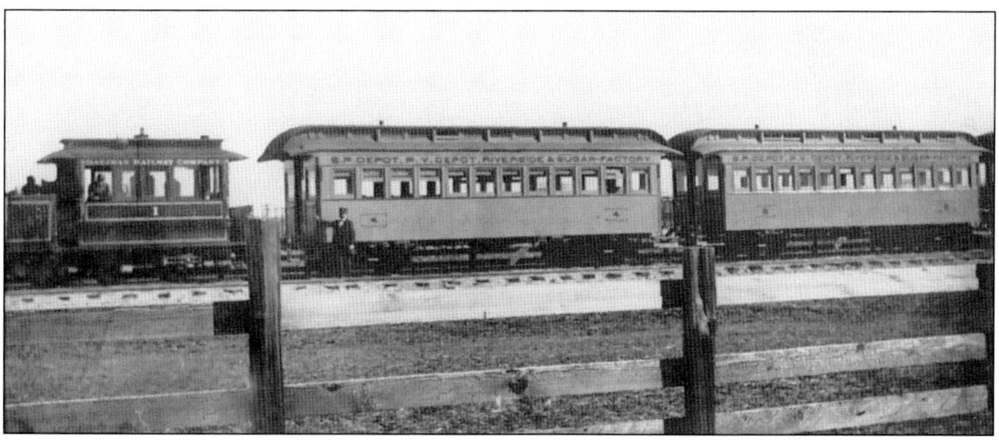

The "dinky," originally used in San Francisco to carry passengers to and from the Cliff House, ran between Spreckels and Salinas. It began at the Spreckels Hotel, ran along Spreckels Boulevard and Monterey Road (now Highway 68), through Main Street, and then west on Market Street as far as the Catholic church. The fare was 15¢ each way.

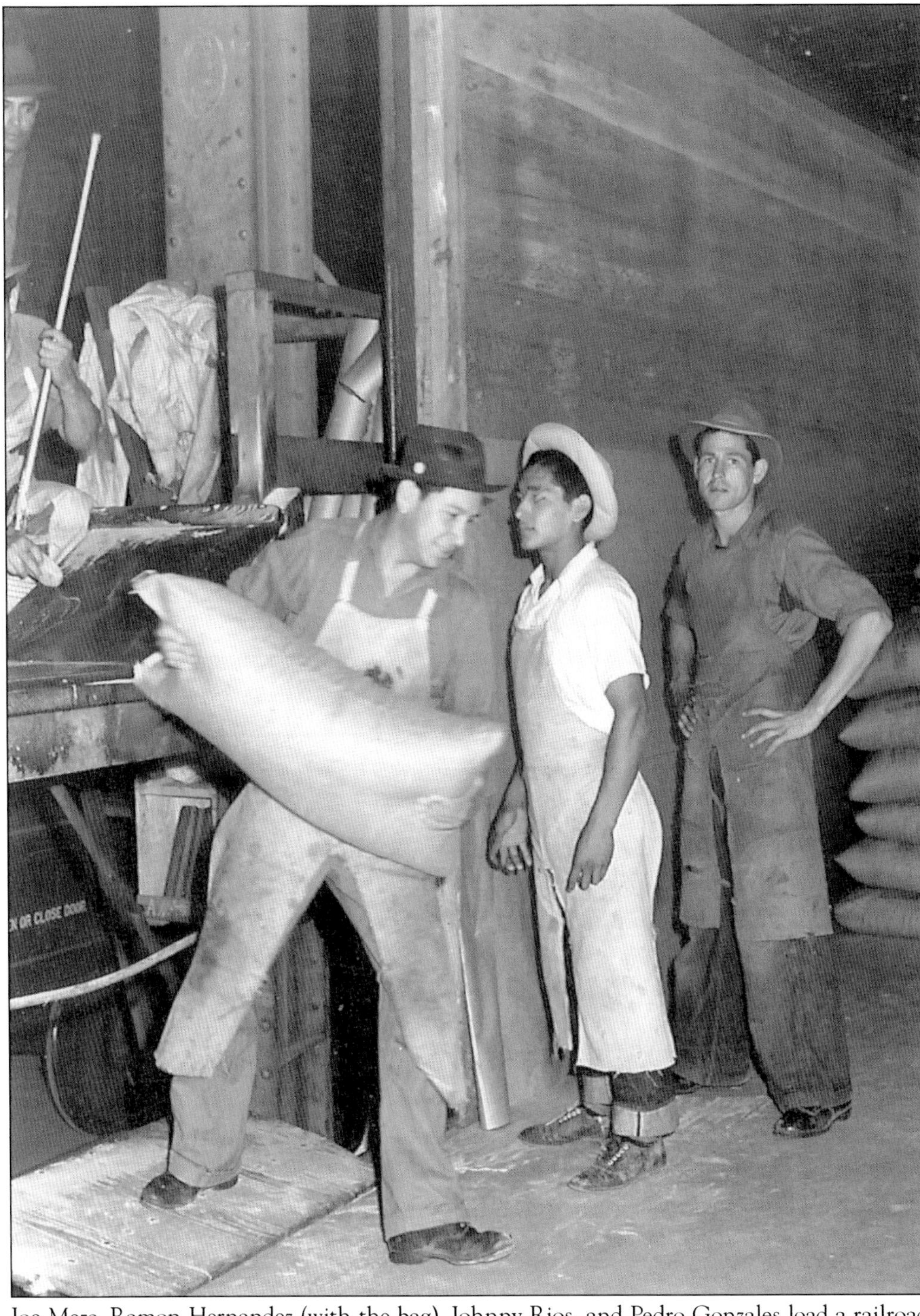

Joe Meza, Ramon Hernandez (with the bag), Johnny Rios, and Pedro Gonzales load a railroad car with 100-pound sacks of sugar the hard way. The final product was loaded into railcars for transit to market. Early Spreckels sugar went via railroad to Moss Landing, where it was loaded onto steamships. (Courtesy of Monterey County Agricultural and Rural Life Museum.)

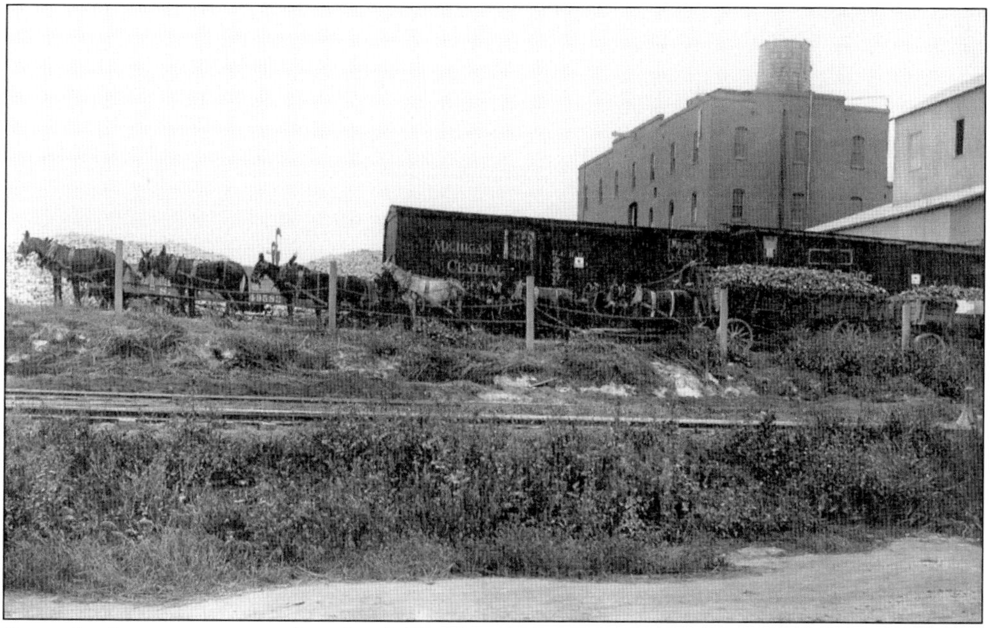

Once the beets were topped in the fields, the race was on to get them to the plant with the highest sugar content possible. Here a 12-mule team hauls their own train of beet-filled wagons in the shadow of the railcars.

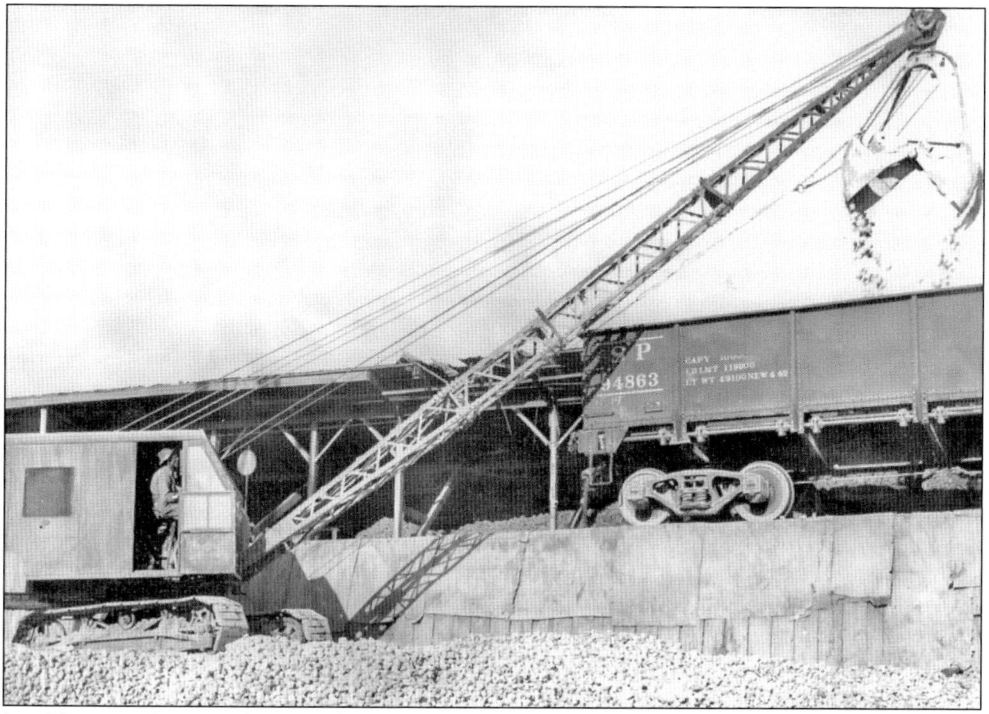

In addition to beets and water, the plant needed many other materials, including lime rock for the Steffen process. Coke (coal) was another important resource, as those boilers used a lot of fuel in processing and also generated electricity for the plant. Here workers are loading lime rock onto railcars. (Courtesy of Monterey County Agricultural and Rural Life Museum.)

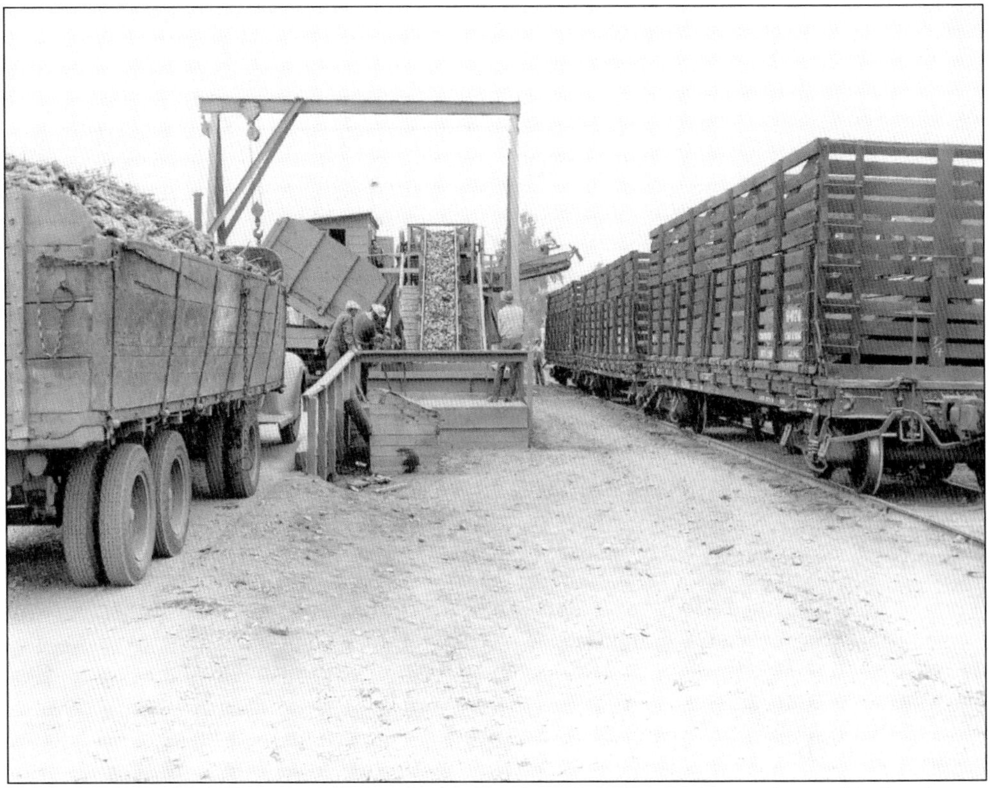

Note that the beets are now being hauled by diesel trucks. The trucks are dumped by hooking a hoist to its underside and tilting the truck bed sideways onto a motorized conveyor belt, which lifted the beets into waiting railcars.

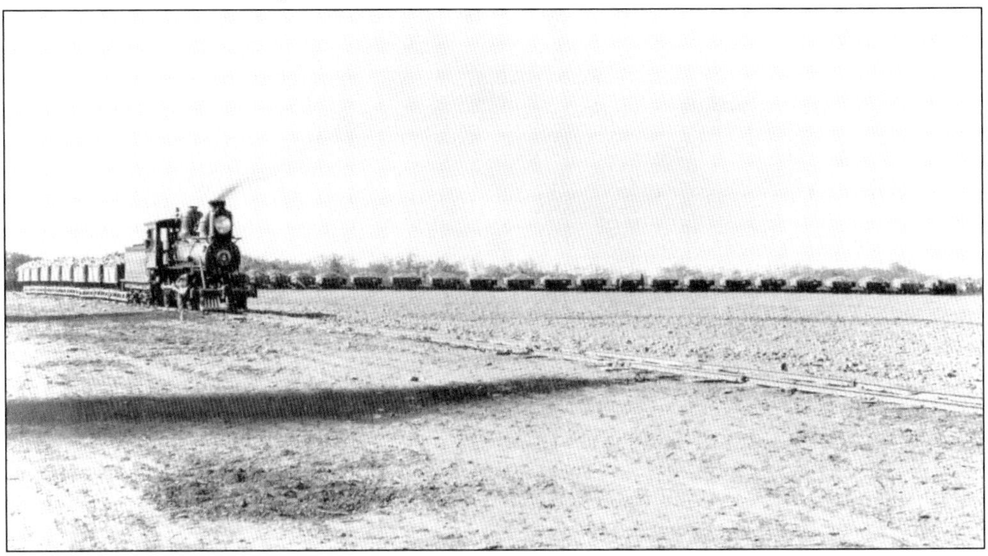

Pajaro Valley No. 2, a Baldwin Mogul class 8-20D, hauls a long line of beet-filled railcars from the Moro Cojo ranch. Note the very simple railroad track bed, which looks more like a dirt road than a track line. Between 1898 and 1920, the railroad was the principal way the beets were hauled to the Spreckels factory.

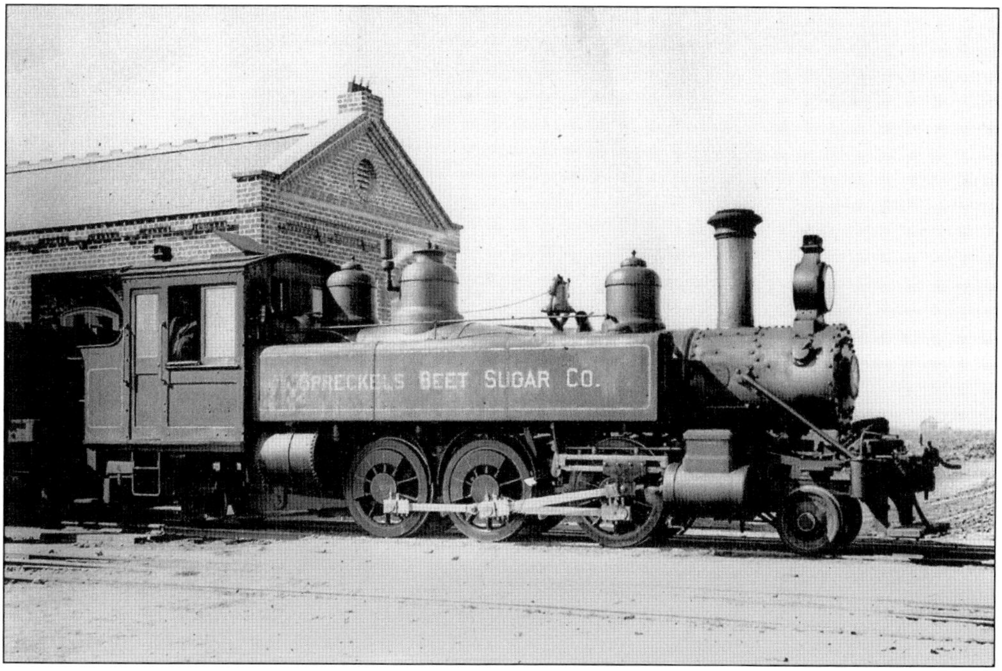

In this view of the Spreckels Beet Sugar Company No. 1, around 1920, one can only imagine the miles and miles these engines traveled, not only around the sugar factory but also to different locations for shipping. Long before the time of the automobile and large trucks, trains were the main form of transportation for all heavy loads.

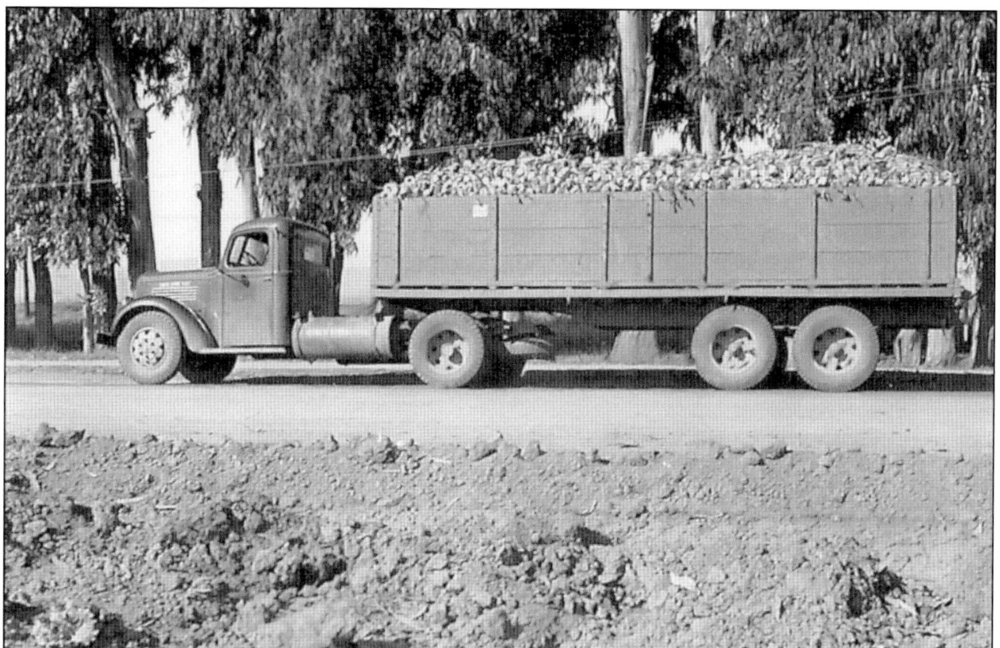

Diesel trucks eventually replaced the horse-drawn wagons and the Pajaro Valley Consolidated Railroad. Once automotive technology and efficient roads were developed, trucks were cheaper and more convenient. (Courtesy of Monterey County Agricultural and Rural Life Museum.)

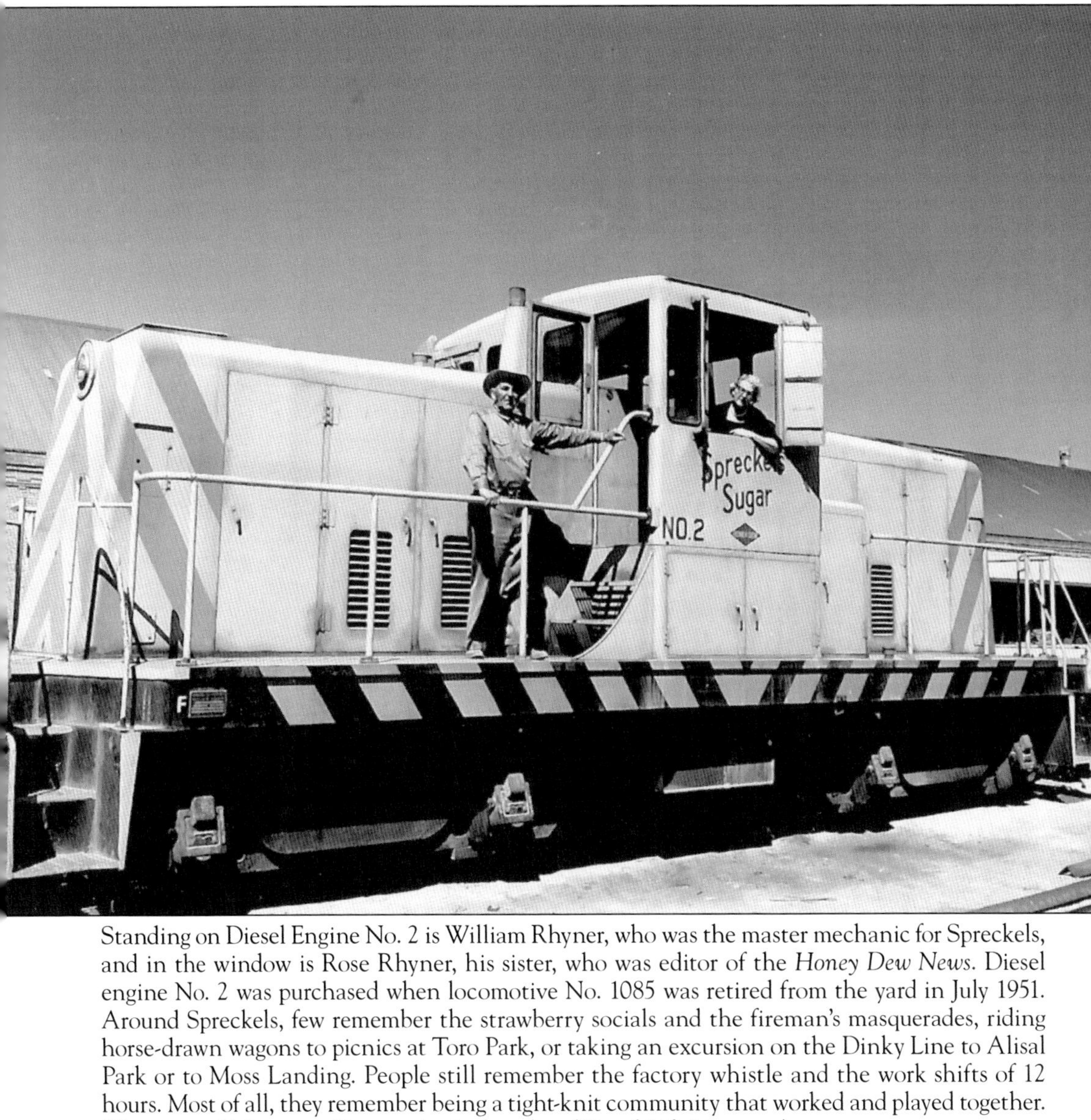

Standing on Diesel Engine No. 2 is William Rhyner, who was the master mechanic for Spreckels, and in the window is Rose Rhyner, his sister, who was editor of the *Honey Dew News*. Diesel engine No. 2 was purchased when locomotive No. 1085 was retired from the yard in July 1951. Around Spreckels, few remember the strawberry socials and the fireman's masquerades, riding horse-drawn wagons to picnics at Toro Park, or taking an excursion on the Dinky Line to Alisal Park or to Moss Landing. People still remember the factory whistle and the work shifts of 12 hours. Most of all, they remember being a tight-knit community that worked and played together. (Courtesy of Monterey County Agricultural and Rural Life Museum.)

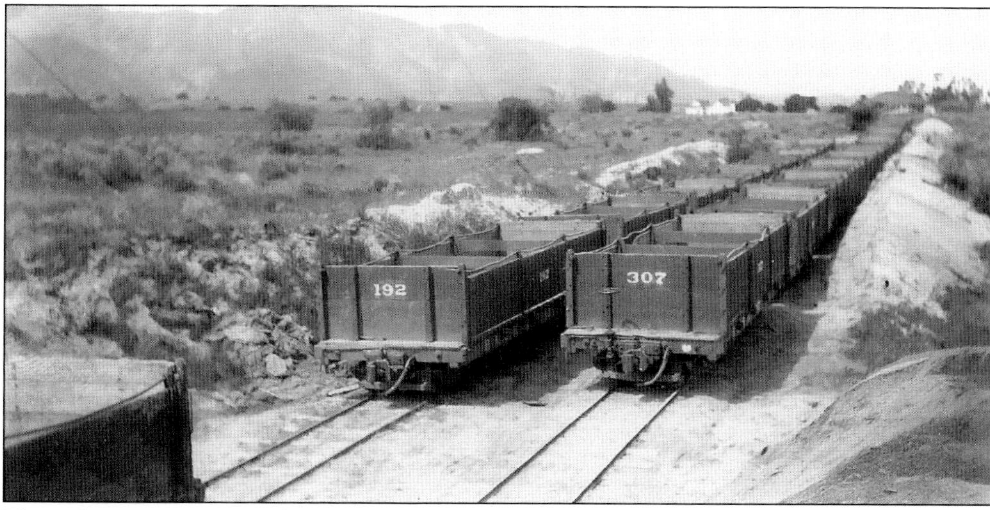

These dump cars were used to transport beets to the Spreckels factory. One of the lesser-known by-products of the sugar-refining process was beet pulp. The spent beet mash was loaded into railcars and transported for use as cattle feed. Carloads of beet mash were often seen parked on railway sidings as the priority was to get fresh beets into the factory. Enterprising itinerants would raid these parked cars to fill burlap sacks with mash, which they then squeezed to make a potent hooch. One story suggests it had plenty of "head" but horrible aftereffects.

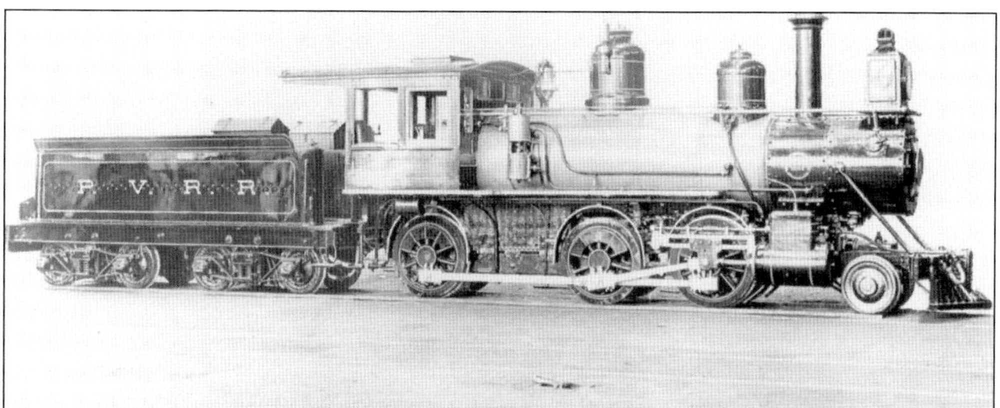

The Pajaro Valley Engine No. 4 was photographed at the Baldwin factory before it was shipped. The Pajaro Valley Railroad was expanded to provide much-needed transportation to the new Spreckels factory and town. When the new track was added, the name was changed to the Pajaro Valley Consolidated Railroad, but it was also called the Dead Beet Railroad and the Dinky Line.

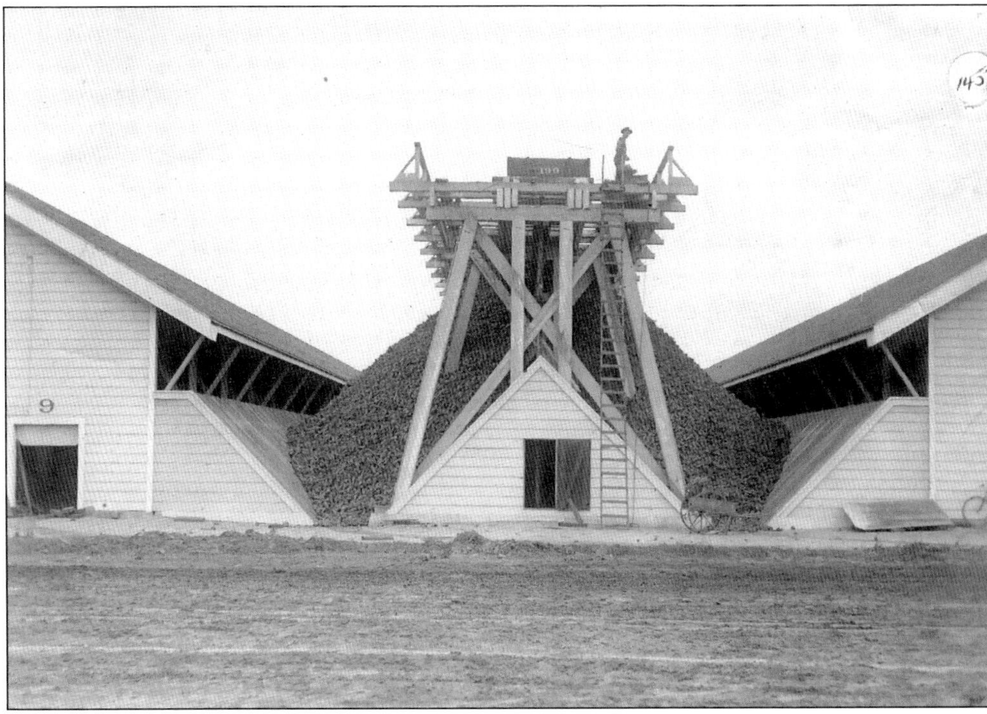

Railcars were run out onto the elevated platform to dump their loads of beets. The beets were moved into the beet bins for storage and then into the flume system, which carried them to the factory for processing.

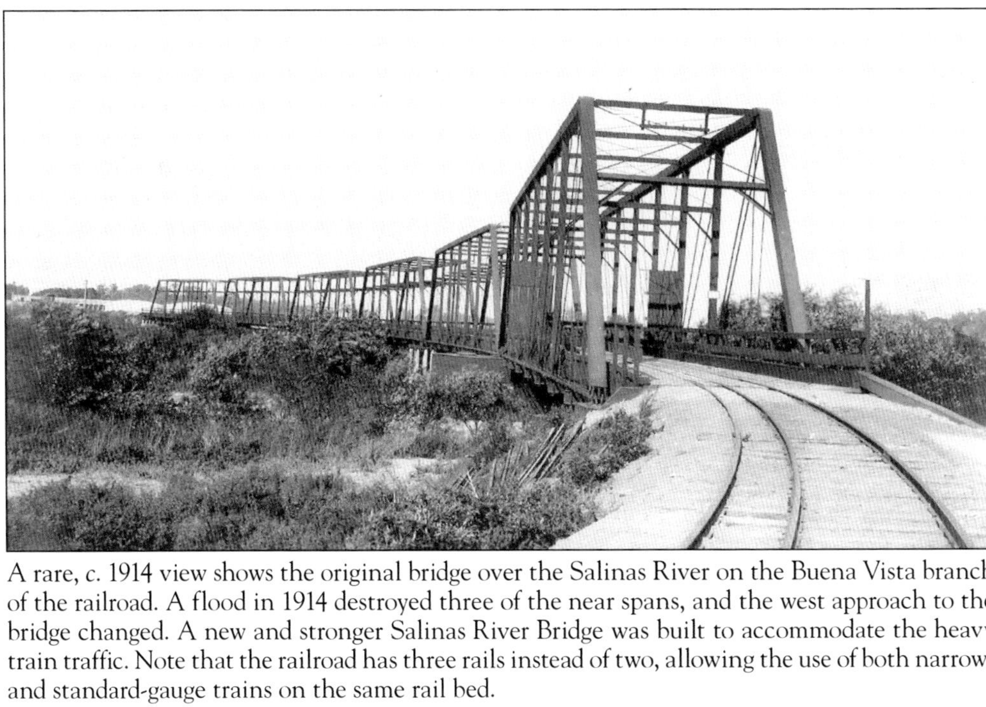

A rare, c. 1914 view shows the original bridge over the Salinas River on the Buena Vista branch of the railroad. A flood in 1914 destroyed three of the near spans, and the west approach to the bridge changed. A new and stronger Salinas River Bridge was built to accommodate the heavy train traffic. Note that the railroad has three rails instead of two, allowing the use of both narrow- and standard-gauge trains on the same rail bed.

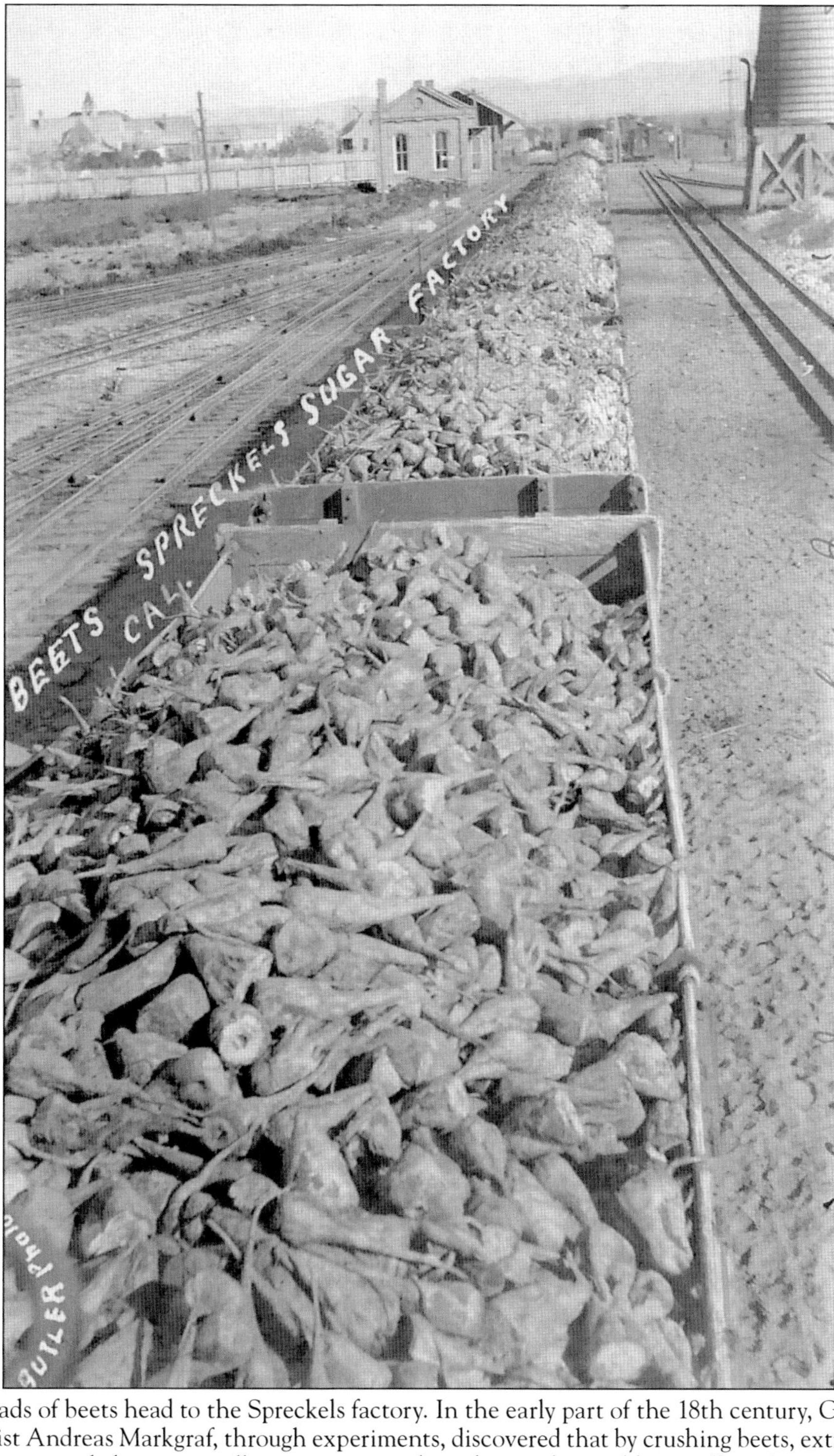

Carloads of beets head to the Spreckels factory. In the early part of the 18th century, German chemist Andreas Markgraf, through experiments, discovered that by crushing beets, extracting the juices, and then using albumen to treat the solution, he could crystallize the extract to make sugar.

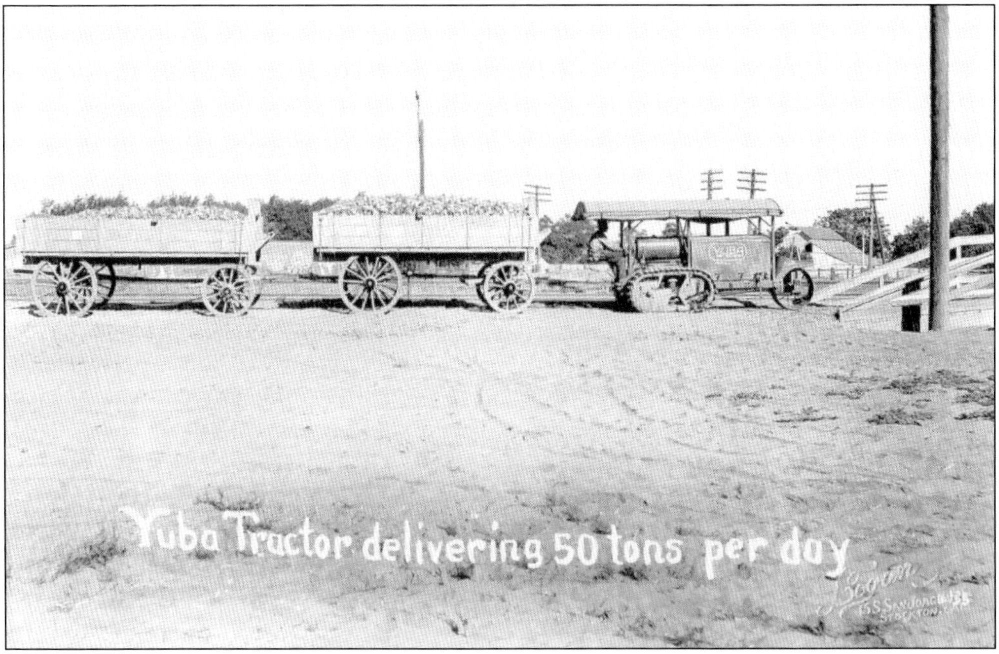

A Yuba tractor delivers 50 tons of beets to the transportation depot. Technology was changing rapidly, and enterprising farmers made the most out of the equipment at hand. All available means were used to get those beets harvested and to the factory. (Courtesy of Monterey County Agricultural and Rural Life Museum.)

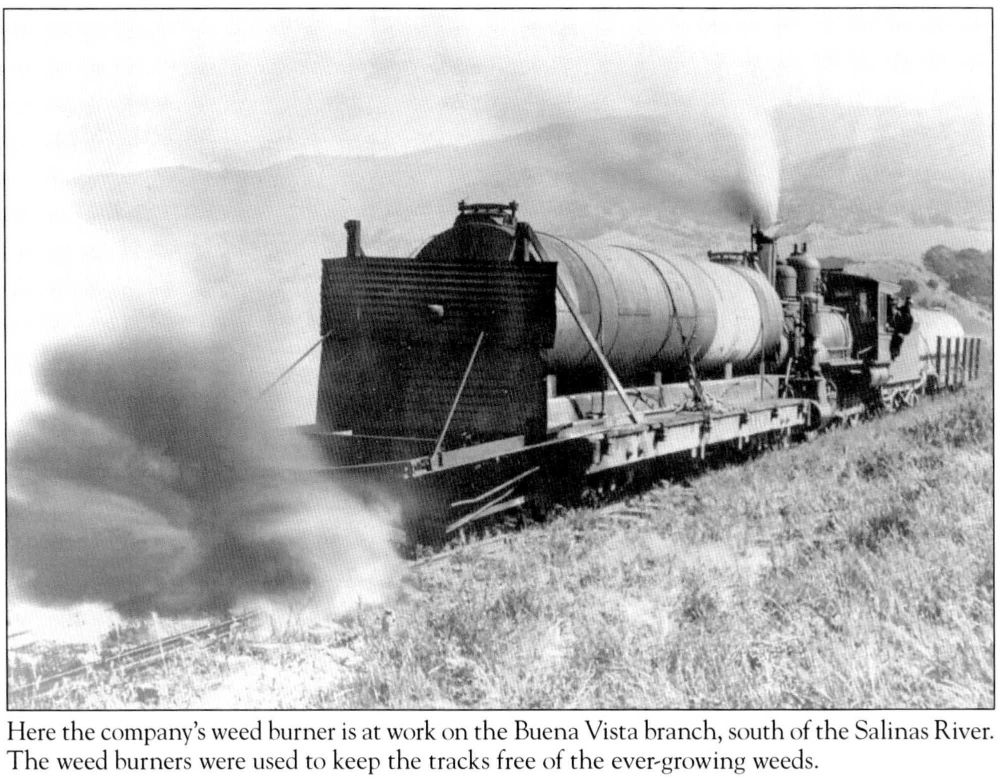

Here the company's weed burner is at work on the Buena Vista branch, south of the Salinas River. The weed burners were used to keep the tracks free of the ever-growing weeds.

Seven

AGRICULTURE AND THE WORKERS

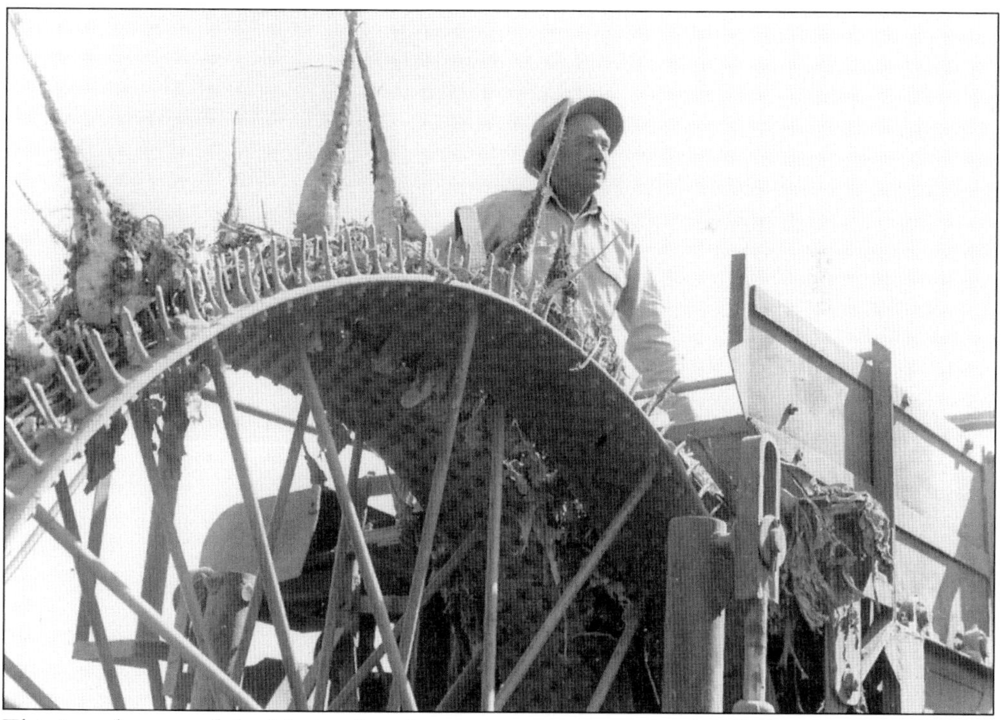

This is a close-up of the Marion beet harvester in operation with Bill Pelisseir operating the machinery. (Courtesy of Monterey County Agricultural and Rural Life Museum.)

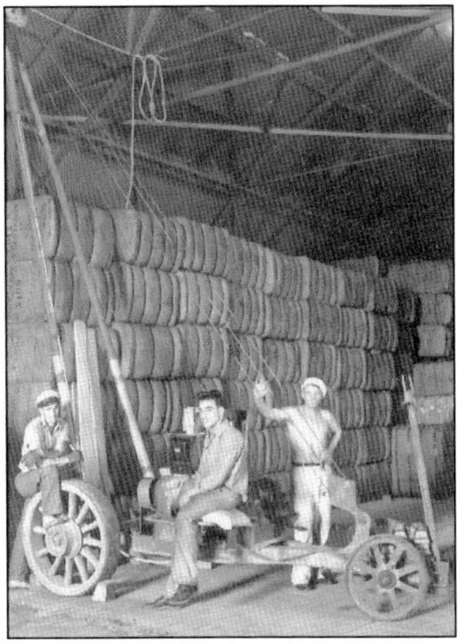

This bag hoist was designed by A. J. McKinley in 1940; clearly an improvement over lifting the weight by hand. Great care had to be taken in many parts of the factory not to have any equipment that would produce a spark, which might start a fire or cause an explosion. The names of the workers are not known. (Courtesy of Monterey County Agricultural and Rural Life Museum.)

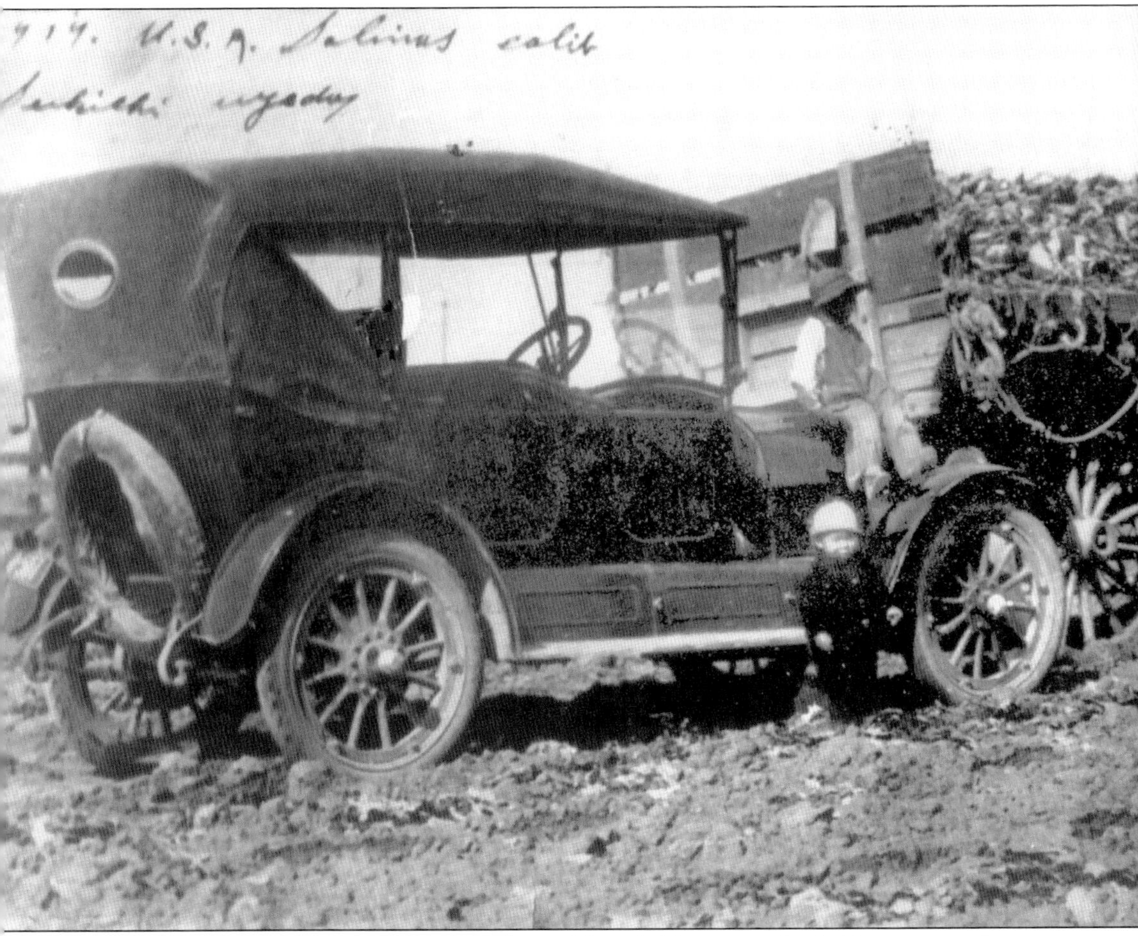

In 1919, Japanese farmer Suhichi Uyaday and his children visit the field operation. Beets were loaded into a wagon using the dump-net technology, in which the empty wagon is first lined with a large net. The wagon was filled with beets by field laborers and taken to a dump station where

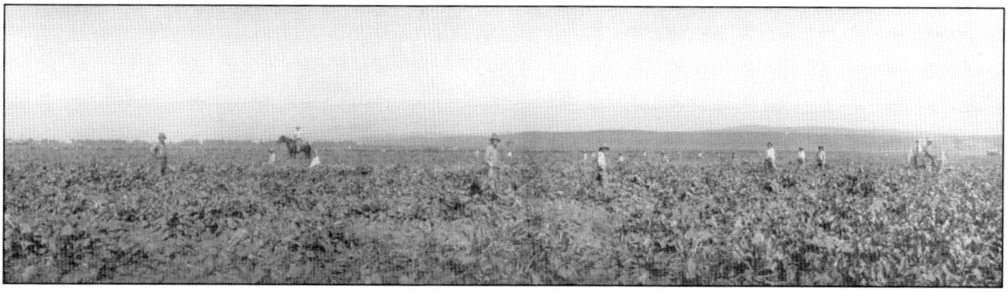

Timing on the beet crop was very important. Payment was based on tonnage and on percentage of sugar present. Large quantities of water were required to grow the beets, but just before harvest, the water would be withdrawn so that the sugar content would concentrate. Weeds and other foreign matter, such as dirt, would bring down the value of the delivered beets.

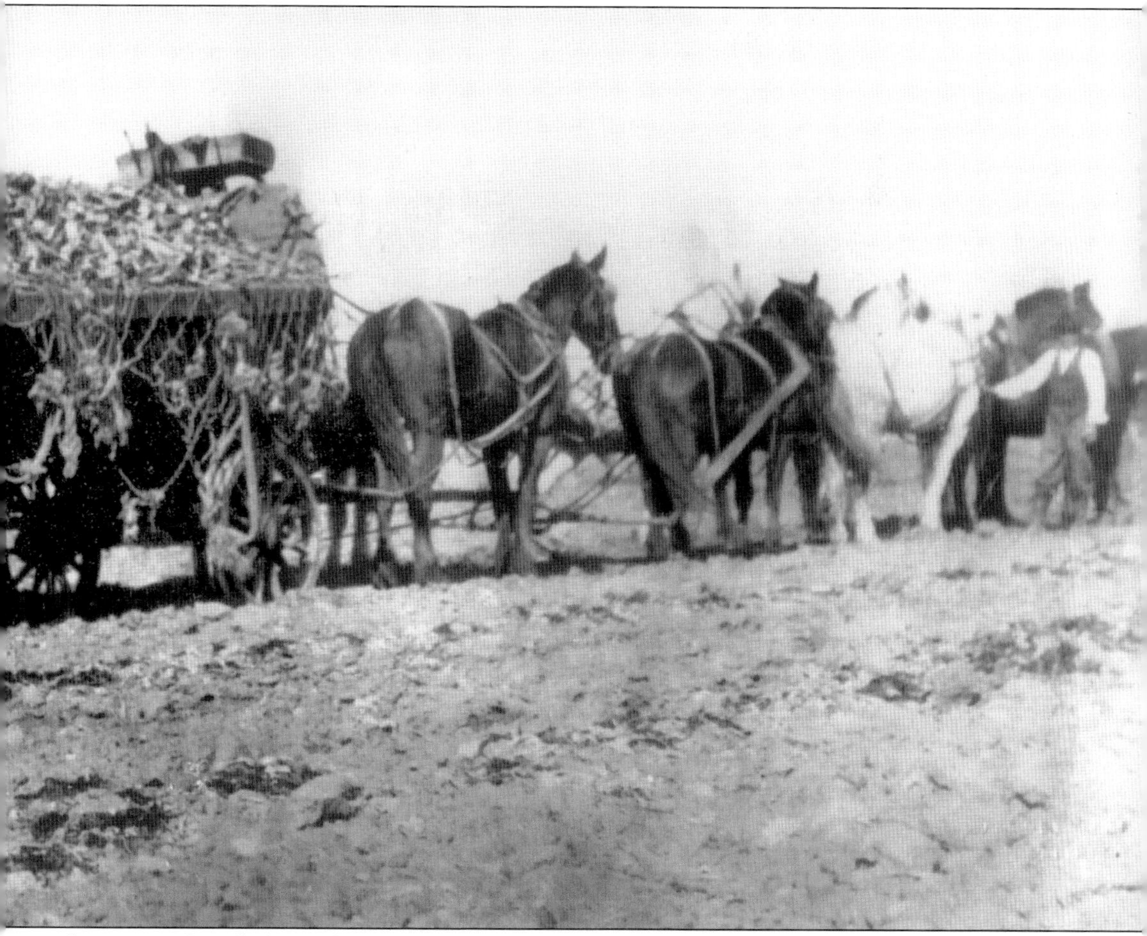

the net was bundled together and hooked to a lift, thereby removing the beets from the wagon and allowing them to be moved to a railway car or into the plant. By this time, Japanese farmers were beginning to play an increasing role in Salinas Valley agricultural operations.

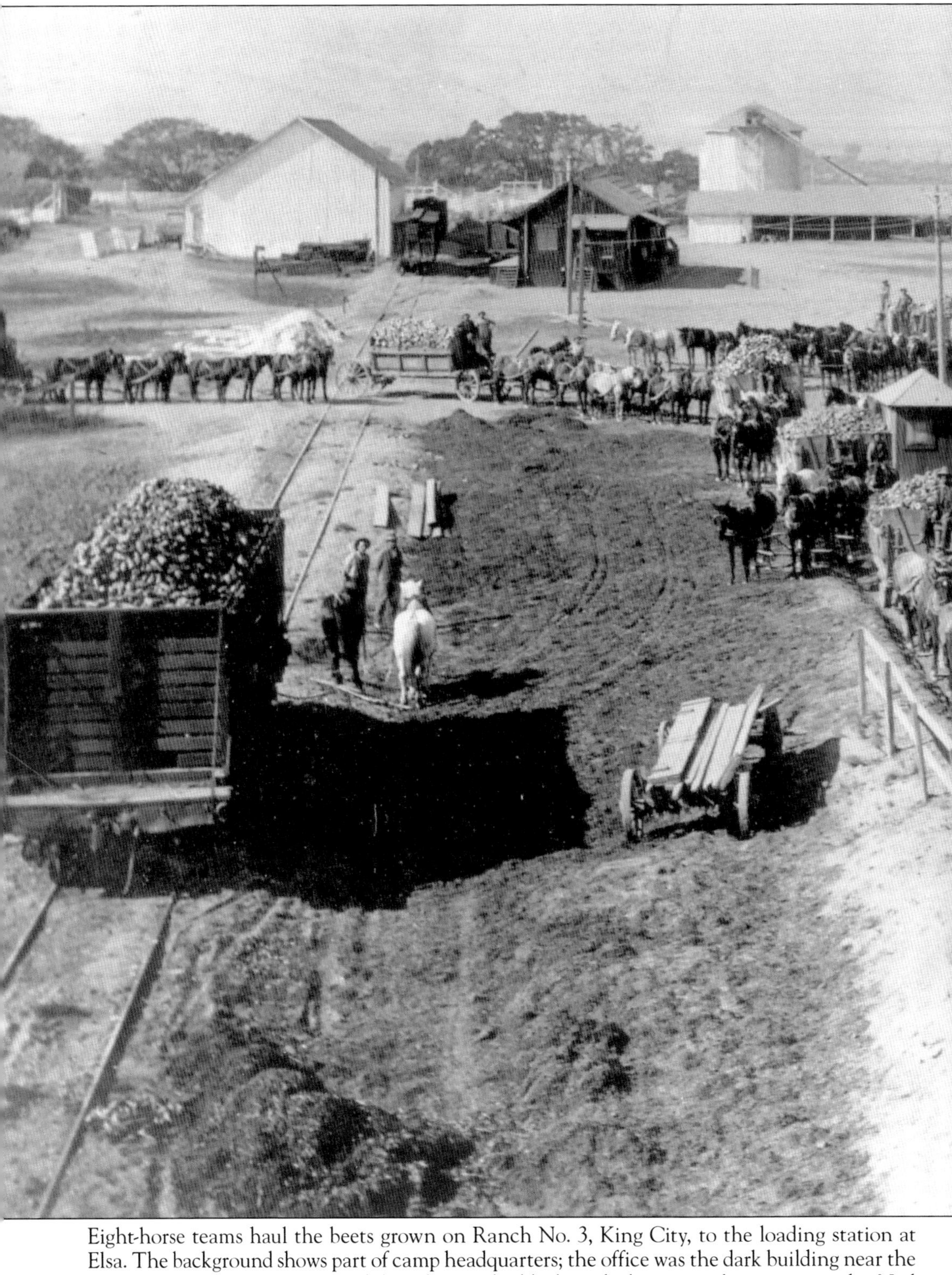

Eight-horse teams haul the beets grown on Ranch No. 3, King City, to the loading station at Elsa. The background shows part of camp headquarters; the office was the dark building near the tracks. To its right is the silo and dairy barn. The blacksmith shop is on the extreme right. Neil

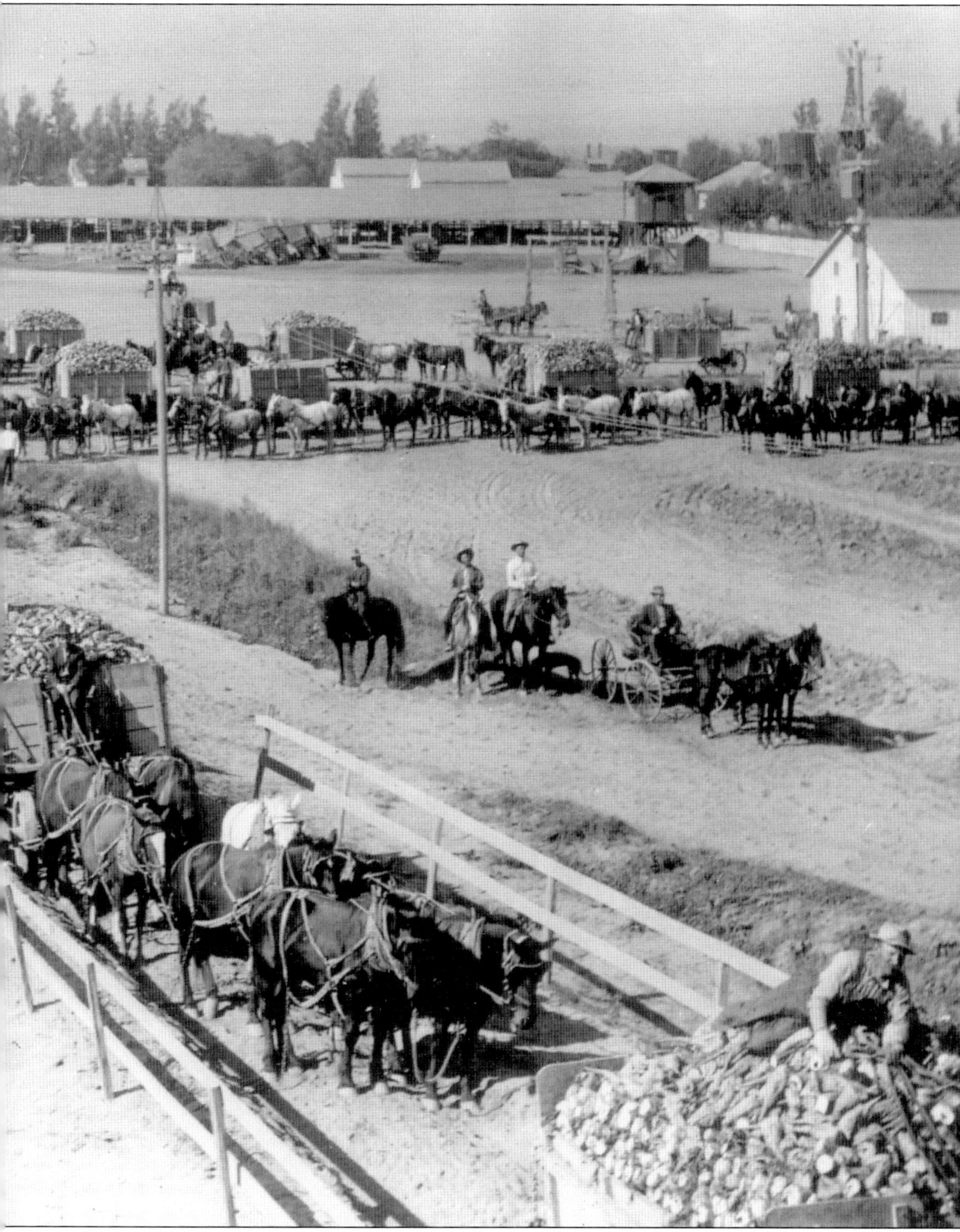

Forden, ranch superintendent, is seated in the buggy, and Bruce Foster, ranch foreman, is the center horseman. At the time the photograph was taken in 1915, the Spreckels Sugar Company had a total of 750 workhorses and mules at Ranch No. 3. (*Honey Dew News*, October 1942).

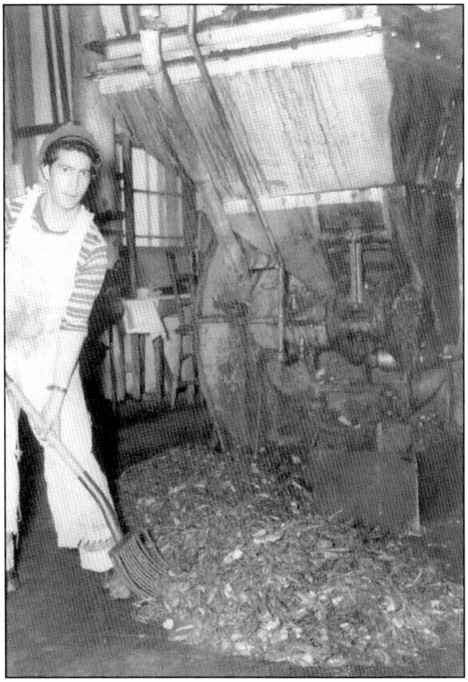

Once the beets were unloaded at the plant, weeds and debris were vibrated off. This cleaning process produced a pile of mostly weeds, which was referred to as "trash." This worker is removing about two hours worth. The weight of the trash was deducted from the payment weight of the beets. (Courtesy of Monterey County Agricultural and Rural Life Museum.)

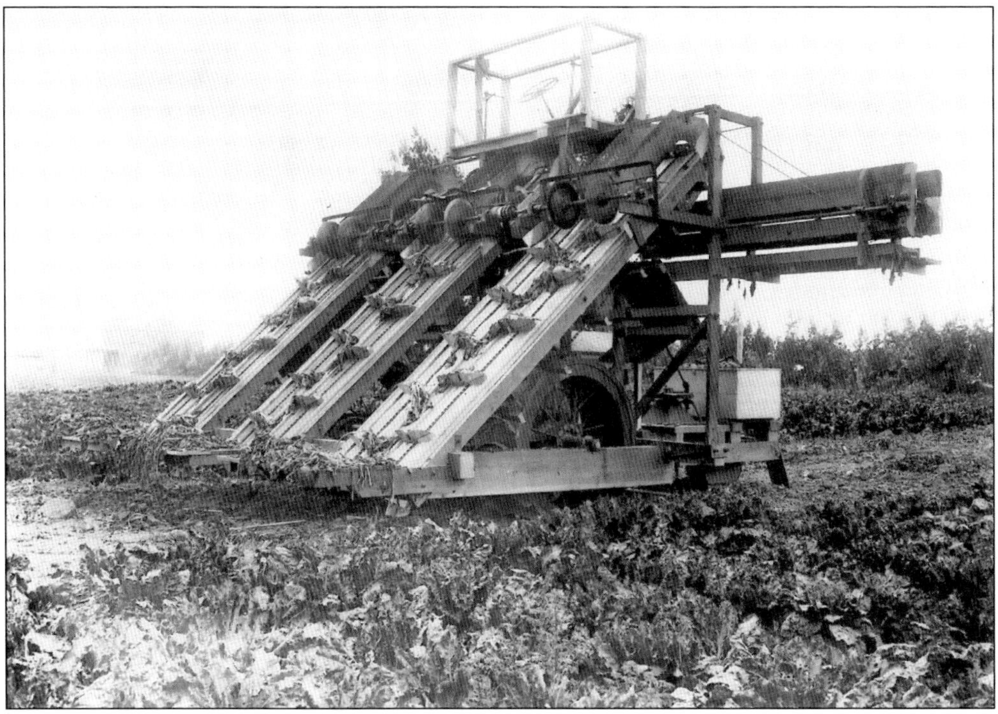

Beet harvesting required enormous amounts of hand labor. This early wooden prototype beet picker was partly the brainchild of Claus Spreckels, although he died in 1908 and this photograph is dated September 26, 1910. The actual design was done by R. H. Moore. According to the *Salinas Californian* on August 16, 1957, by the late 1950s, 98 percent of all sugar beets were harvested mechanically.

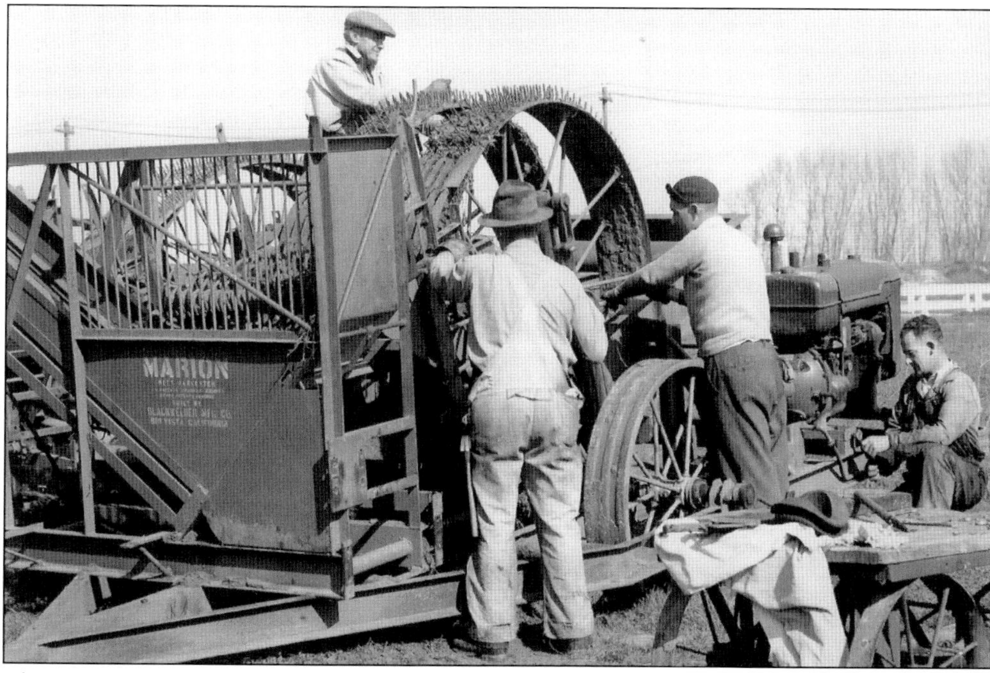

The Marion double picker was designed by sugar crews in the Central Valley to compensate for the severe labor shortage caused by the war effort. The harvester lifts beets from the soil, tops them, and loads them on the truck. Many of these harvesters were purchased by the Spreckels Sugar Company and then rented to the growers. Two of these individuals are identified as Ted Morris and George Mowery. (Courtesy of Monterey County Agricultural and Rural Life Museum.)

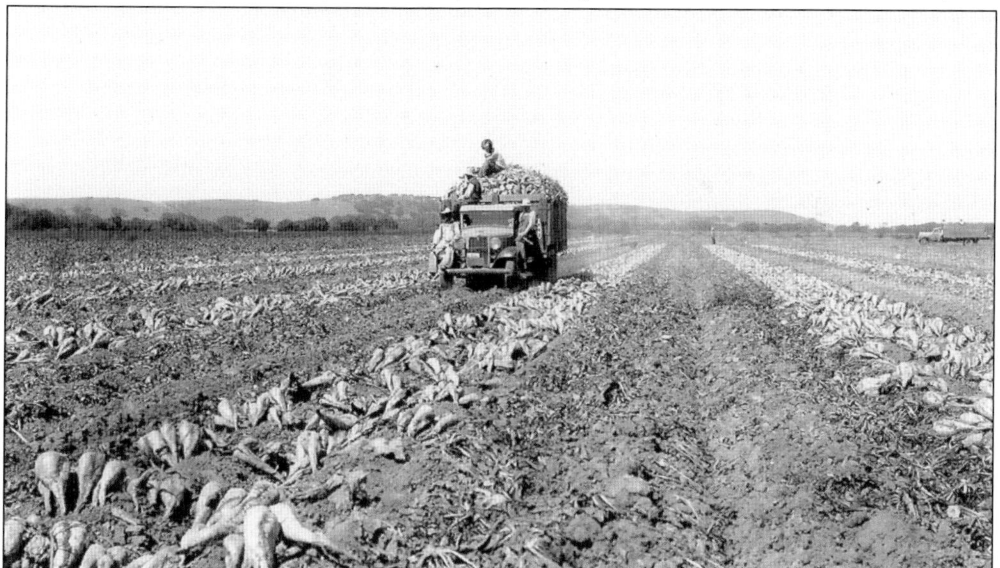

There are at least four field hands catching a ride on the outside of this truck—on the load of beets, on the truck roof, on the right front fender, and on the driver's side running board. People could get away with it in those days. This truck was photographed on the McFadden brothers ranch in Blanco, southwest of Salinas, in 1937. (Courtesy of Monterey County Agricultural and Rural Life Museum.)

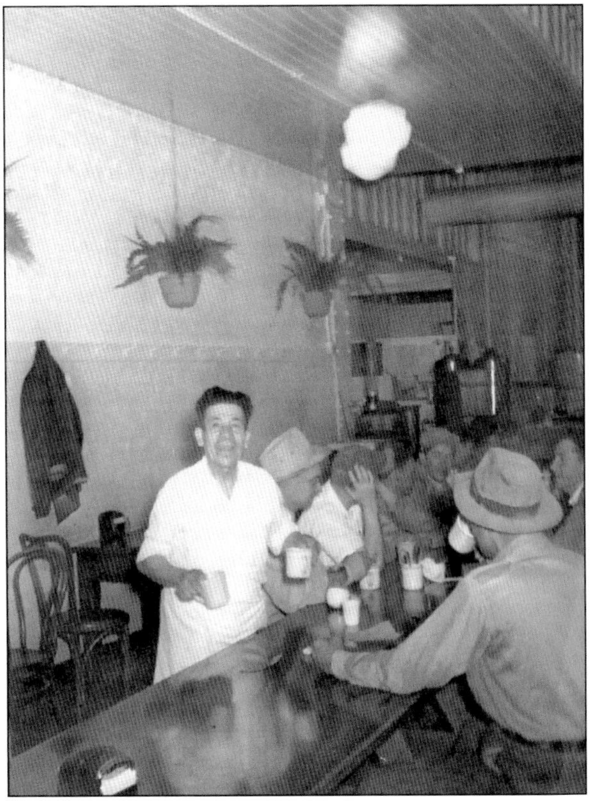

Isidore Gutierrez, a lunchroom attendant, was known for his efficiency in the lunchroom and at his height of five feet two inches, seeing "eye to eye" with the figures at the cash register. (Courtesy of Monterey County Agricultural and Rural Life Museum.)

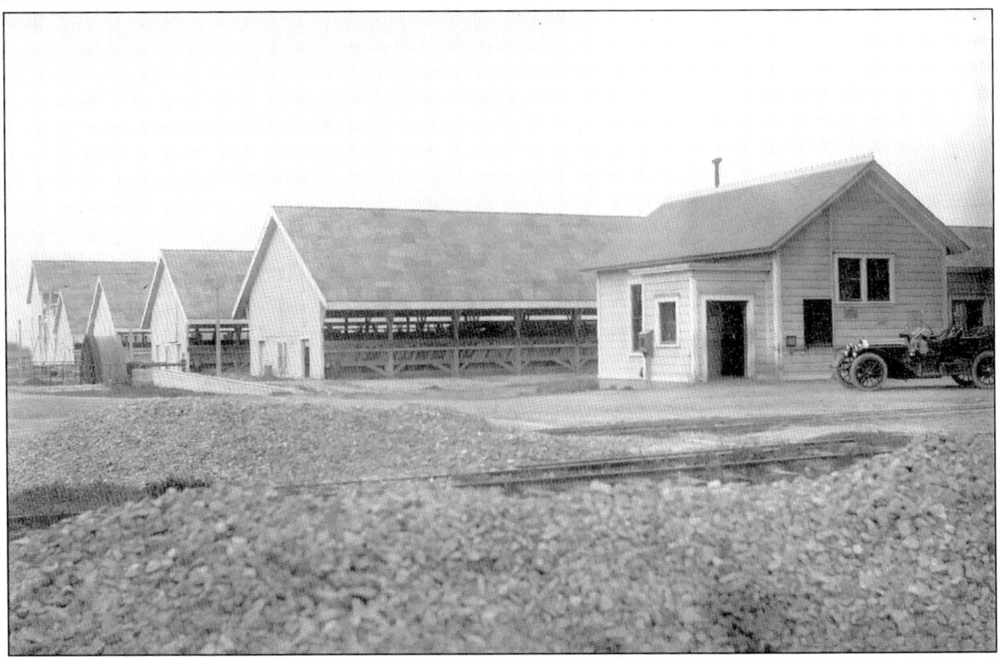

Beets were stored in these bins while waiting to enter the processing cycle. The aim was to keep all of the equipment in the plant running 24 hours a day. The plant was a hungry giant when it was built, and its capacity continued to increase as its equipment was upgraded.

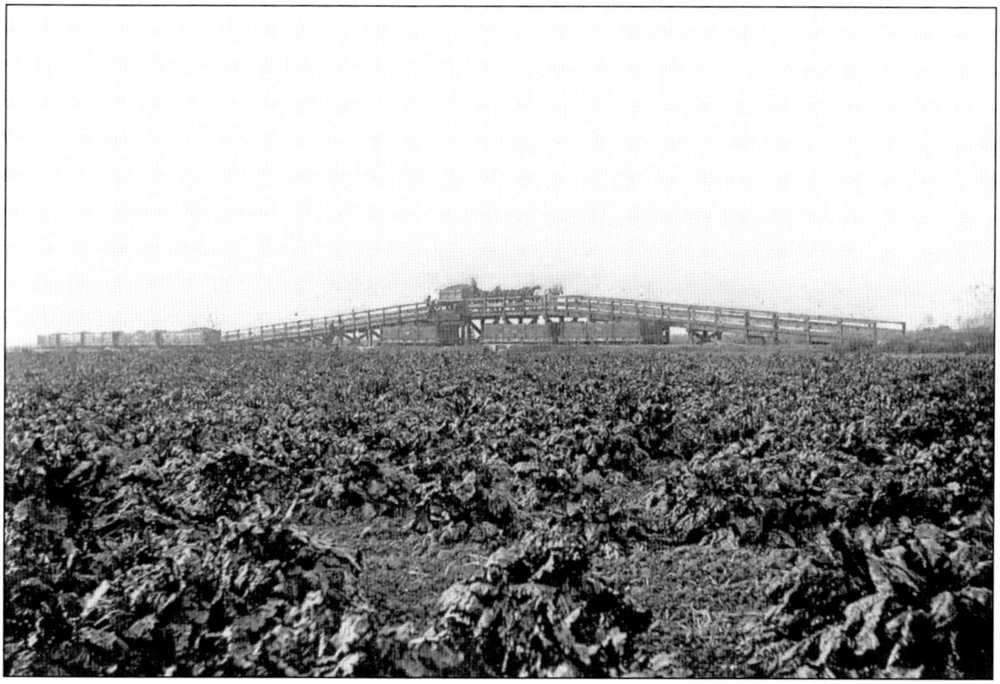

Beets from these fields were loaded onto railway cars for the trip to the Spreckels plant. This photograph, dated November 1, 1907, shows the loading station of Ranch No. 1 in Spreckels. A dump chute was used to load the railroad cars.

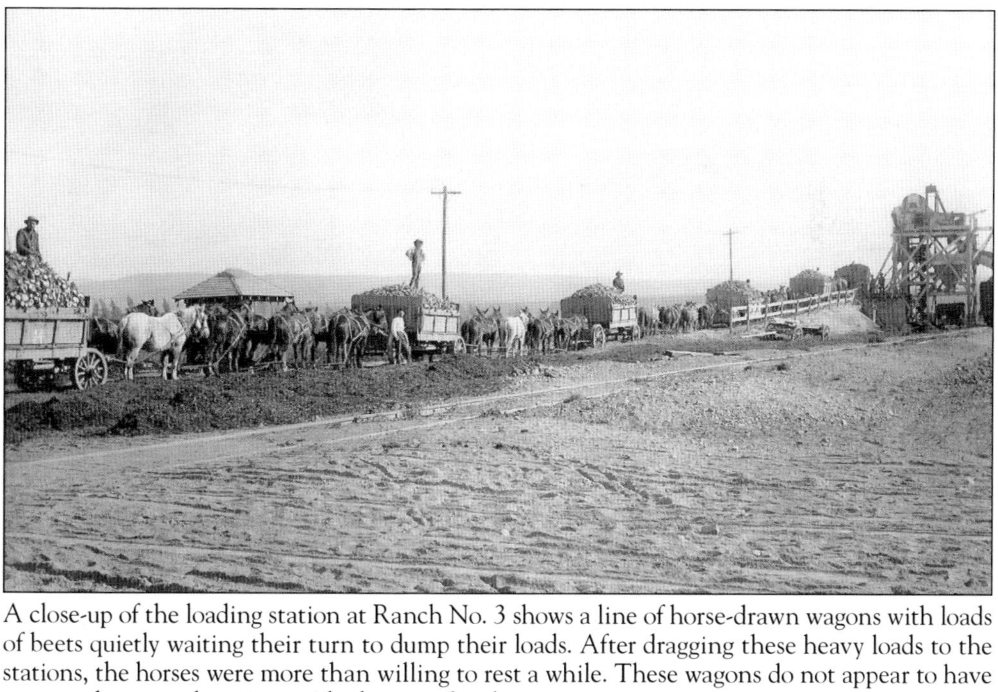

A close-up of the loading station at Ranch No. 3 shows a line of horse-drawn wagons with loads of beets quietly waiting their turn to dump their loads. After dragging these heavy loads to the stations, the horses were more than willing to rest a while. These wagons do not appear to have nets, so they must be using a side-dump technology.

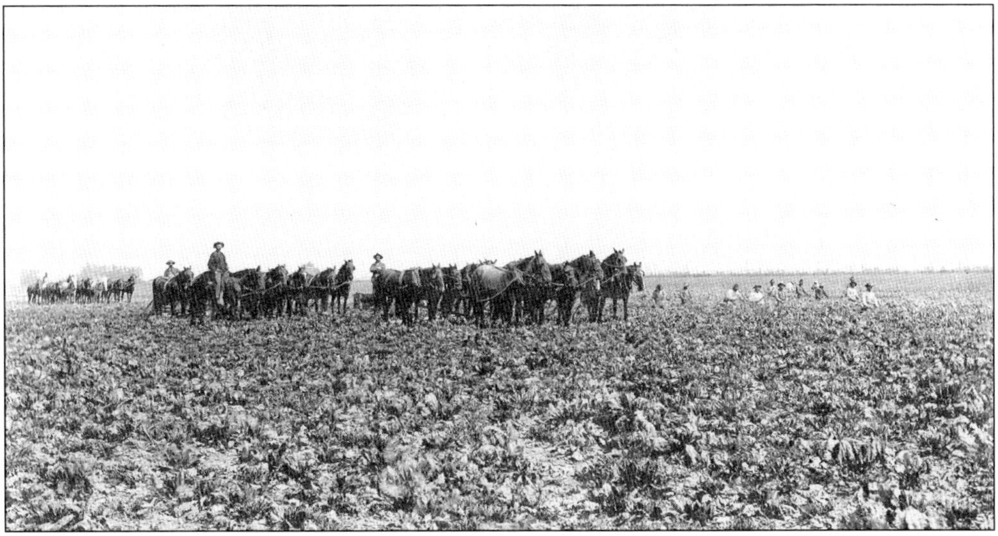

Plow teams were used for beet production in the 1890s. The *Salinas Index*, on February 2, 1897, notes that on the south side of the Salinas River, beets are being grown by Hiram Corey, J. D. Thompson, Herb Tittamore, Sullivan, Graves, Johnston, Craine, Craft, Carey, Clark, Lent, and Quong Wo.

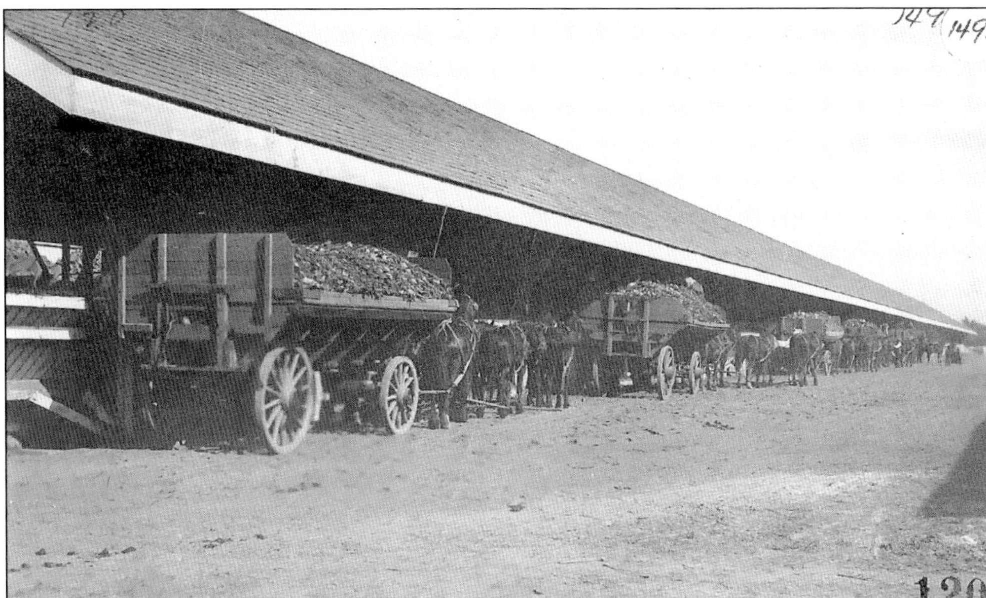

Wagons loaded with sugar beets are lined up next to a storage bin. At the factory, beets were deposited into these bins, where they waited to enter the flume system, which carried them into the factory for processing. There were also outlying beet dumps where farmers could transfer their beets to the company.

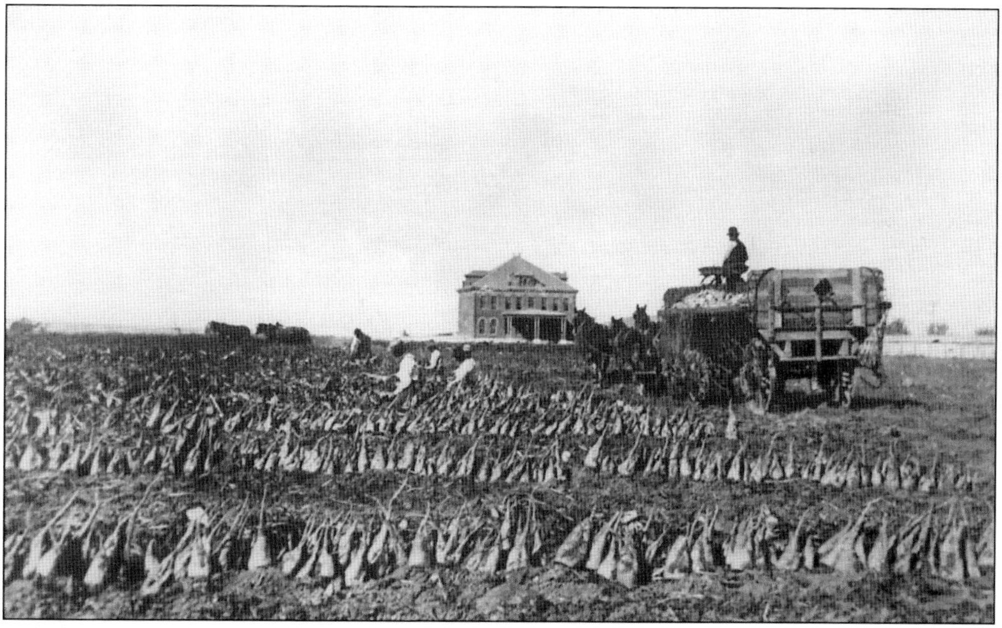

To help ensure a steady supply of beets, even land immediately adjacent to the factory was put into production. This field was next to the main office, which can be seen in the background. Some of these fields were later used for the experimental plots associated with the research lab.

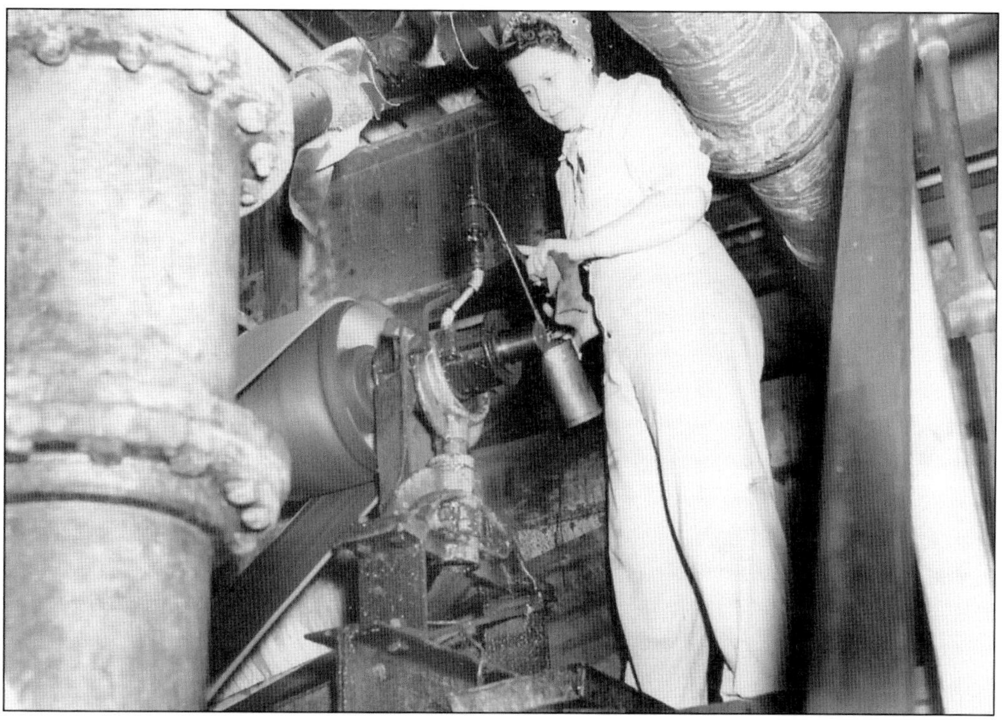

Inez Case tends the maze of machinery that needed constant monitoring to keep running properly. A breakdown of one part could shut down the entire factory. (Courtesy of Monterey County Agricultural and Rural Life Museum.)

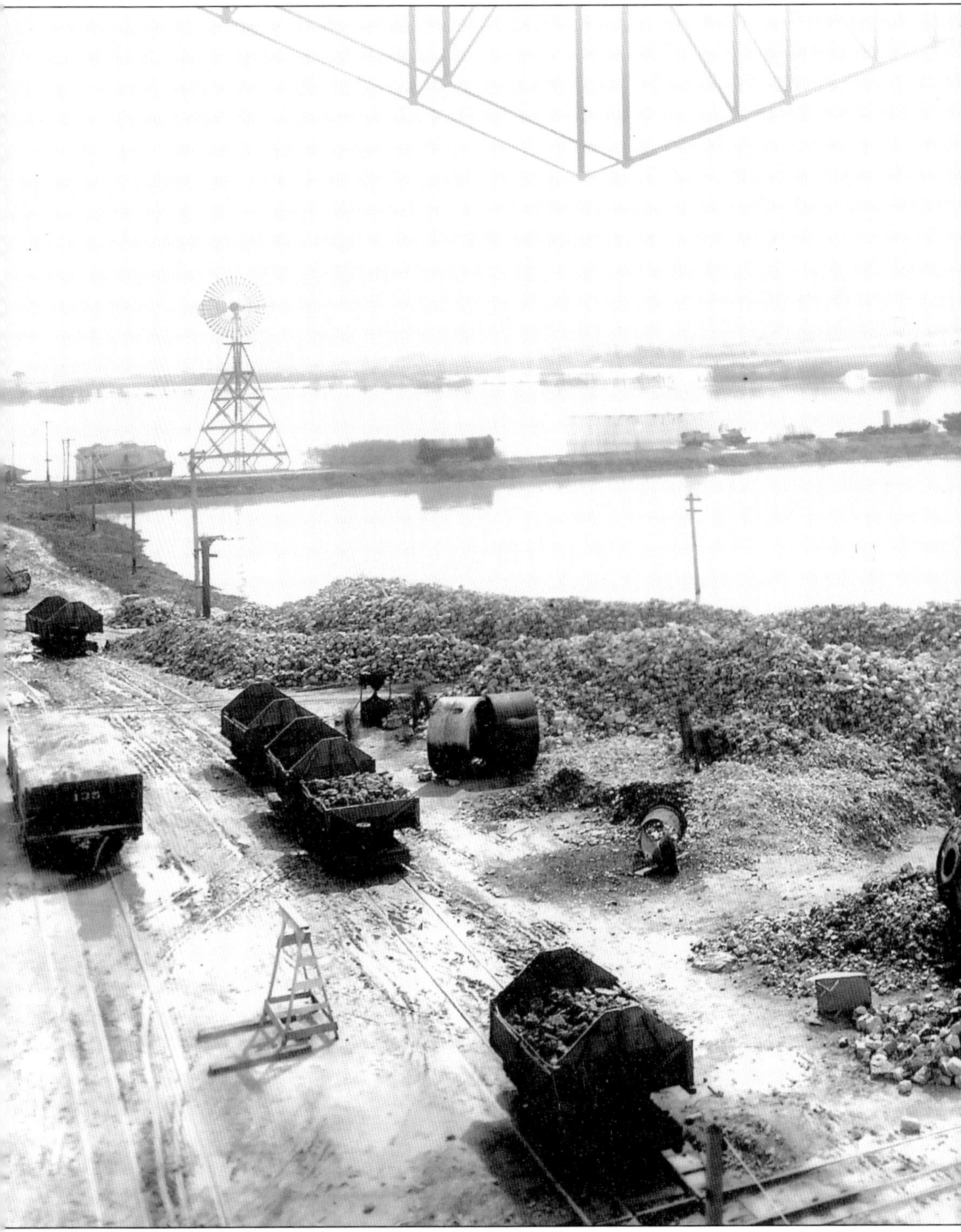

In addition to beets, the factory imported great quantities of lime rock from the Alisal Canyon and other quarries. Here piles of lime rock wait to be lifted to the kiln and the crusher to be made into lime milk. In the background, there is an outbound trail headed for the bridge over

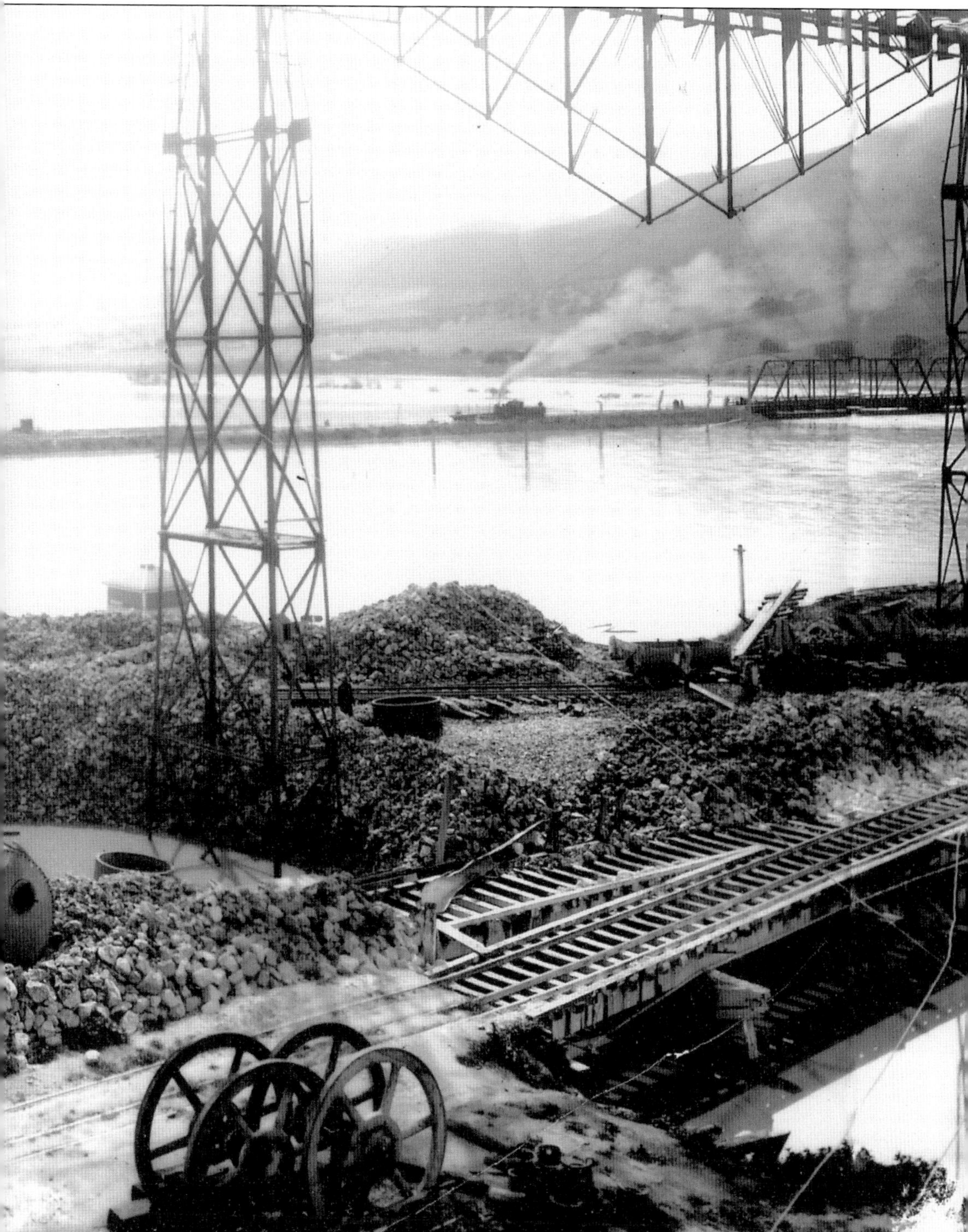

the Salinas River. On the other side of the river, the tracks paralleled what is now River Road for several miles, connecting to a quarry and additional beet fields.

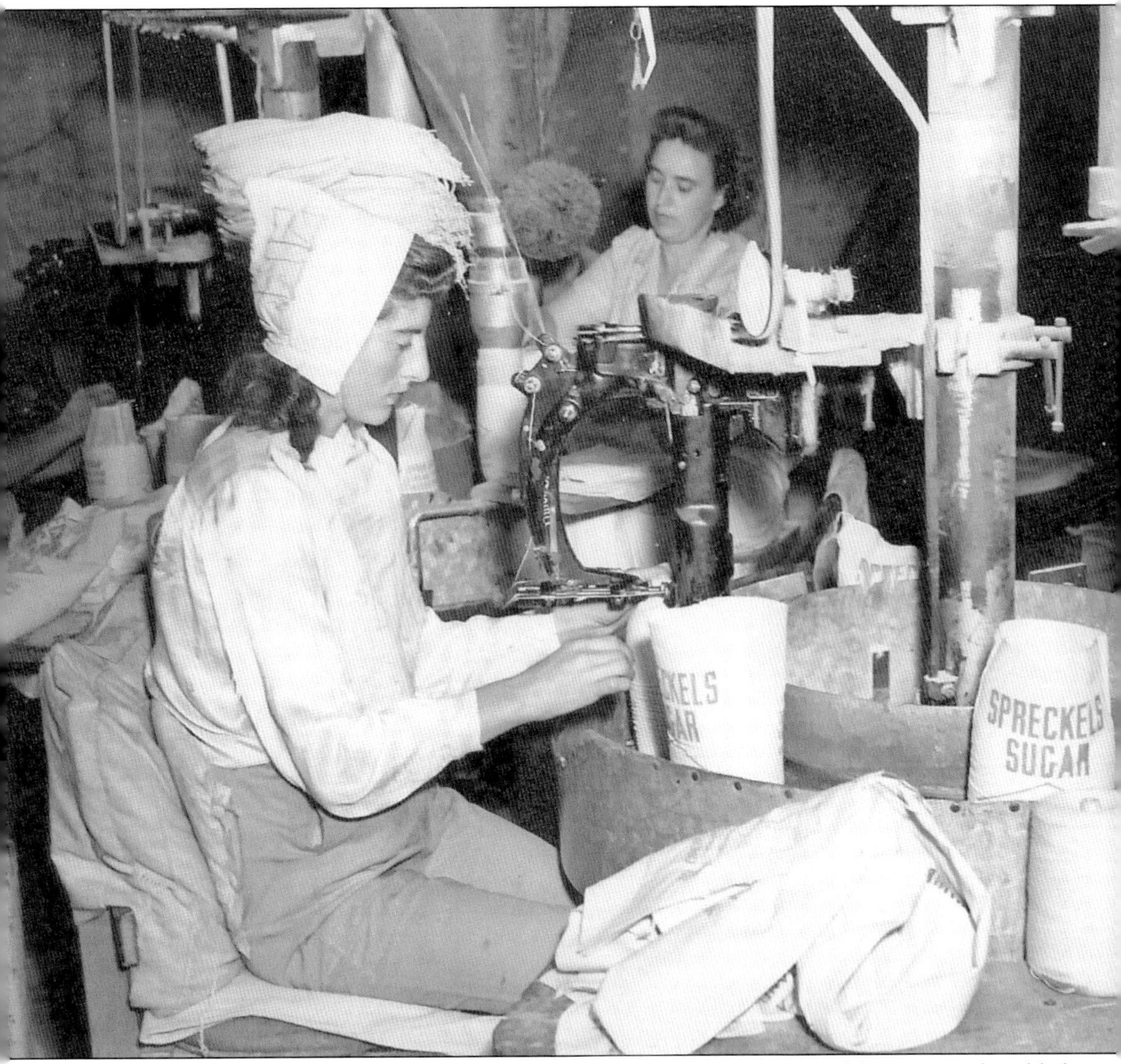

Katherine McHaney and Mrs. M. Prescott are in the sewing room. One of the many unheralded jobs at the factory was sewing the bags that held the sugar. The sewing room was located on the fourth floor of the main building, and about 15 women stitched white sugar sacks for packaging sugar and burlap bags for packing beet pulp. For raw materials, they used heavy bolts of white cloth, canvas, and bales of burlap. Depending on the type of bag that was needed, women were expected to produce the following: 4,000 white sacks a day, 3,750 burlap sacks for industrial use, or 2,000 beet pulp sacks. By 1945, at the end of World War II, sugar production was four times what it had been during the first campaign of 1899. (Courtesy of Monterey County Agricultural and Rural Life Museum.)

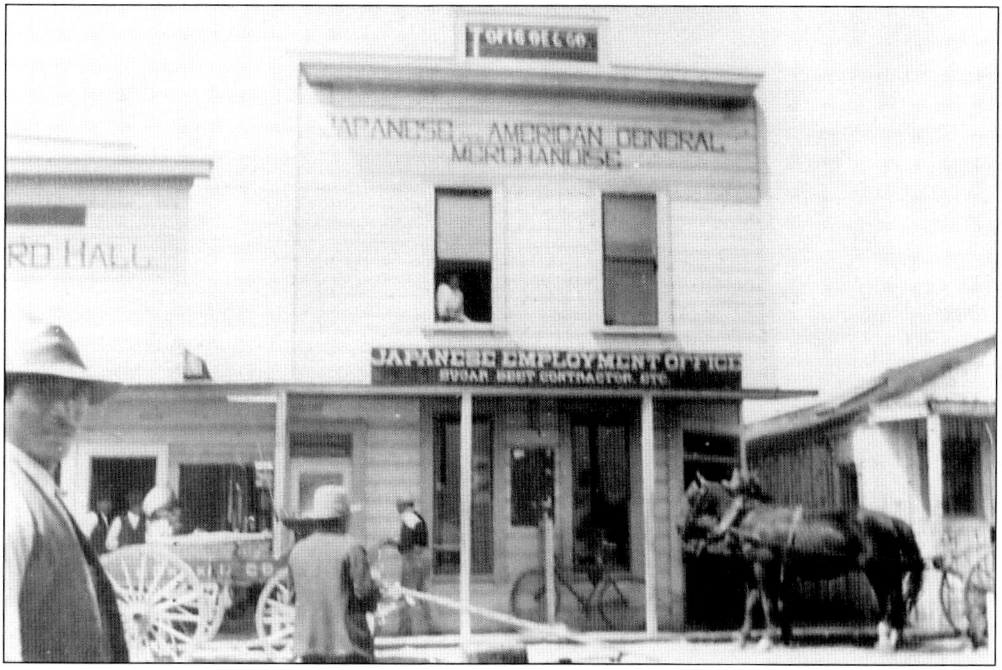

In the early 1900s, the Japanese became a major force in sugar-beet labor, overtaking the Chinese beet workers. The Japanese, to establish themselves in the local market, had to work for less money than their Chinese competitors. However, as Chinese workers grew scarce, the Japanese took on more of the work and were able to raise their rates. The men found jobs by joining organized "clubs" run by Japanese contractors.

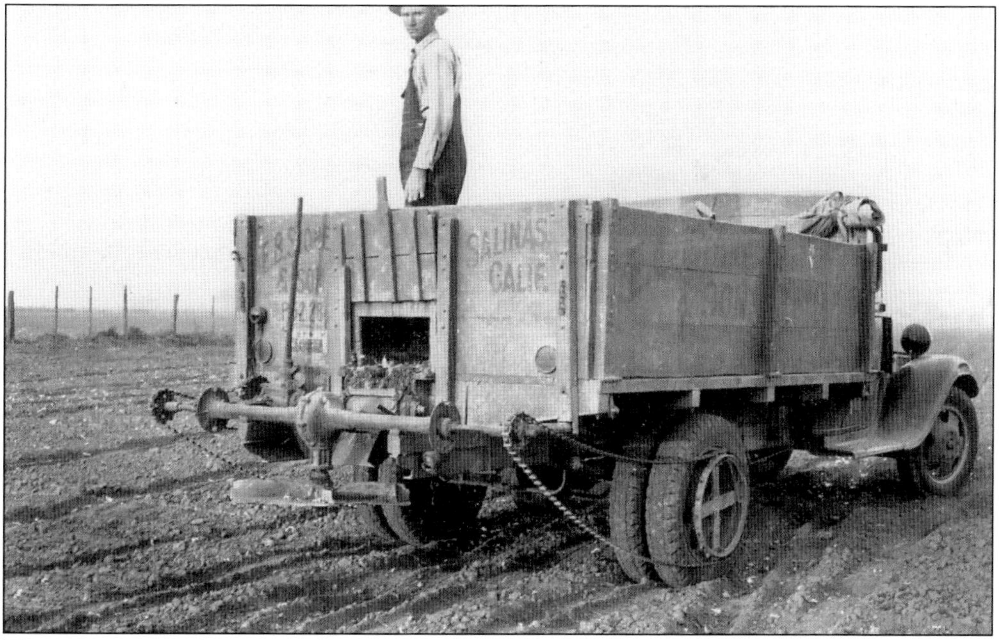

This manure spreader, pictured here around 1938, was operated by a chain drive to the outside of the rear truck wheels, so spreading occurred while the truck was in motion. (Courtesy of Monterey County Agricultural and Rural Life Museum.)

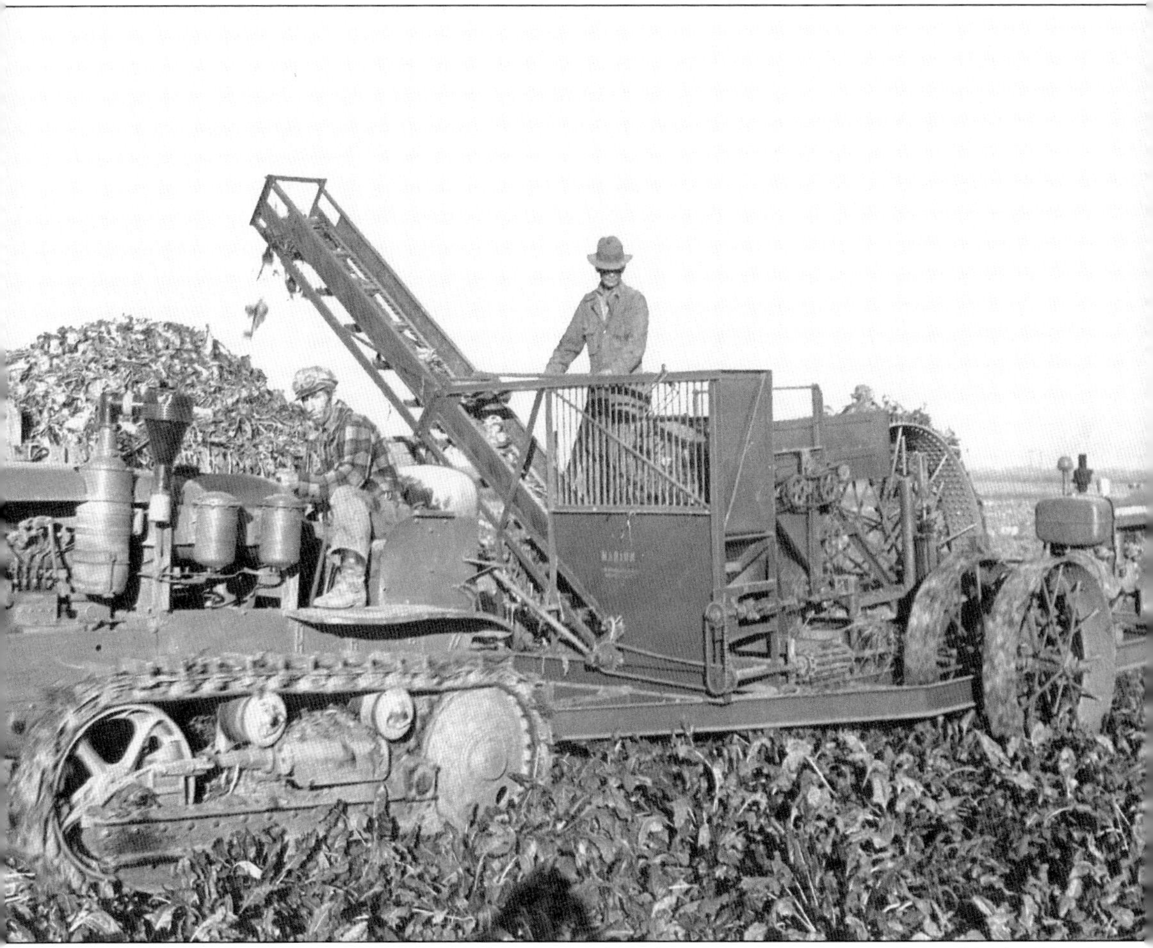

Burton Anderson writes, "The Marbeet sugar beet harvester was invented in 1939 by Lloyd Schmidt in conjunction with his partners, Luke Schmidt, Claude Loucks, Albert Jongengeel, and the Gordon-Hansen International implement dealer of Rio Vista, California. The machine was named after Albert's wife, Marion, and shortened to 'Marbeet.' Ernie Blackwelder of Rio Vista was licensed by the Marbeet Company to build the machine and it was sold by the Gordon-Hansen Company. This was a significant development because the harvester replaced hand topping and loading of beets, one of the hardest field jobs in agriculture. It also partially relieved a critical farm labor shortage in beet harvesting, and sugar was vital to the war effort. The War Production Board granted Blackwelder a priority to obtain steel to build the machine."

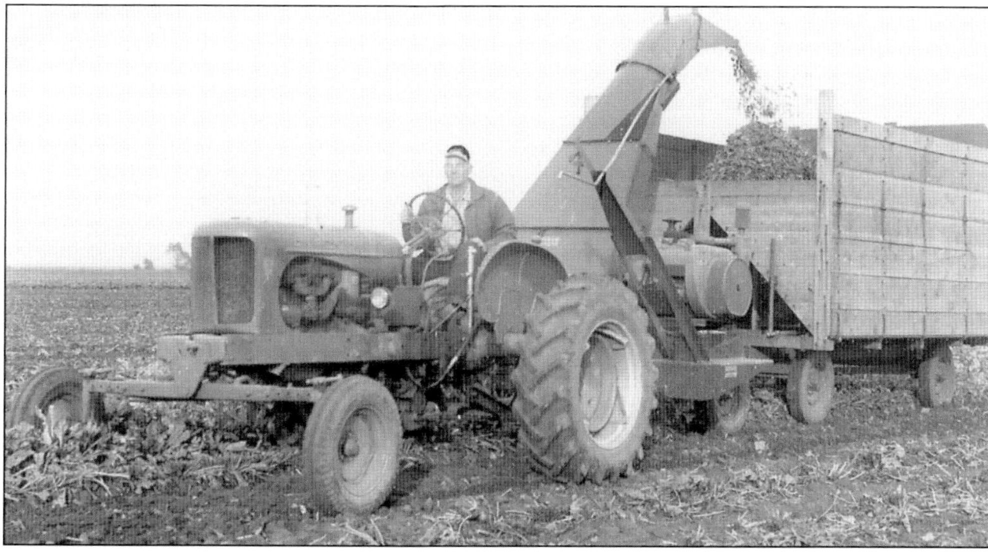

Beets were topped in the field, as only the clean bulb was supposed to be transported to the factory. Originally the topping was done by hand, but because of chronic labor shortages, mechanization soon took over the task. (Courtesy of Monterey County Agricultural and Rural Life Museum.)

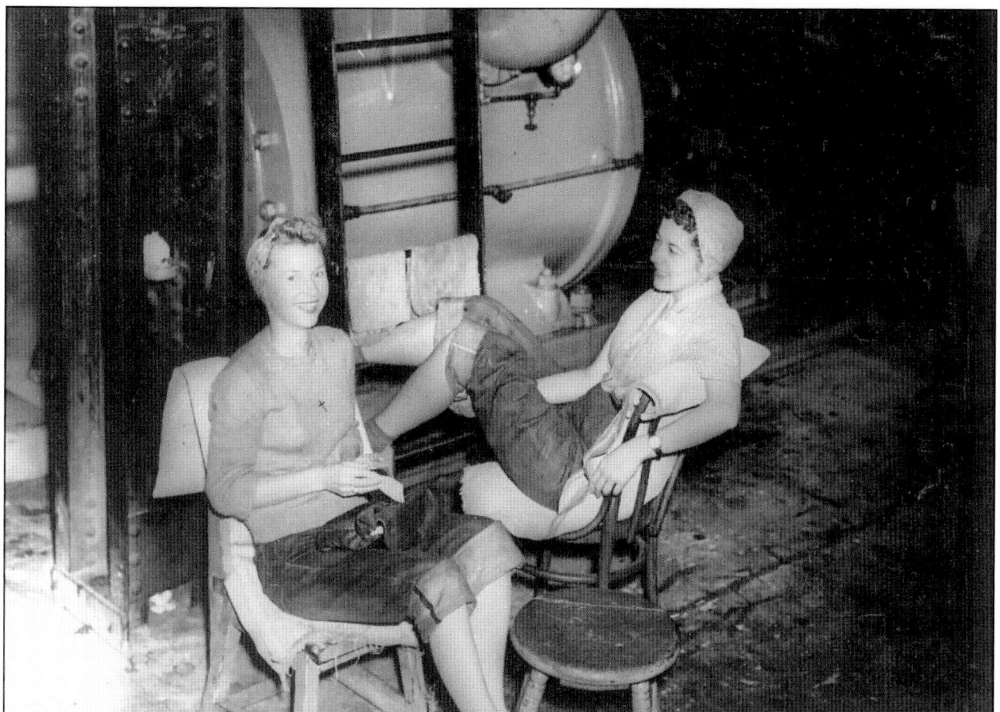

Davida Douglas and Emma Stolz worked at the factory during World War II. When the men went off to war for the first time in 40 years, women became an important part of the continued production of sugar. They worked every job within the plant. In time, the company found that the women were more particular in the operation of the equipment, and there were fewer industrial injuries. The women were not allowed to wear dresses or jewelry, and only comfortable shoes were allowed. (Courtesy of Monterey County Agricultural and Rural Life Museum.)

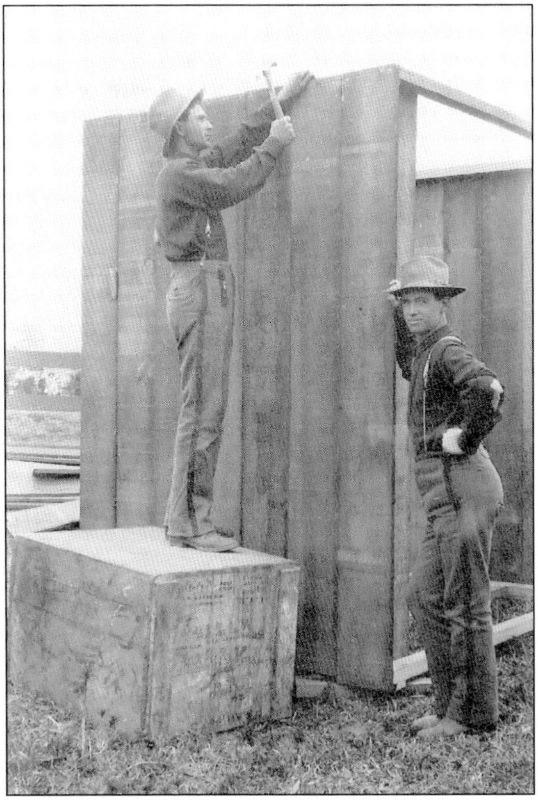

Ray Bullene, with the hammer, and Dan Dougherty help hold the structure steady. They had a lot to do, as there was an entire town and factory to build. (Courtesy of Monterey County Agricultural and Rural Life Museum.)

Ernestine Salas works on the sugar scrolls. (Courtesy of Monterey County Agricultural and Rural Life Museum.)

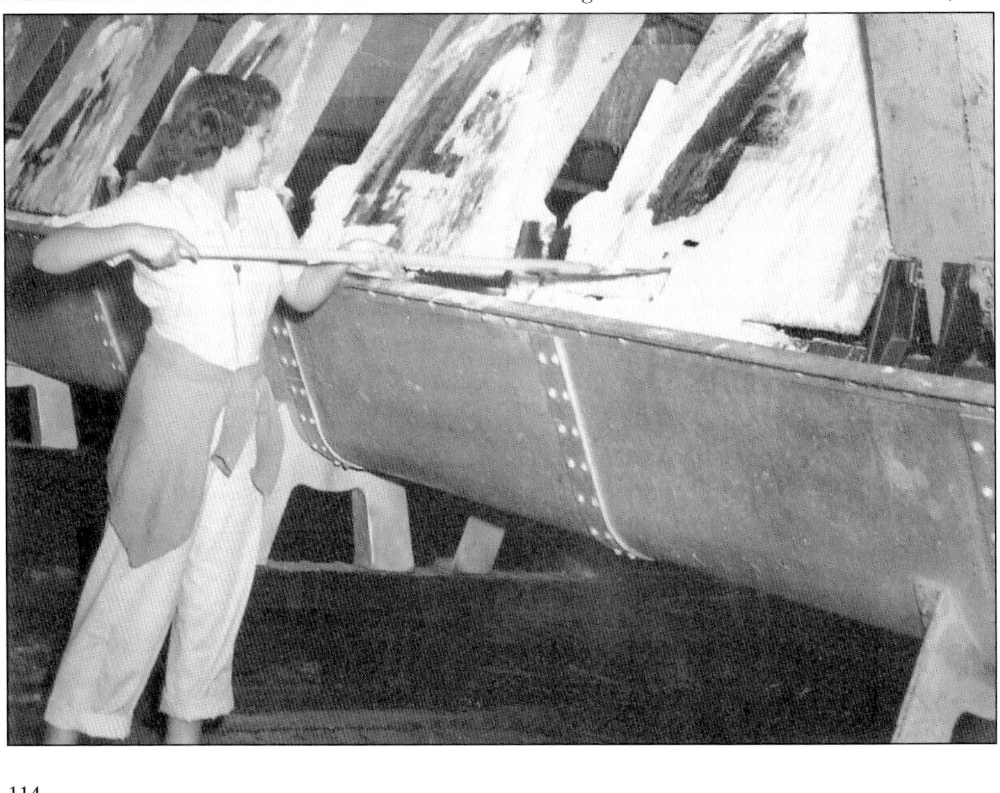

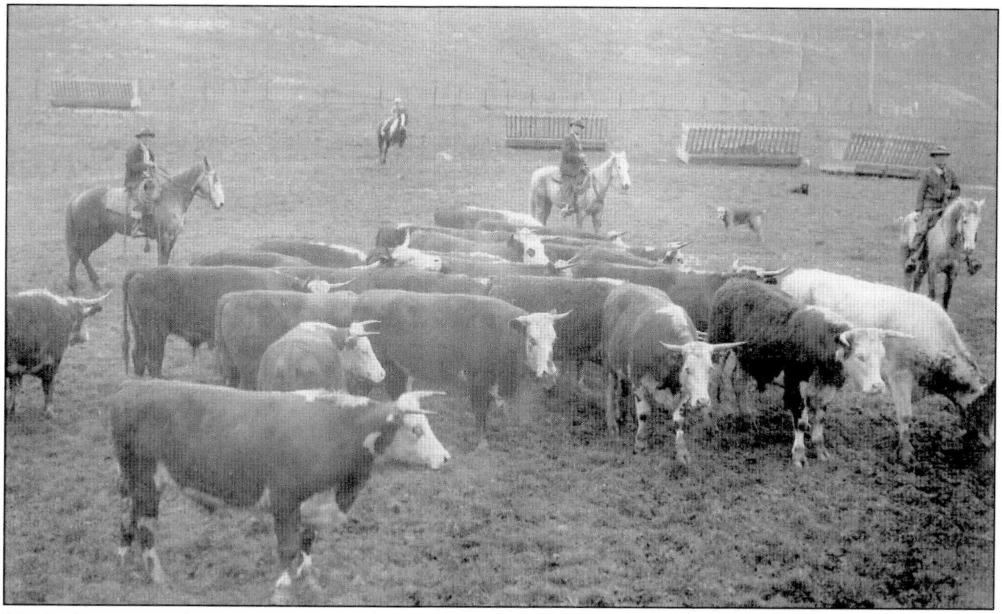

With the onset of operations at Spreckels, beef cattle were pushed out of the valley, though the cattle continued to occupy the hillsides surrounding the valley as this operation in the Toro area shows. One benefit of the beet process was a new cattle feed: beet pulp. The Spreckels plant produced large quantities of wet beet pulp, which was hauled away and fed to the cattle. After driers were added, dried beet pulp was bagged for sale. (Courtesy of Monterey County Agricultural and Rural Life Museum.)

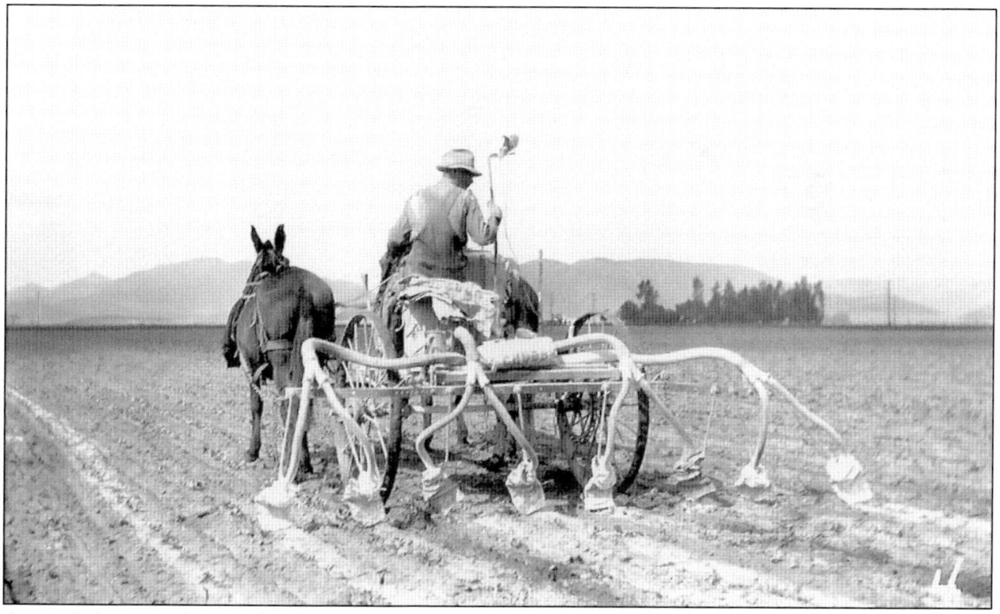

An early lime applicator fertilizes a beet field. Although the equipment has changed considerably, the process is still basically the same. With more modern machinery, yields increased and labor decreased considerably. (Courtesy of Monterey County Agricultural and Rural Life Museum.)

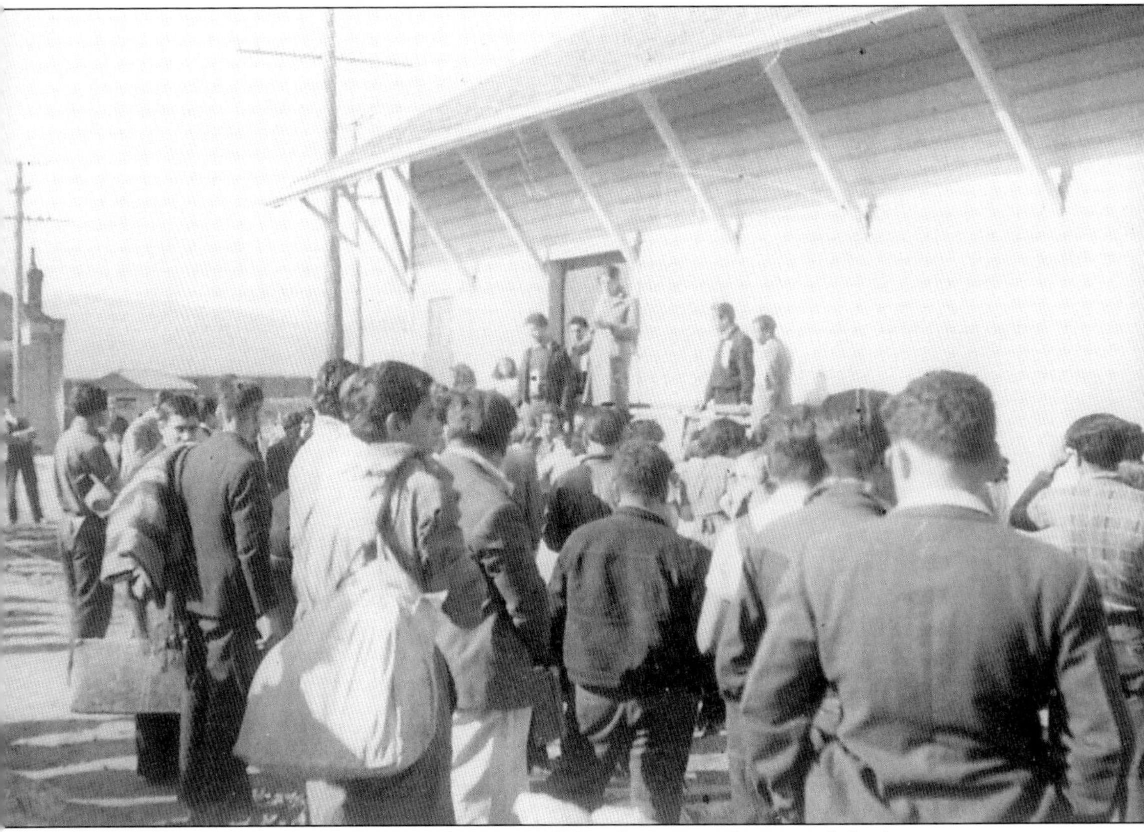

During World War II, there was a shortage of labor for growing beets, and the factory was operating at only half capacity. This was quite a drop from 1940, when a record of 696,303 tons of beets were made into 2,322,000 100-pound bags of sugar and 876,873 bags of beet pulp. To help relieve the labor shortage, permission was obtained to bring 3,000 workers from Mexico. From the second trainload, 621 men arrived in King City on October 5, 1942. Sixty men were left at Guadalupe, 180 at King City, and the rest came to Spreckels. Mexico was not in a position to supply munitions for the war effort, but Mexican officials told the laborers that each worker should regard himself as a fighter for democracy and to conduct himself as a soldier of the Allies on the battlefront. Assembled in front of the Southern Pacific warehouse, facing the Stars and Stripes and the flag of Mexico, they joined in singing the national anthem of Mexico. (Courtesy of Monterey County Agricultural and Rural Life Museum.)

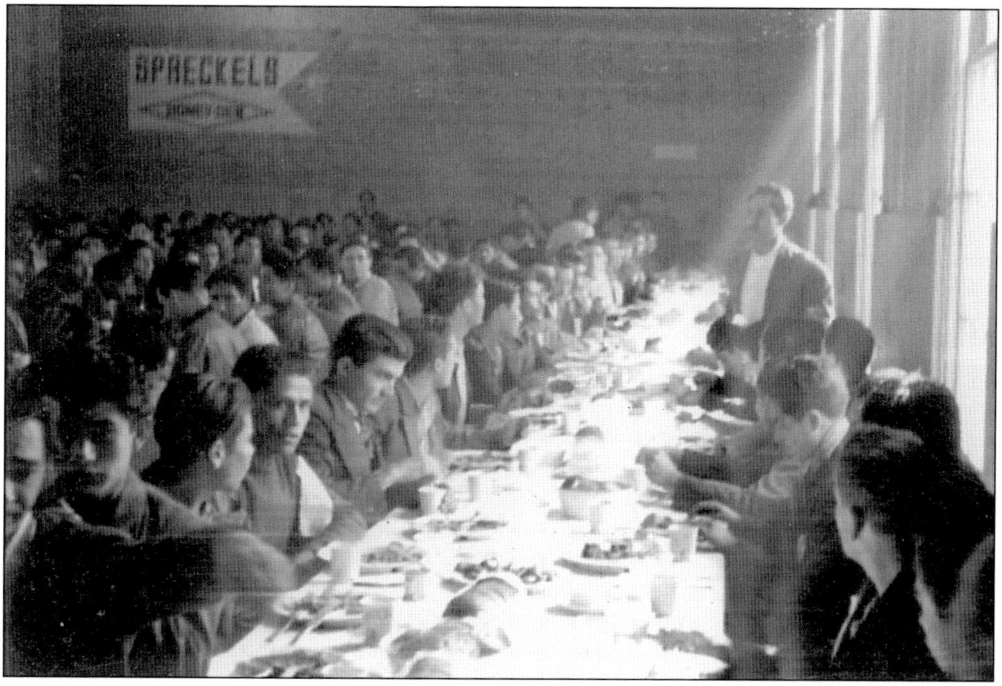

When the singing of the Mexican anthem and the briefing was completed, 120 of the men were taken to Scout House and the rest to the recreation building for a welcoming meal before being sent to their respective camps. In this photograph, a "Jefe del Grupo" responds to the speeches of welcome. The complete story of this event is found in the *Honey Dew News*, October 1942. (Courtesy of Monterey County Agricultural and Rural Life Museum.)

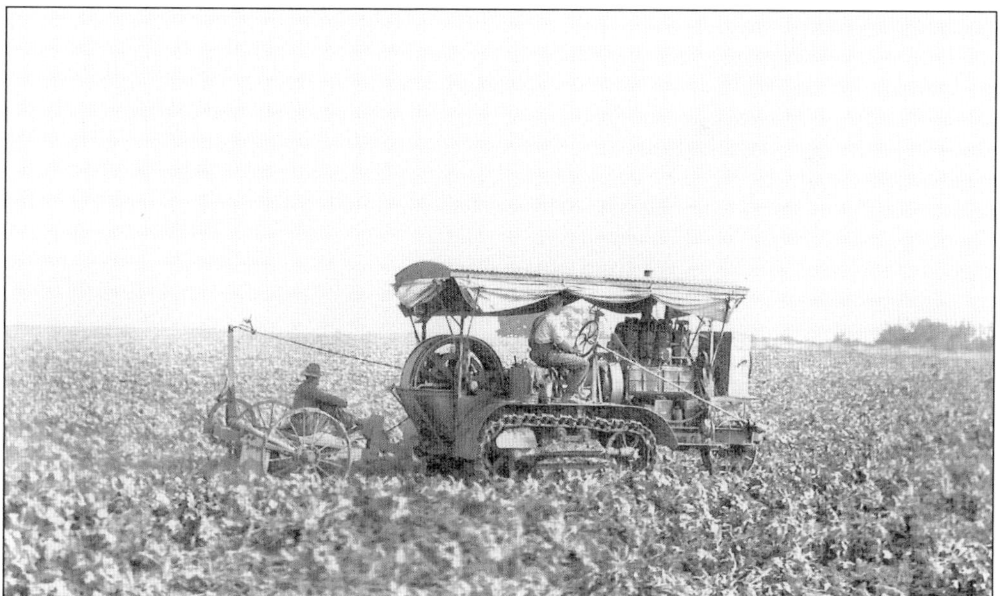

The deep ripper chisel was an early method used for loosening the beetroots before harvesting. (Courtesy of Monterey County Agricultural and Rural Life Museum.)

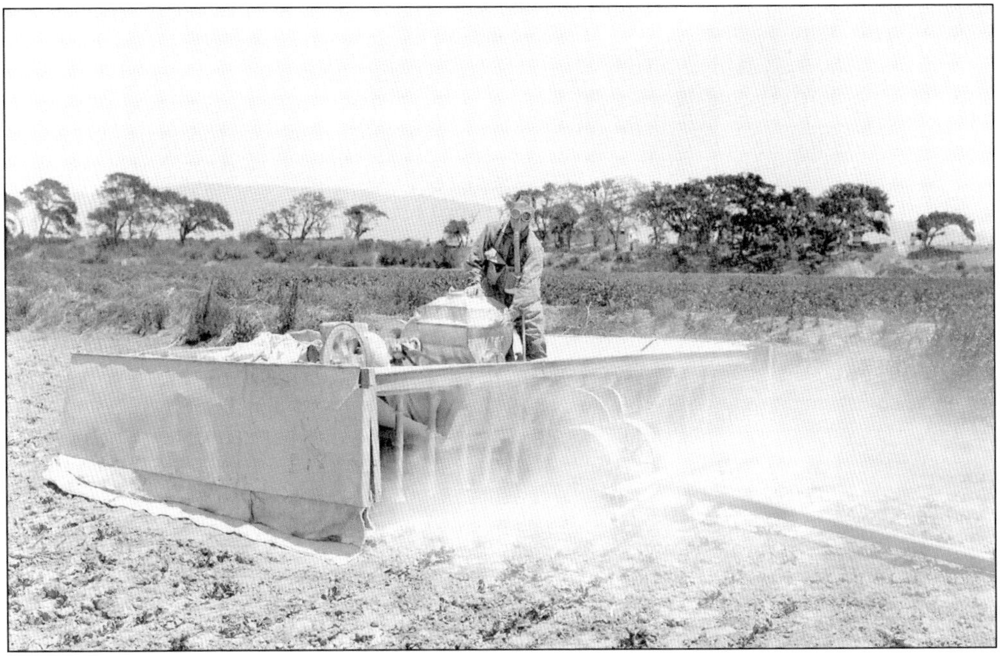

Lime rock was used as a part of the sugar-refining process. Waste lime was sent via a flume system to settling ponds near the factory. Periodically the ponds were drained and the lime was collected for use in the fields. (Courtesy of Monterey County Agricultural and Rural Life Museum.)

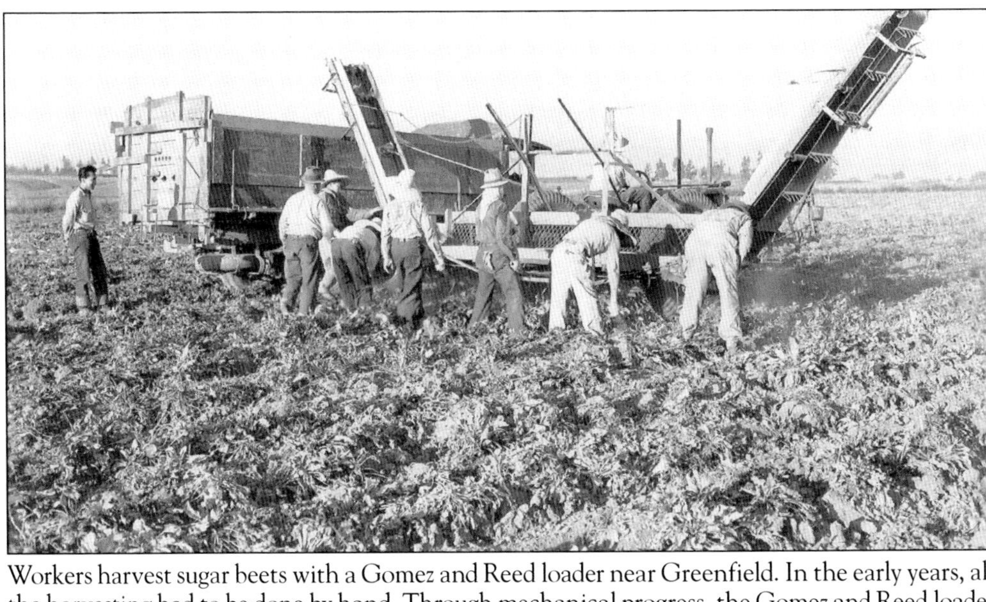

Workers harvest sugar beets with a Gomez and Reed loader near Greenfield. In the early years, all the harvesting had to be done by hand. Through mechanical progress, the Gomez and Reed loader topped the sugar beets, but hand labor was still required to load them. (Courtesy of Monterey County Agricultural and Rural Life Museum.)

Charles Smiley proudly displays a portion of his beet crop in 1917. Tenant farmers were leaseholders who paid rent and the costs associated with the production and harvest of crops, including the payment to farm labor to help with the harvest and transport of the beets to the nearest beet dump, to a landlord.

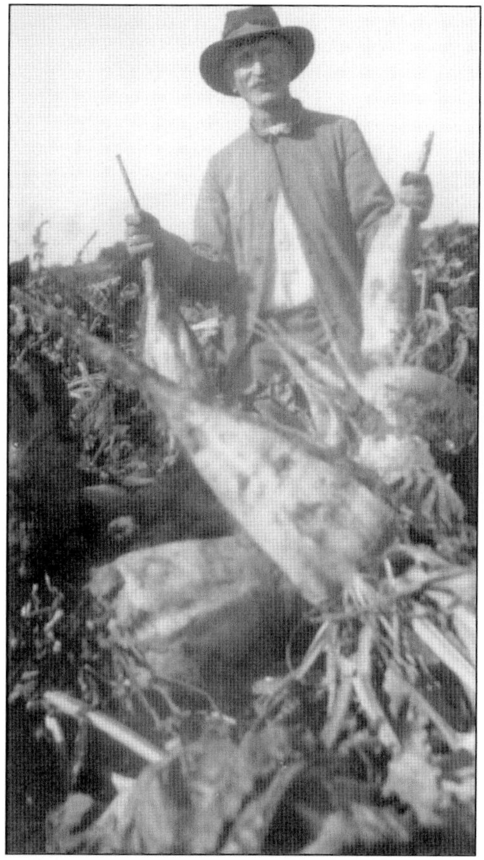

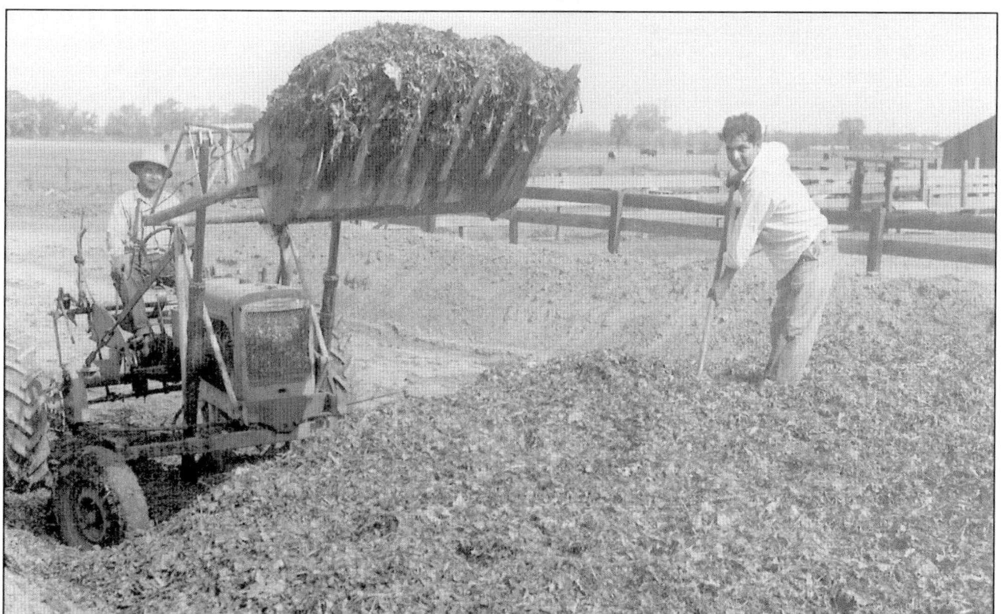

This early John Deere tractor is turning and moving beet tops or pulp. Beet waste products were used for cattle feed. (Courtesy of Monterey County Agricultural and Rural Life Museum.)

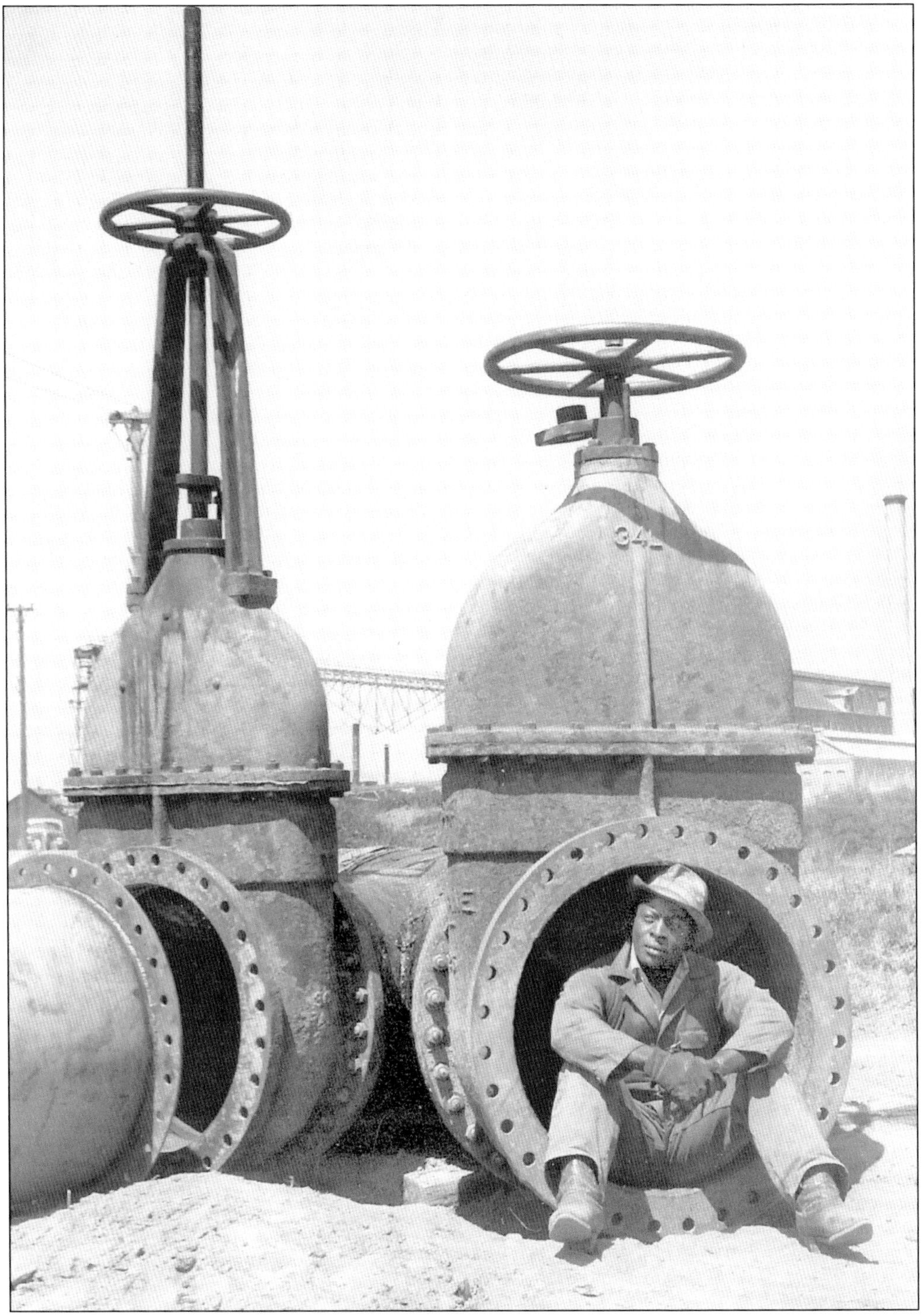

J. S. Dixon, at the request of Ray Sens, a photographer for the *Honey Dew News*, poses in a large pipe called the "Big Inch" to illustrate its size of 36 inches. Dixon assisted in laying the pipeline, which was part of the wastewater piping for Spreckels. (Courtesy of Monterey County Agricultural and Rural Life Museum.)

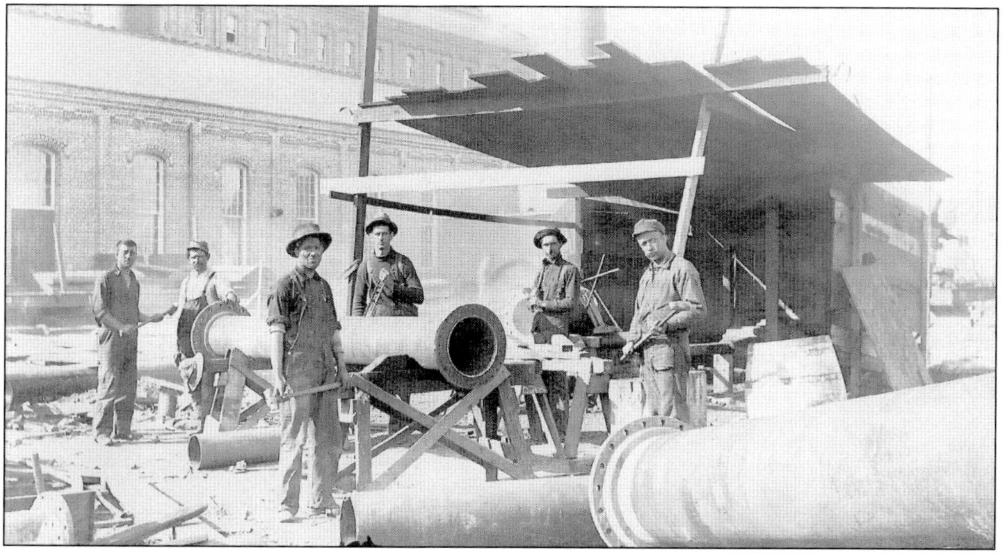

Workers are pictured here with iron pipes. The plant required miles of pipe to be laid in order to access the water needed to run the processing operation. Pipes ran from the factory across the bridge to the reservoir on the hill south of the Salinas River. It had a storage capacity of 1.3 million gallons. (Courtesy of Monterey County Agricultural and Rural Life Museum.)

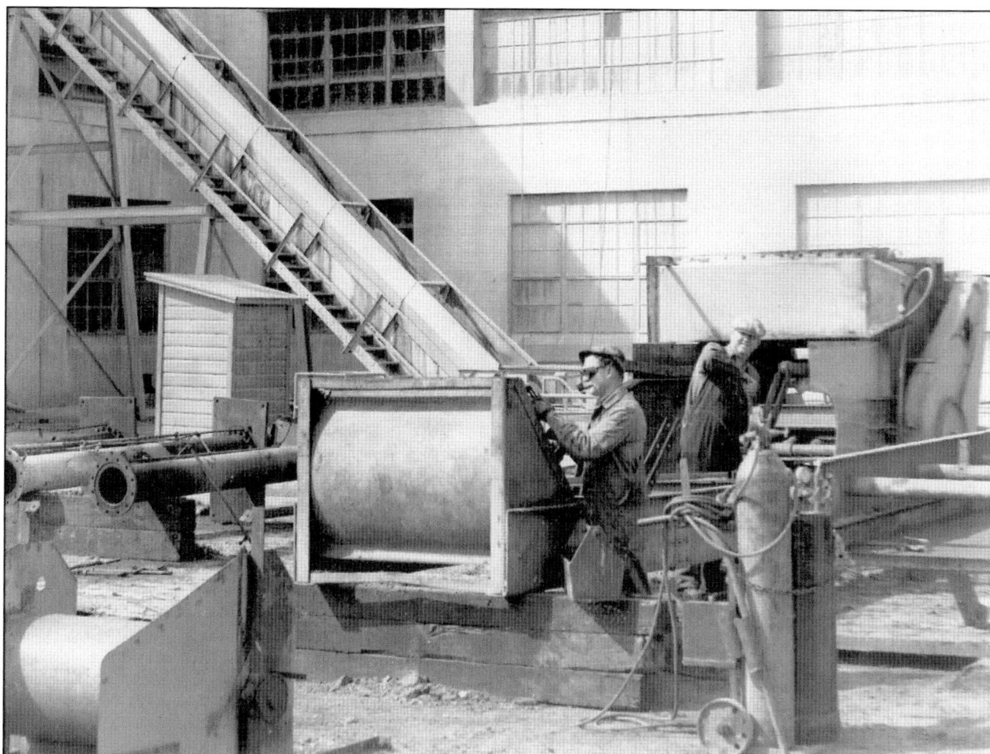

Lowell Davis and George Hutching are at work at the factory. The gas tanks indicate they are either cutting or welding. This type of equipment maintenance, or periodic upgrades, was a constant part of factory life. (Courtesy of Monterey County Agricultural and Rural Life Museum.)

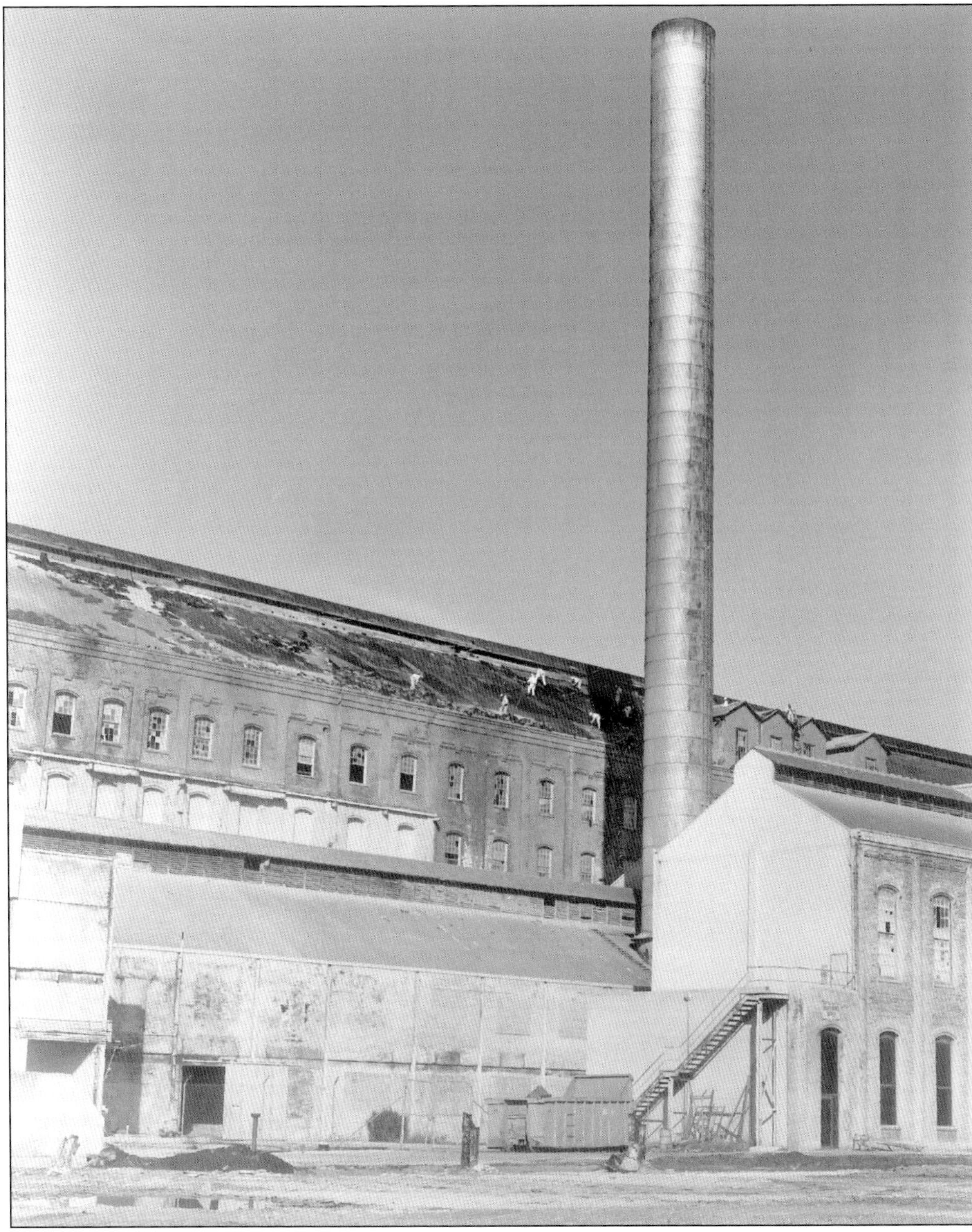

On October 17, 1989, the main factory building suffered extensive structural damage as a result of the magnitude 7.1 Loma Prieta earthquake. There were no injuries, as the main building had been idle for several years, and the asbestos and hazardous chemicals had already been removed. Beginning in the early 1980s, the Spreckels facility had been used only as a packaging plant as a division of AMSTAR Corporation. In 1987, the facility was taken private under the name of the Spreckels Sugar Company. Demolition work on the interior began in 1990 and continued through 1992. Between March and August 1993, the factory itself was demolished—after 95 years. In 1996, Spreckels Sugar Company merged with Holly Sugar Corporation, a division of Imperial Holly Corporation, and ceased to exist as a separate company. (For a sense of scale, note the demolition workers on the roof.)

Eight

END OF AN ERA

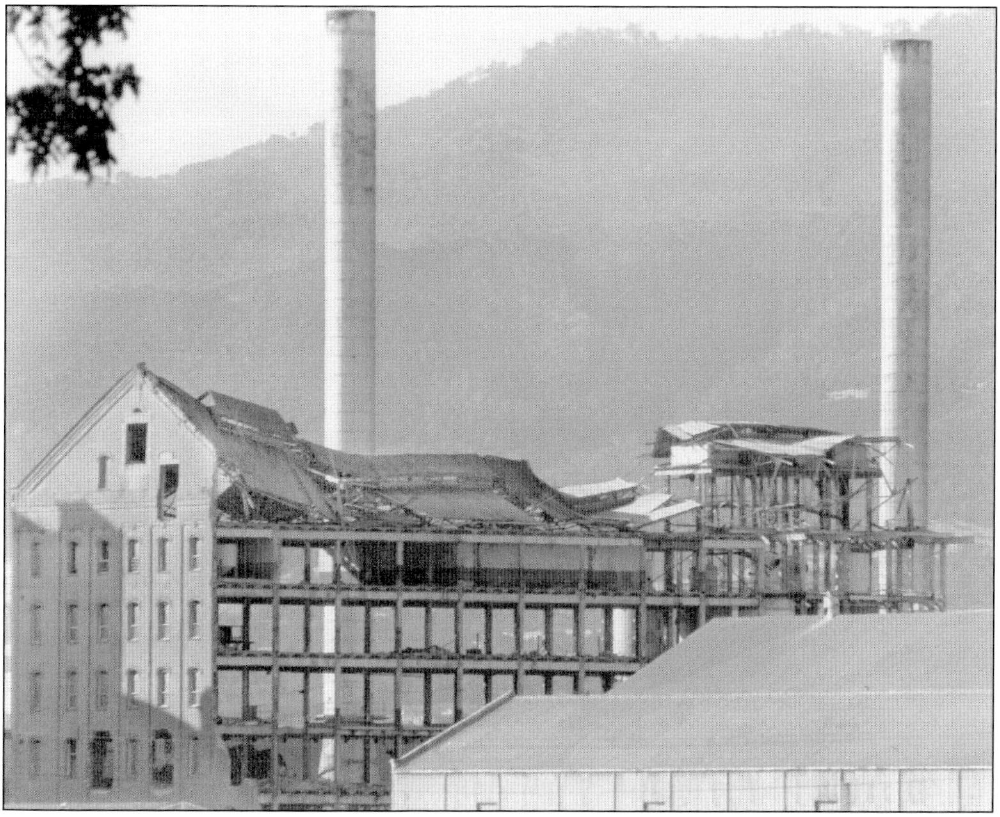

In this view of the demolition, the roof is mostly gone and the brick sides have been removed. The red bricks, numbering some four million in all, were imported from Germany in 1898. Because of their weight, they were used as ballast in the ships that carried them. When the factory was demolished, the Spreckels Sugar Company donated several thousand bricks to the Monterey County Historical Society. While these cannot be used as structural materials, they are being used for walkways and other ornamental landscaping and will be preserved as a commemoration of Claus Spreckels, the Sugar King, and the largest sugar refinery in the world.

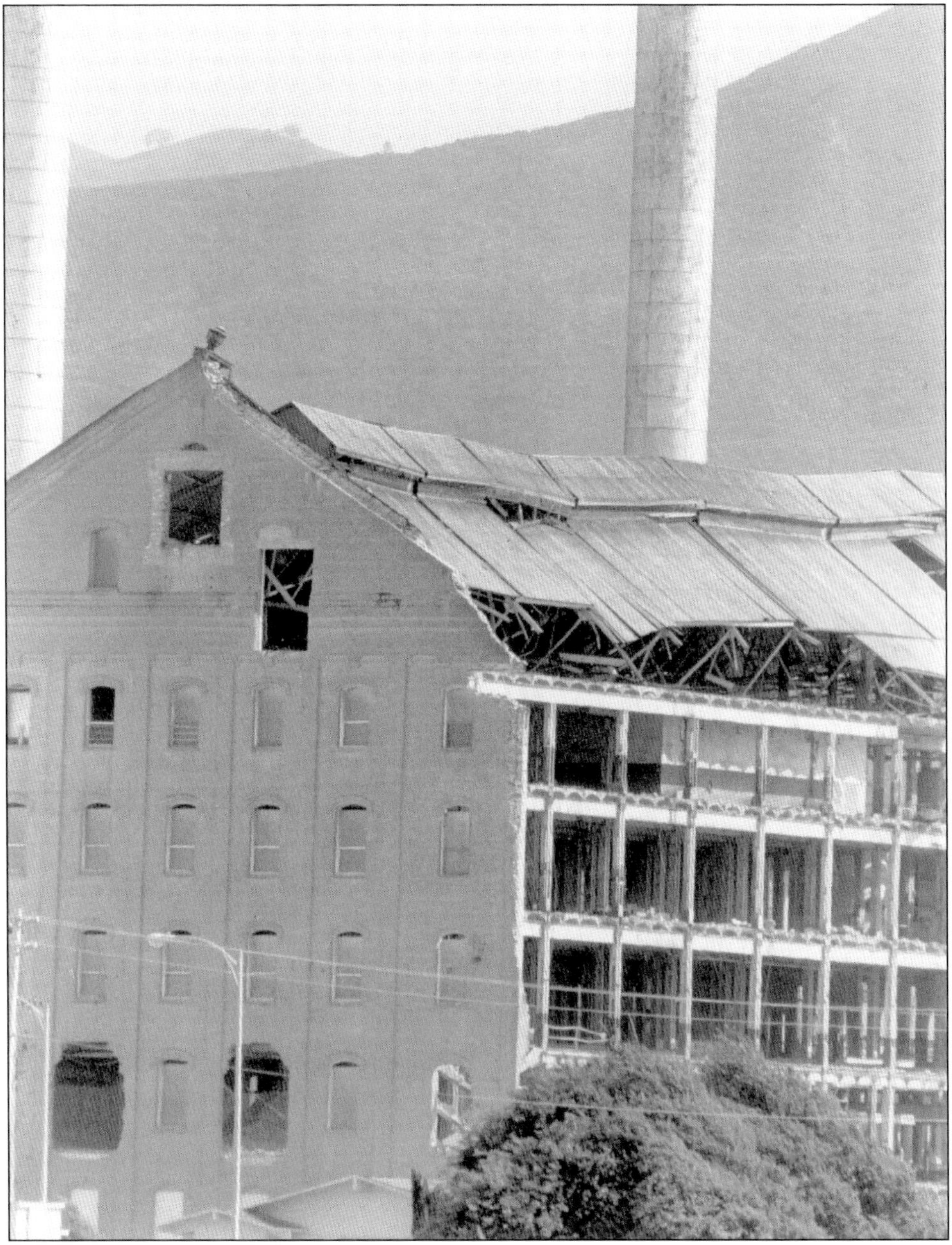

After the Loma Prieta earthquake, Monterey County building officials declared the old factory unsafe for occupancy, and the Spreckels Sugar Company applied for a permit to demolish it and four other buildings. A group, Friends of Spreckels, was quickly formed to pursue preservation alternatives. The Monterey County Historical Society assisted in the effort. However, there were many problems. First was the sheer size of the main building and the difficulty of finding an economically viable use for such an immense structure. After seven years of standing idle, the roof, along with the trusses and diagonal bracing, were in poor condition. The corrosive action of water and sugar had weakened the structural steel frame, and numerous shear cracks had weakened the walls. Because of these, and other problems, efforts to preserve the buildings were unsuccessful.

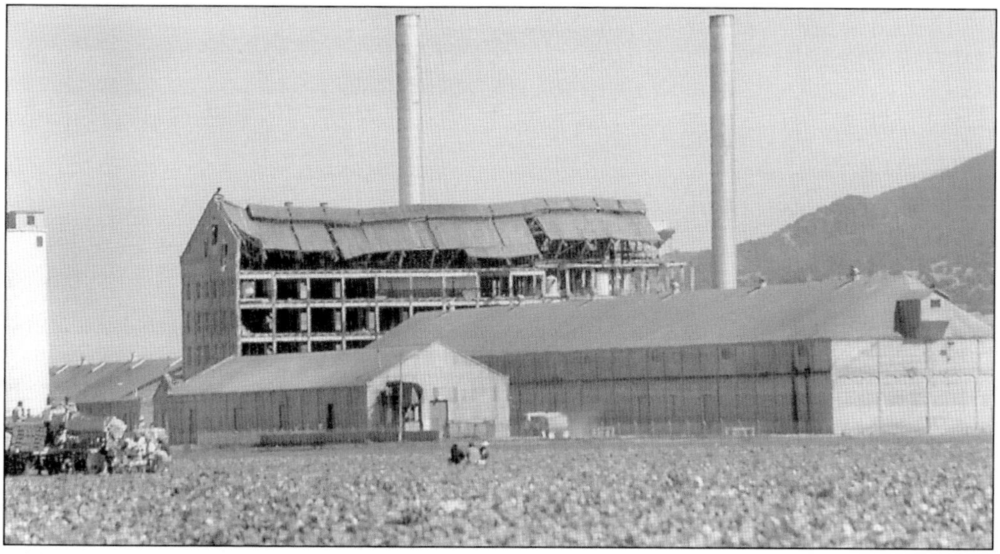

Although the Spreckels Sugar Company is no longer shipping sugar from the old factory, another company, Tanimura and Antle, has opened their headquarters just a few hundred yards from the main building. Located on the far side of the factory building, the company represents two pioneering agricultural families who are carrying on the Spreckels tradition in Spreckels.

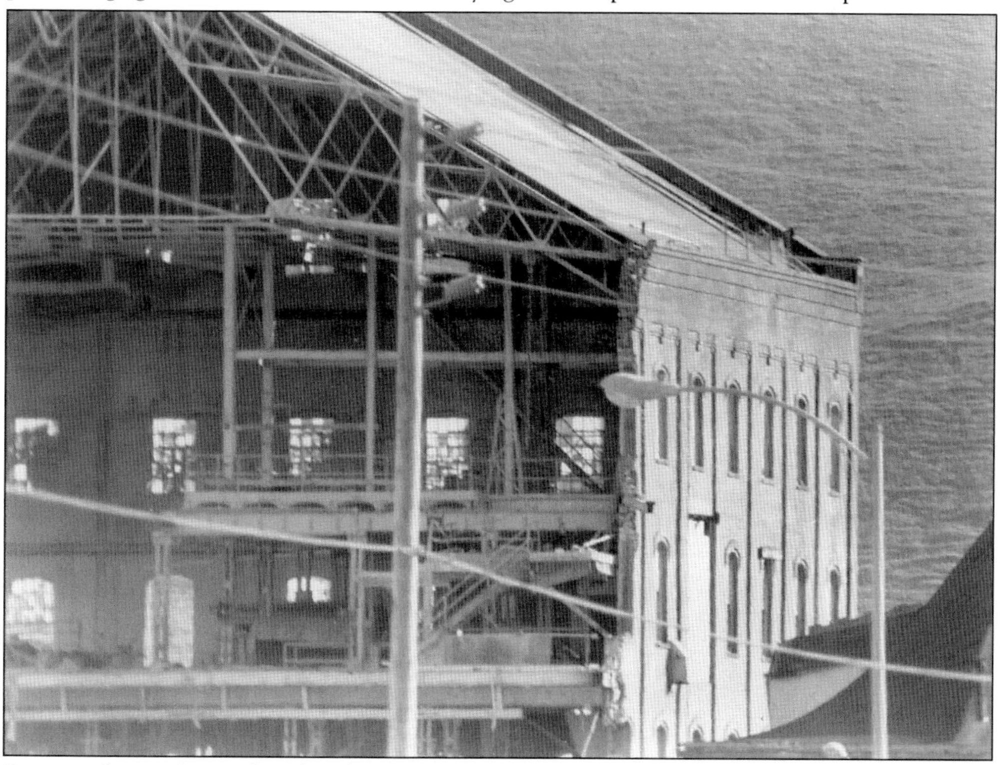

Prior to closing down their local operations and selling them, the Spreckels Sugar Company donated significant portions of their historical files, including photographs, blueprints, maps, and other documents, to the Monterey County Historical Society. These documents are being preserved in the archival vault and assisted greatly in the preparation of this book.

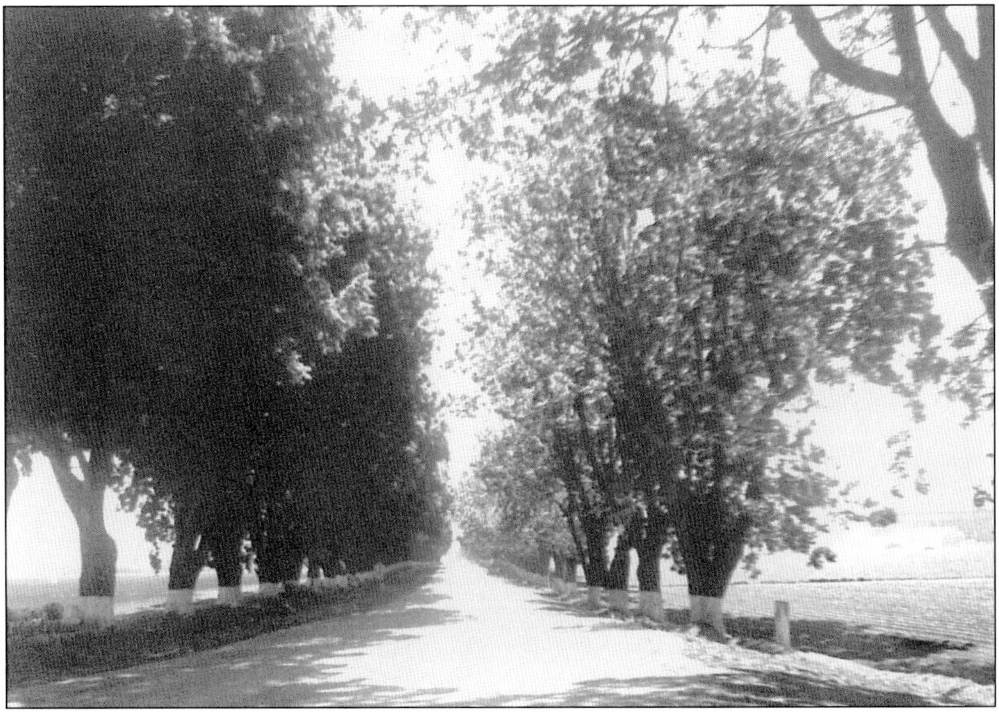

Black walnut trees line Spreckels Boulevard. Somehow a single almond tree became a part of the grove. According to *The Courier* on September 27, 1913, "The almond crop and the consequent profit of harvesting it seems to have escaped the attention of the company until the boys had gathered and sold well nigh everything in sight."

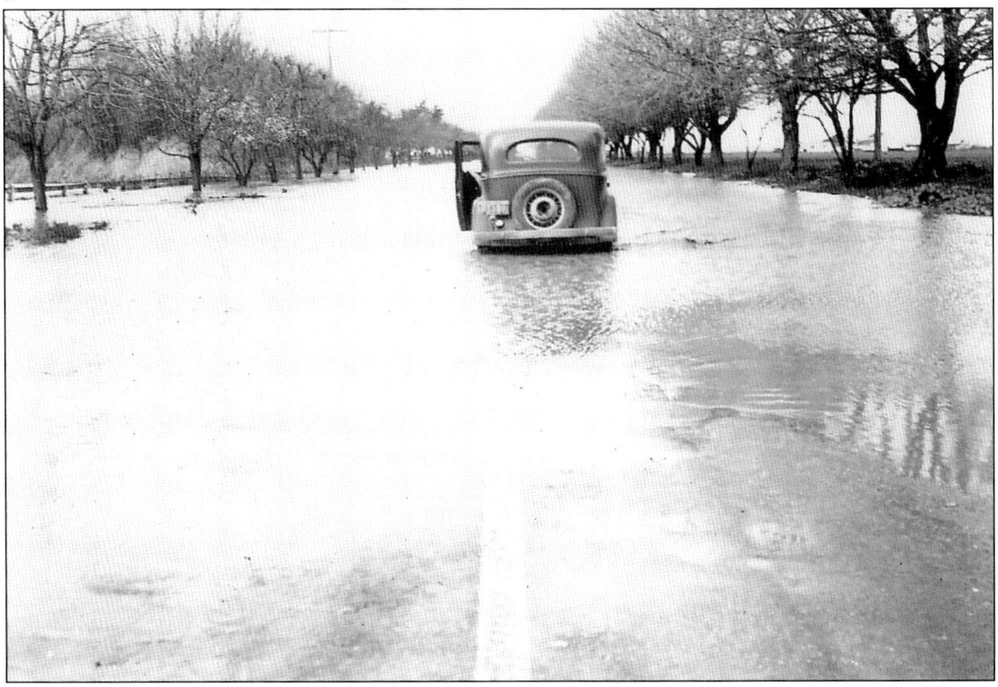

The end. (Courtesy of Monterey County Agricultural and Rural Life Museum.)

BIBLIOGRAPHY

Abbott, Carlisle S. *Recollections of a California Pioneer.* New York: The Neale Publishing Company, 1917.

Adler, Jacob. *Claus Spreckels: The Sugar King in Hawaii.* Honolulu: Mutual Publishing Paperback Series, 1966.

Anderson, Burton. *America's Salad Bowl: An Agricultural History of the Salinas Valley.* Salinas, CA: Monterey County Historical Society, Inc., 2000.

Binsacca, Leslie, ed. *Sweet Nostalgia: Spreckels Sugar, Spreckels, CA, 1898–1982.* Spreckels, CA: Spreckels Sugar, 1982.

Cordray, William Woodrow. *Claus Spreckels of California.* Doctoral dissertation, Department of History, University of Southern California, 1955.

Fabing, Horace W. and Rick Hamman. *Steinbeck Country Narrow Gauge.* Boulder, CO: Pruett Publishing Company, 1985.

Monterey County Planning and Building Inspection Department. *Spreckels, California: Design Guidelines.* Salinas, CA: Monterey County Planning and Building Inspection Department, 1999.

Page and Turnbull, Inc. Modified HABS/HAER Report, Spreckels Sugar Company Factory No. 1, Spreckels, California. Prepared for Spreckels Sugar Company, Inc., Pleasanton, California, 1993.

Tunzi, Matt. "The Birth of a Town." *Salinas Californian.* September 17, 1977.